Educational Research

A Practical Approach

Delmar Publishers' Online Services

To access Delmar on the World Wide Web, point your browser to:
        http://www.delmar.com/delmar.html
To access through Gopher:
        gopher://gopher.delmar.com
(Delmar Online is part of "thomson.com", an Internet site with information on more than 30 publishers of the International Thomson Publishing organization.)
For more information on our products and services:
        email: info@delmar.com or call 800-347-7707

Educational Research

Research

A Practical Approach

George R. Bieger, Ph.D.

Gail J. Gerlach, Ed.D.

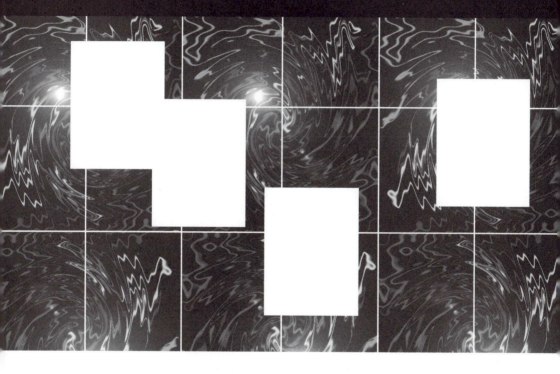

Delmar Publishers

I T P

Albany • Bonn • Boston • Cincinnati • Detroit • London • Madrid • Melbourne
Mexico City • New York • Pacific Grove • Paris • San Francisco • Singapore • Tokyo
Toronto • Washington

Cover Design: Timothy J. Conners

Delmar Staff
Associate Editor: Erin O'Connor Traylor
Production Editor: Marah Bellegarde
Editorial Assistant: Glenna Stanfield

COPYRIGHT © 1996
By Delmar Publishers
a division of International Thomson Publishing Inc.

The ITP logo is a trademark under license.

Printed in the United States of America

For more information, contact:

Delmar Publishers
3 Columbia Circle, Box 15015
Albany, New York 12212-5015

International Thomson Publishing Europe
Berkshire House 168-173
High Holborn
London, WC1V 7AA
England

Thomas Nelson Australia
102 Dodds Street
South Melbourne, 3205
Victoria, Australia

Nelson Canada
1120 Birchmont Road
Scarborough, Ontario
Canada, M1K 5G4

International Thomson Editores
Campos Eliseos 385, Piso 7
Col Polanco
11560 Mexico D F Mexico

International Thomson Publishing GmbH
Konigswinterer Strasse 418
53227 Bonn
Germany

International Thomson Publishing Asia
221 Henderson Road
#05-10 Henderson Building
Singapore 0315

International Thomson Publishing—Japan
Hirakawacho Kyowa Building, 3F
2-2-1 Hirakawacho
Chiyoda-ku, Tokyo 102
Japan

1 2 3 4 5 6 7 8 9 10 XXX 01 00 99 98 97 96

Library of Congress Cataloging-in-Publication Data

Bieger, George R.
  Educational research: a practical approach/George R. Bieger,
Gail J. Gerlach.
    p.   cm.
  Includes index.
  ISBN 0-8273-6834-8
  1. Education—Research—Methodology. 2. Report writing.
I. Gerlach, Gail J.   II. Title.
LB1028.B473 1996
370'.78—dc20   95-42816
                                                    CIP

C O N T E N T S

PREFACE

Our experience, as teachers of research methods courses, is that students are typically anxious about research methodology. Their anxiety, which interferes with their ability to learn and master the content of this subject, is often exacerbated by the mathematical, technical, and/or theoretical orientation and tone of many research texts. Students frequently ask for practice exercises or practical applications for the various concepts and topics covered in research courses.

This book is intended to provide relevant, practical, and clear exercises in applying the various concepts and techniques that are usually taught in research courses at the graduate and advanced undergraduate levels. The teaching/practice strategy for each topic includes a brief introduction of the topic/chapter, a list of specific learning competencies for each topic/chapter, specific scenarios and questions to which students will respond, and well-explained answers for students to use to evaluate their own responses. The exercises provided in this book could be the basis for direct instruction and, with the detailed responses, could provide the content for classroom discussions.

WHAT RESEARCH IS AND WHAT IT IS NOT

In order for a professional educator to be effective, he or she must demonstrate the ability to deal effectively with the myriad of problems that occurs in educational settings. Success in solving problems depends, to a large extent, on one's ability to

1. Identify problems and propose solutions in a systematic fashion

2. Generate new knowledge needed for formulating potential solutions to problems

3. Evaluate proposed explanations and solutions from a knowledgeable perspective

These three interrelated abilities constitute the basis for scientific research, not just in education but in any discipline. They are, in abbreviated form, the components of the scientific method that we all learned (or at least were taught) somewhere around the junior high school level.

Because the discipline of education is most properly considered as one of the social sciences, it is not surprising that the methods of science have become one of the principal ways by which educators acquire knowledge and test ideas. The rigor of the scientific method, its insistence on logic and rationality, and its use of accepted and replicable procedures all combine to provide a powerful tool for the acquisition and testing of knowledge and theories. The application of the scientific method to problems or questions is the essence of research.

The term "research" is often used to mean many things, including conducting experiments, trial-and-error testing of different techniques or methods, or using the library and similar resources to review documents on a topic. All of these activities might be considered research, but they do not capture the essential qualities of the research enterprise. Research is, at its essence, a systematic and empirical approach to answering questions. By systematic, we mean that the research is carried out in a way that is well planned and organized, and follows certain procedural standards that will increase the likelihood that the results will be reliable and valid. By empirical, we mean that the research process involves observation, either directly or indirectly. The products of observations are called data, which may take many forms, such as test scores or observation notes. The researcher processes these data in a variety of ways such as organizing the data or statistically analyzing the data.

Sometimes research is described as some sort of idealistic "search for the truth," or someone might say that a researcher is trying to prove something. These conceptions of research, while common, reflect a point of view different from ours. The search for "truth," however noble that may be, is not the point of research, nor is the attempt to prove something. The research enterprise is concerned, rather, with understanding a phenomenon, within the context of our theories and experiences regarding that phenomenon. Theories are constructed to try to explain various aspects of our world, and research is a process whereby we test the adequacy of those theories.

Research, then, is a process for using empirical data to answer questions in a systematic fashion.

There are two types of people with respect to research: consumers, those who read and perhaps use research, and producers, those who conduct research.

CRITICALLY ANALYZING RESEARCH STUDIES

The purpose of this book is to help you become a knowledgeable consumer of research. When reading a research article many people read the introduction, skip "all that stuff" in the middle, and read the discussion and conclusions. We hope that after you finish this book you will want to read "all that stuff" in the middle, or at least be able to understand "all that stuff."

DESIGNING RESEARCH STUDIES

It is sometimes easy to be critical of research, finding all of the things that a researcher should have done or could have done better. It is quite another matter to design good research studies. Part of this book will help you understand the difficult decisions that researchers often must make as they try to balance the hope for a quality study with the demands of reality. By making certain research design decisions, and considering the consequences of those decisions, you will become a better consumer of research.

SUMMARY

We hope that you will find this approach to educational research both stimulating and useful. It is our view that the value of research

ACKNOWLEDGMENTS

We are appreciative of the following researchers who granted permission to have their studies included in this book. Their contributions added authenticity to the exercises. A special thank-you to Dennis Ausel, Karen Bauer, Marian Beckman, Janet Fleischauer, Gloria Gerbracht, Gregory Hofstetter, Celine Kandala, Edward Meshanko, Cheryl Ralston, Derry Stufft, Dorothy Touvell, and Donald Tylinski.

In addition, we would like to thank the thirty-five students who were enrolled in *GR 615—Elements of Research* during the second summer session of 1995. Their help in testing an earlier draft of the manuscript for this book helped us during the revision process. Their patience is appreciated.

Our appreciation is extended to the reviewers enlisted through Delmar for their constructive criticism and helpful suggestions. They include Richard Antonak, Ph.D., University of North Carolina, Charlotte, NC; John Bruno, Ph.D., State College, Buffalo, NY; P. J. Karr-Kidwell, Ph.D., Texas Women's University, Denton, TX.

1 | IDENTIFYING RESEARCH PROBLEMS

INTRODUCTION

The first task, for both consumers and producers of research, is to identify the research problem, or purpose for the study. This task includes

- Specifying the problem statement
- Identifying the variables to be manipulated, measured, or otherwise used in the study
- Operationally defining the variables used in the study
- Stating specific experimental hypotheses and/or research questions

PROBLEM STATEMENTS

A problem statement identifies the purpose of the study, and should include the following characteristics (Tuckman, 1988):

1. It should refer to a connection between (or among) two or more variables.

2. It should be stated clearly and unambiguously.

3. It should be testable using empirical methods. In other words, it should be possible and feasible to collect data to address directly the stated problem.

A good problem statement is a concise declaration of the purpose of a research study. It should be clear from the problem statement what the researcher is studying and problem statements should be directly linked to research hypotheses.

VARIABLES

A variable is a characteristic that may take on different values (Wiersma, 1991). Classification of variables depends on their role in the research. Researchers may identify variables using different terminology.

The most commonly used classifications of variables include **independent, dependent, intervening, control** and **moderator variables.** These variables are used in experimental research. Wiersma (1991) defines these variables as follows:

> Independent variable: A variable that affects (or is assumed to affect) the dependent variable under study and is included in the research design so that its effect can be determined.

> Dependent variable: The variable being affected or assumed to be affected by the independent variable.

> Intervening variable: A variable whose existence is inferred but that cannot always be manipulated or measured.

> Control variable: A variable, other than the independent variable(s) of primary interest, whose effects are determined by the researcher.

> Moderator variable: A variable that may or may not be controlled but has an effect on the research situation.

Independent variables have been further categorized by various authors (e.g., Kerlinger, 1986) according to the extent to which they are manipulable by the researcher. In this book we will not make distinctions among types of independent variables, but will use the term independent variable to refer to any variable that is presumed to be a "cause" of a change in another variable.

Wiersma (1995) observes, "If a moderator variable is uncontrolled, it is essentially an intervening variable. If it is controlled—that is, its effects have been determined—it becomes a control variable" (p. 37). When a researcher becomes aware of the existence of a possible moderator variable, he or she may try to manipulate or measure that variable to assess its effect on the dependent variable. In such cases, we will classify that variable as a control variable. If, on the other hand, the researcher chooses not to, or is unable to manipulate or measure the potential moderator variable, we will classify it as an intervening variable. For the purpose of answering the exercises in this book, the term intervening variable will also be used when the actions of a researcher concerning that variable are not known because they are not mentioned in the description of the research situation.

When using various correlational statistical techniques such as linear regression analysis, two variables not mentioned previously are identified. These are **predictor** and **criterion variables.** According to Popham and Sirotnik (1967), the variable that is predicted is the criterion variable (dependent variable) and the variable from which the prediction is being made is the predictor variable (independent variable). For example, when Scholastic Aptitude Test (SAT) scores are used as indicators of success in college, which in turn is measured by grade point average (GPA) at the end of the first year, SAT score is the predictor variable and GPA is the criterion variable.

The specific variables described here do not constitute an exhaustive list. Many other kinds of variables are defined and described by the authors of various research texts (e.g., confounding variables, extraneous variables, organismic variables). For a more complete discussion of these kinds of variables, we suggest consulting several primary research texts.

OPERATIONAL DEFINITIONS

When researchers describe the problem to be studied in a problem statement, they usually describe it in conceptual, rather than measurable, terms. For example, a researcher might state that the purpose of a study is to determine the relationship between self-concept and intelligence. The terms "self-concept" and "intelligence" refer to concepts that have been defined in various ways by different theorists. It is therefore essential for the researcher to specify how these terms will be defined in the study. **Operational definitions** are based on the observable or measurable characteristics of what is being defined (Tuckman, 1988). For example, "intelligence" could be operationally defined as a score from a widely accepted standardized test such as the Stanford-Binet-Revised or the Wechsler Intelligence Scale for Children-III, and "socioeconomic status" might be defined by whether a student is eligible for free or reduced lunch or not.

Since hypotheses, discussed in the next section, are specific testable predictions, they require observable or measurable definitions for the variables involved. Operational definitions for all concepts mentioned in the problem statement are an important aspect of planning research studies.

HYPOTHESES

A research hypothesis is usually a predictive statement that represents a very specific proposed answer to the problem statement. The hypothesis must be stated in an empirically testable form, and should indicate the specific nature of the connection (usually a difference or a relationship) between or among variables that was initially identified in the problem statement.

Research hypotheses are logically deduced from relevant theories, or logically induced from prior related research and may be stated in either the **null** or the **alternative** form.

A **null hypothesis,** which is primarily used for statistical purposes, is a statement that we expect that there will be *no* connection among variables. An **alternative hypothesis,** which is used for research purposes, states the nature of the connection between or among variables that we expect, based on theory and/or prior research. The reasons for stating hypotheses in the null form or the alternative form are primarily related to the logic of inferential reasoning and are not relevant to the discussion here. For a comprehensive discussion of this topic, refer to Sir Ronald Fisher's book entitled *The Design of Experiments* (1951).

Another way of categorizing a research (or alternative) hypothesis deals with the specificity, or directionality, of the hypothesis. **Nondirectional** hypotheses state that a connection among variables exists, whereas **directional** hypotheses state the particular nature of the connection (Gay, 1992). For example, a nondirectional hypothesis might state that there will be a difference between elementary and secondary teachers in the amount of professional reading that they do, whereas a directional hypothesis might state not only that there will be a difference but also that secondary teachers do more professional reading than their elementary counterparts. The

null hypothesis in this example would state that there will be *no* difference between elementary and secondary teachers in the amount of professional reading that they do.

Since testing hypotheses is really what the research enterprise is all about, careful and precise statement of the research hypotheses is essential for the research project to be worthwhile.

COMPETENCIES

After completing the exercises in this chapter, you will be able to

- Identify the problem statement in a research study

- Write a succinct, clear, testable problem statement for a proposed research study

- Explain and identify the following items in a research study:
  Independent variable
  Dependent variable
  Predictor variable
  Criterion variable
  Intervening variable
  Control variable
  Moderating variable

- Identify operational definitions of variables in a research study

- Write operational definitions for variables in a proposed research study

- Identify the hypothesis or hypotheses for a research study

- Classify the hypothesis or hypotheses in a research study as either in the null or alternative (research) form

- Write hypotheses in both the null and the alternative form for a proposed research study

- Classify the hypothesis or hypotheses in a research study as either nondirectional or directional

- Write both nondirectional and directional hypotheses for a proposed research study

RESEARCH PROBLEM EXERCISES

Two types of exercises are included in this chapter. The first is intended to provide practice in analyzing research situations and in identifying and classifying problem statements, variables, and hypotheses. The second is intended to provide practice in writing relevant problem statements, operational definitions, and hypotheses.

For the purpose of answering these exercises, none of the variables should be classified as moderator variables. If the problem or scenario mentions a variable that, while not the major focus of the study, is measured or controlled by the researcher, that variable should be classified as a control variable. For other variables, if the actions of the researcher concerning a variable are not known because they are not mentioned in the description of the research situation, those variables should be classified as intervening variables.

Exercises in Analyzing Research Situations

In each of the following exercises, carefully read the description of the research situation. Base your response only on the information given in the description.

✎ **Exercise 1–1**   A researcher is interested in determining whether or not there are differences in students' classroom participation as a result of the kind of feedback provided by the teacher. Being aware of prior research indicating that boys and girls participate at different levels, the researcher will make sure that the sample consists of approximately equal numbers of third-grade boys and girls. The data will consist of the observed frequency with which students will volunteer to participate or respond during class activities. The sample will be divided into three groups, which will differ in the kind of feedback the teacher provides to the students. One group will receive oral feedback only, the second group will receive written feedback only, and the third group will receive oral and written feedback. The researcher will compare the frequency of students' voluntary participation among the three groups after the feedback treatment has been used for three weeks.

1. Mark the sentence or clause that contains the problem statement for this research.

2. From the following list of possible variables, classify them as *independent, dependent, intervening, control, predictor,* or *criterion* variables.

    a.   Gender of teacher
    b.   Gender of student
    c.   Frequency of voluntary participation
    d.   Feedback group
    e.   Age of student
    f.   Student's enthusiasm for the subject

3.   Of the possible variables listed in item 2, identify the variables that need to be operationally defined.

4.   Based on the problem statement alone, indicate whether or not each of the following hypotheses is relevant; if relevant, indicate whether the hypothesis is written in the null or the alternative form. If the hypothesis is in the alternative form, further indicate if it is directional or nondirectional.

    a.   There will be no difference between students taught by male teachers and those taught by female teachers in frequency of students' voluntary participation.
    b.   Female students will volunteer to participate more frequently than males.
    c.   Students who receive more feedback will attain achievement test scores different from those who receive less feedback.
    d.   There will be no difference among the three feedback groups in the frequency of students' voluntary participation.
    e.   The students receiving oral and written feedback will volunteer to participate more frequently than students in either of the other groups.
    f.   Highly enthusiastic students will receive more feedback than less enthusiastic students.

✎ **Exercise 1–2**   The transportation director of a large school district has received numerous complaints from parents, students, and teachers about the frequent lateness of several school buses. Additional complaints have been made about the distance that students, especially the elementary students, must walk to reach their bus stops. The transportation director has considered using a computer-based bus scheduling and routing program to redesign the bus schedule but would like to test the program before purchasing it. Two regions of the school district are selected to conduct the test, one of which will have the schedule arranged "manually" while the other will implement a computerized bus schedule. The transportation director plans to determine whether or not the computerized system results in fewer complaints. The results will also be analyzed to see if there is any difference in the number of complaints for elementary versus secondary students.

1. Mark the sentence or clause that contains the problem statement for this research.

2. From the following list of possible variables, classify them as *independent, dependent, intervening, control, predictor,* or *criterion* variables.
   a. Bus driver's experience
   b. Bus driver's age
   c. Student's educational level (i.e., elementary or secondary)
   d. Method of scheduling
   e. Number of complaints
   f. Parents' income

3. Of the possible variables listed in item 2, identify the variables that need to be operationally defined.

4. Based on the problem statement alone, indicate whether or not each of the following hypotheses is relevant; if relevant, indicate whether the hypothesis is written in the null or the alternative form. If the hypothesis is in the alternative form, further indicate if it is directional or nondirectional.
   a. There will be fewer complaints using the computerized scheduling system.
   b. There will be a negative correlation between parents' income and number of complaints.
   c. There will be fewer complaints for more experienced drivers.
   d. There will be no difference in the number of complaints for older bus drivers compared with younger drivers.
   e. There will be no difference in the number of complaints between the regions using the computerized versus the manual scheduling system.
   f. There will be no relationship among the following: parents' income, driver's age, number of complaints, student's level, and driver's experience.

✎ **Exercise 1–3** Students being educated to be teachers at a large state university are given several field experiences prior to student teaching. In the first field experience, each student has a choice of either participating as a tutor in an after-school tutoring program in a local school district or serving as a classroom teacher aide in a local school district. The coordinator of university field experiences will conduct a research study to determine whether one program or the other leads to greater enthusiasm for teaching as a career. Of secondary interest is whether or not there are differences in enthusiasm between elementary and secondary majors. A "self-report" questionnaire, the Teaching Enthusiasm Inventory, will be sent to students participating in both programs, and the responses from students in the two field experience groups will be compared.

1. Mark the sentence or clause that contains the problem statement for this research.

2. From the following list of possible variables, classify them as *independent, dependent, intervening, control, predictor,* or *criterion* variables.
    a. Gender of the student
    b. Field experience group
    c. Student's age
    d. Amount of prior experience working with children
    e. Level of enthusiasm
    f. Student's major (elementary or secondary education)

3. Of the possible variables listed in item 2, identify the variables that need to be operationally defined.

4. Based on the problem statement alone, indicate whether or not each of the following hypotheses is relevant; if relevant, indicate whether the hypothesis is written in the null or the alternative form. If the hypothesis is in the alternative form, further indicate if it is directional or nondirectional.
    a. There will be no difference in the level of enthusiasm between male and female students.
    b. Elementary education majors will have higher levels of enthusiasm than secondary education majors.
    c. There will be no difference in the level of enthusiasm between students in the two field experience groups.
    d. There will be a correlation (either positive or negative) between the amount of prior experience working with children and level of enthusiasm (i.e., the more experience a student has had, the more enthusiastic he or she is likely to be).
    e. Students participating in the tutoring program will differ in enthusiasm compared with students participating in the classroom aide program.
    f. Older students will express greater enthusiasm for the tutoring program than will younger students.

✎ **Exercise 1–4**   Being familiar with a theoretical perspective that argues for the superiority of a science program that emphasizes a process orientation rather than memorization of science facts, a teacher hopes to determine if a "hands-on" science process curriculum will produce higher achievement and more favorable attitudes toward science than a conventional "text-based" curriculum. The teacher will obtain science attitude and achievement data from a large number of students, about half of whom had been taught science using each of the two types of curriculum, and consisting of approximately equal numbers of females and males.

1. Mark the sentence or clause that contains the problem statement for this research.

2. From the following list of possible variables, classify them as *independent, dependent, intervening, control, predictor,* or *criterion* variables.
    a. Student's science achievement score
    b. Student's IQ score
    c. Science curriculum
    d. Teacher effectiveness
    e. Student's attitude toward science
    f. Student's gender

3. Of the possible variables listed in item 2, identify the variables that need to be operationally defined.

4. Based on the problem statement alone, indicate whether or not each of the following hypotheses is relevant; if relevant, indicate whether the hypothesis is written in the null or the alternative form. If the hypothesis is in the alternative form, further indicate if it is directional or nondirectional.
    a. There will be a positive correlation between students' attitudes toward science and students' science achievement scores.
    b. Students in the "hands-on" curriculum will differ from students in the text curriculum in their achievement scores and in their attitudes toward science.
    c. There will be a correlation between teacher effectiveness rating and students' science achievement and attitude toward science scores.
    d. There will be a positive correlation between students' IQ scores and their science achievement scores, and a negative correlation between students' IQ scores and their attitudes toward science scores.
    e. There will be no difference in the science achievement scores or attitudes toward science scores as a function of teachers' attitudes toward science.
    f. There will be no difference in the science achievement scores or attitudes toward science scores between students in the two curriculum groups.

✎ **Exercise 1–5**   A researcher is interested in studying the effects on student test performance of different types of preparation for the National Teachers Examination (Praxis Series) offered by a statewide commercial learning center. The learning center provides 10 one-hour sessions using a trained tutor to review the content for the Special Area Test for the certification area, elementary education. On the day of the administration of the exam, students at all administration sites across the state will be asked to complete a questionnaire that assesses how they prepared for the exam. The questionnaire will be completed anonymously, but it requests specific demographic data, such as gender, region of the state, and class designation in college. Students will be asked to identify the major type of preparation for the exam. Some of the major types listed are commercial learning center, self-study, group study, no study, published workbooks, and computer software.

1. Mark the sentence or clause that contains the problem statement.

2. From the following list of possible variables, classify them as *independent, dependent, intervening, control, predictor,* or *criterion* variables.
    a. Gender of student
    b. Type of preparation
    c. Region of the state
    d. Class designation
    e. Student performance on the exam
    f. Number of times the student took the exam

3. Of the possible variables listed in item 2, identify the variables that need to be operationally defined.

4. Based on the problem statement alone, indicate whether or not each of the following hypotheses is relevant; if relevant, indicate whether the hypothesis is written in the null or the alternative form. If the hypothesis is in the alternative form, further indicate if it is directional or nondirectional.
    a. There will be no difference in test scores among students receiving different types of preparation for the National Teachers Exam.
    b. Female students will score higher than male students on the Special Area Test of the National Teachers Examination (Praxis Series).
    c. Students who attend universities with fewer than five hundred students in the College of Education will score higher on the Special Area Test of the National Teachers Exam than students who attend universities with more than five hundred students in the College of Education.

d.   There will be a difference in test scores among students receiving different types of preparation for the Special Area Test of the National Teachers Examination (Praxis Series).

e.   There will be no difference in the performance on the Special Area Test of the National Teachers Examination (Praxis Series) of elementary education majors and special education majors.

f.   Commercial learning center preparation for the Special Area Exam of the National Teachers Examination (Praxis Series) will yield higher scores than preparation by self-study.

Exercise 1–6   A college of education is interested in determining whether or not the portfolio that students have to prepare is being used in the initial screening interviews, and how the use (or non-use) of the portfolio influences the interaction during the interview. A large school district tends to hire many teachers who have graduated from the university. The school district has agreed to participate in the study. During the interview, data will be collected by an interviewer/researcher. The data collected will include the following: whether or not the portfolio is used in the interview; what question/comment prompted the use of the portfolio; and the interaction that occurred between the interviewer and the interviewee regarding the portfolio.

1.   Mark the sentence or clause that contains the problem statement.

2.   From the following list of possible variables, classify them as *independent, dependent, intervening, control, predictor,* or *criterion* variables.
    a.   Quality of the portfolio
    b.   Interaction of the dyad
    c.   Training of interviewer/researcher
    d.   Question/comment that prompted the use of the portfolio
    e.   Gender of the interviewer
    f.   Gender of the interviewee

3.   Of the possible variables listed in item 2, identify the variables that need to be operationally defined.

4.   Based on the problem statement alone, indicate whether or not each of the following hypotheses is relevant; if relevant, indicate whether the hypothesis is written in the null or the alternative form. If the hypothesis is in the alternative form, further indicate if it is directional or nondirectional.
    a.   There will be a specific type of question that triggers the use of the portfolio.
    b.   Female students will use the portfolio in the interview more often than male students.

   c.   Interviewees who use the portfolio in the interview as compared with interviewees who do not use the portfolio more often are offered a teaching position.

   d.   There will be a difference in who (interviewer or interviewee) most often initiates discussion of the portfolio.

   e.   More interviewees will use the portfolio in the interview than not use the portfolio in the interview.

✎ **Exercise 1–7**   An elementary school principal is interested in assessing parent satisfaction with the flow of information from the school under two plans. Traditionally, parents have had the opportunity for two conferences with the child's teacher each year. In addition, student papers have been sent home with each child as soon as they have been checked. In one school, an alternate plan for communicating with parents will be implemented. The two parent-teacher conferences will be retained; however, sending home papers as checked will be replaced with a folio of work sent home at the end of each week.

1.   Mark the sentence or clause that contains the problem statement.

2.   From the following list of possible variables, classify them as *independent, dependent, intervening, control, predictor,* or *criterion* variables.
   a.   Flow of information
   b.   Parent-teacher conferences
   c.   Papers sent home as checked
   d.   Folio of papers sent home at the end of the week
   e.   Parent satisfaction

3.   Of the possible variables listed in item 2, identify the variables that need to be operationally defined.

4.   Based on the problem statement alone, indicate whether or not each of the following hypotheses is relevant; if relevant, indicate whether the hypothesis is written in the null or the alternative form. If the hypothesis is in the alternative form, further indicate if it is directional or nondirectional.
   a.   Parents will express greater satisfaction with the portfolio of information than with the checked paper flow of information.
   b.   There will be no difference in parental satisfaction regarding the type of information given to them about their children's progress.
   c.   A parent who works outside of the home will show greater satisfaction with the type of information received on the child's progress than will the parent who does not work outside of the home.

    d.   There will be no difference in parental satisfaction between parents with one child and parents with more than one child in the school regarding the type of information given about the child's/children's progress.

    e.   Male parents more so than female parents will express greater satisfaction with the checked paper flow of information than with the portfolio flow of information.

Exercise 1–8   Two affluent school districts regularly upgrade technology for use in the classroom. If a teacher in either district supports the use of new technology, the district will purchase the technology with all of the needed components. The districts share a director of technology, so both districts always receive the same technology. The director of technology believes that a crucial issue in terms of whether teachers use the technology is in-service training. District A provides in-service training with all new technology purchased; District B does not. To assess the impact of in-service training, the director of technology decides to track the checkout of equipment from the technology room at both schools. The assumption is that if an item is checked out, it is being used.

1.   Mark the sentence or clause that contains the problem statement.

2.   From the following list of possible variables, classify them as *independent, dependent, intervening, control, predictor,* or *criterion* variables.
    a.   School district
    b.   Gender of the teacher
    c.   Type of technology
    d.   In-service training
    e.   Checkout of equipment

3.   Of the possible variables listed in item 2, identify the variables that need to be operationally defined.

4.   Based on the problem statement alone, indicate whether or not each of the following hypotheses is relevant; if relevant, indicate whether the hypothesis is written in the null or the alternative form. If the hypothesis is in the alternative form, further indicate if it is directional or nondirectional.
    a.   Training in the use of technology will increase the frequency of its use.
    b.   Male teachers will use technology more often than female teachers.
    c.   There will be no difference in the use of easy-to-use technology as compared with more-difficult-to-use technology.
    d.   There will be no difference in the frequency of use of older technology and recently purchased technology.
    e.   There will be a difference in frequency of use of technology between districts that provide in-service training and those that do not.

✎ **Exercise 1–9**   A high school principal is interested in finding out whether or not there is any connection between the extent of students' participation in extracurricular activities and their academic grades. For each student, the principal will record the following data: class (ninth grade, tenth grade, etc.), gender, GPA, IQ, type of extracurricular activity, and number of hours per week of participation in each type of activity.

1.   Mark the sentence or clause that contains the problem statement for this research.

2.   From the following list of possible variables, classify them as *independent, dependent, intervening, control, predictor,* or *criterion* variables.
  a.   Academic grades
  b.   Students' IQ scores
  c.   Gender of student
  d.   Parents' income
  e.   Type of extracurricular activity
  f.   Number of hours of extracurricular participation

3.   Of the possible variables listed in item 2, identify the variables that need to be operationally defined.

4.   Based on the problem statement alone, indicate whether or not each of the following hypotheses is relevant; if relevant, indicate whether the hypothesis is written in the null or the alternative form. If the hypothesis is in the alternative form, further indicate if it is directional or nondirectional.
  a.   There will be no correlation between the extent of students' participation in extracurricular activities and academic grades.
  b.   Female students who participate in extracurricular activities will have higher grades than nonparticipating female students; male students who participate in extracurricular activities will have lower grades than nonparticipating male students.
  c.   There will be a negative correlation among the following: students' IQ scores, parents' income, and extent of participation in extracurricular activities.
  d.   There will be no correlation among the following: students' IQ scores, parents' income, and extent of participation in extracurricular activities.
  e.   There will be significant differences between male and female students in the extent of their participation in extracurricular activities.
  f.   There will be a positive correlation between the extent of students' participation in extracurricular activities and academic grades.

✎ **Exercise 1–10**   The director of reading in a school district believes that knowledge of the alphabet and chronological age at entry into first grade are important factors in predicting success in reading. He proposes a research project to test his beliefs. He will assess all male and female first graders on their knowledge of the alphabet and determine the chronological age of each child as of September 1. In May, he will obtain reading data from the district's standardized reading test.

1. Mark the sentence or clause that contains the problem statement.

2. From the following list of possible variables, classify them as *independent, dependent, intervening, control, predictor,* or *criterion* variables.
   a. Gender of the student
   b. Socioeconomic status
   c. Kindergarten experiences
   d. Knowledge of the alphabet
   e. Chronological age in September
   f. Reading achievement score in May

3. Of the possible variables listed in item 2, identify the variables that need to be operationally defined.

4. Based on the problem statement alone, indicate whether or not each of the following hypotheses is relevant; if relevant, indicate whether the hypothesis is written in the null or the alternative form. If the hypothesis is in the alternative form, further indicate if it is directional or nondirectional.
   a. High knowledge of the alphabet and higher chronological age will predict higher reading achievement.
   b. Knowledge of the alphabet and chronological age will not be related to reading achievement.
   c. Better knowledge of the alphabet will occur with older children.
   d. Lower chronological age will predict lower knowledge of the alphabet.
   e. There will be a relationship between knowledge of the alphabet and chronological age and reading achievement.

Exercises in Writing Research Problems

In each of the following exercises, carefully read the description of the situation. Based only on the information given in the description, answer each of the questions.

✎ **Exercise 1–11**   An instructor has reason to believe that certain information could be presented more effectively in pictures rather than in text. That is, it is the instructor's belief that a pictorial presentation of this information will lead to better comprehension and longer retention than will a textual presentation of the same information.

1. Write a problem statement for this research.

2. Identify the relevant variables and label them as *independent, dependent, intervening, control, predictor,* or *criterion* variables.

3. From the set of variables listed in item 2, identify all of the terms that need to be operationally defined. Operationally define any two of these terms.

4. Write one hypothesis for this research based on the problem statement. Write the hypothesis first in the null form, then in an alternative nondirectional form, and finally in an alternative directional form.

✎ **Exercise 1–12**   A middle school mathematics teacher wonders about the usefulness of assigning, grading, and reviewing homework every day. She is willing and eager to continue the practice if it leads to improved mathematics learning for her students, improves their attitudes toward mathematics, or makes them more confident of their mathematics ability. However, if it makes no difference she feels she can use her time and energy more wisely. She plans a research study to explore this question.

1. Write a problem statement for this research.

2. Identify the relevant variables and label them as *independent, dependent, intervening, control, predictor,* or *criterion* variables.

3. From the set of variables listed in item 2, identify all terms that need to be operationally defined. Operationally define any two of these terms.

4. Write one hypothesis for this research based on the problem statement. Write the hypothesis first in the null form, then in an alternative nondirectional form, and finally in an alternative directional form.

✎ **Exercise 1–13**   A teacher is curious about what factors lead to a student being elected as a homeroom representative to the student council. The teacher decides to examine the characteristics and background (e.g., grades, extent of participation in extracurricular activities, popularity) of all of the representatives and of those who were nominated but not elected to see if there is any connection between the various characteristics and background and the outcome of the election.

1. Write a problem statement for this research.

2. Identify the relevant variables and label them as *independent, dependent, intervening, control, predictor,* or *criterion* variables.

3. From the set of variables listed in item 2, identify all terms that need to be operationally defined. Operationally define any two of these terms.

4. Write one hypothesis for this research based on the problem statement. Write the hypothesis first in the null form, then in an alternative nondirectional form, and finally in an alternative directional form.

✎ **Exercise 1–14**   A school board member feels strongly that the process of bidding for contracts for school supplies is not saving money in the long run for a large district. She believes that the district could save more money by establishing a relationship with a local school supply company. She presents her idea to the school board, and the board agrees to split the school supply orders in two parts—half will be purchased from the local supplier and the other half will be put up for bid. An ongoing cost analysis will occur, with a recommendation to be made at the end of the two-year period.

1. Write a problem statement for this research.

2. Identify the relevant variables and label them as *independent, dependent, intervening, control, predictor,* or *criterion* variables.

3. From the set of variables listed in item 2, identify all of the terms that need to be operationally defined. Operationally define any two of these terms.

4. Write one hypothesis for this research based on the problem statement. Write the hypothesis first in the null form, then in an alternative nondirectional form, and finally in an alternative directional form.

✎ **Exercise 1–15**   A high school band director believes that playing in the band influences interest in the type of music that the band plays. He decides to conduct a written survey at the beginning of the school year in music classes to assess the type of music that students choose for leisure listening. This survey will be administered to all band and non-band students. The focus on music for the band for the academic year will be jazz. At the end of the year, both students who play in the band and students who are not in the band will be surveyed again to assess their preferences in music for leisure listening.

1. Write a problem statement for this research.

2. Identify the relevant variables and label them as *independent, dependent, intervening, control, predictor,* or *criterion* variables.

3. From the set of variables listed in item 2, identify all of the terms that need to be operationally defined. Operationally define any two of these terms.

4. Write one hypothesis for this research based on the problem statement. Write the hypothesis first in the null form, then in an alternative nondirectional form, and finally in an alternative directional form.

✎ **Exercise 1–16** After reading articles in several professional magazines about how teachers in many school classrooms treat girls differently from boys, a middle school principal decides to explore whether or not that situation exists in her school. Since a few of the articles pointed out that the differential treatment of boys and girls is more pronounced in mathematics and science classes, the principal plans to compare how teachers' treatment of girls differs from the treatment of boys, and further to compare that treatment across different subjects. Specifically, the principal will count the number of times girls and boys are called on in class, the number of times girls and boys are given feedback for a response, the number of times a teacher stands "near to" a student (i.e., proximity), and the number of times girls and boys are given individualized help with schoolwork.

1. Write a problem statement for this research.

2. Identify the relevant variables and label them as *independent, dependent, intervening, control, predictor,* or *criterion* variables.

3. From the set of variables listed in item 2, identify all terms that need to be operationally defined. Operationally define any two of these terms.

4. Write one hypothesis for this research based on the problem statement. Write the hypothesis first in the null form, then in an alternative nondirectional form, and finally in an alternative directional form.

✎ **Exercise 1–17** The supervisor of the school lunch program believes that the way the servers interact with the students as they go through the lunch line may affect the students' attitudes toward the meal and may influence the students' verbal behavior toward the servers and the amount of food they actually eat. The supervisor decides to observe as the servers help two fourth-grade classes. The supervisor intends to record the number of server-initiated positive verbal comments to each student and the student verbal comments to or about the servers. The supervisor will also record the amount of food remaining on each lunch tray when it is returned to the kitchen by the student. The record of server comments, student comments, and the record of food thrown away will then be correlated.

1. Write a problem statement for this research.

2. Identify the relevant variables and label them as *independent, dependent, intervening, control, predictor,* or *criterion* variables.

3. From the set of variables listed in item 2, identify all terms that need to be operationally defined. Operationally define any two of these terms.

4. Write one hypothesis for this research based on the problem statement. Write the hypothesis first in the null form, then in an alternative nondirectional form, and finally in an alternative directional form.

✎ **Exercise 1–18** Undergraduate students are considering buying the student store at their university. Traditionally, the student store has been owned and operated by the university; however, the university has offered to sell the store to the students. The student congress is concerned about its ability to run the store at a profit. Its members decide to study universities that are similar in size to theirs where students own and operate the student store profitably. The student congress will survey student stores that typically sell the types of items which it is interested in selling—books, school supplies, computers, and imprint items. From these universities, it will gather information on economic status of students according to annual income reported on student loan information and the number of competing off-campus student stores. This information will be used to determine if the student congress can expect to earn a profit, if it were to purchase the student store.

1. Write a problem statement for this research.

2. Identify the relevant variables and label them as *independent, dependent, intervening, control, predictor,* or *criterion* variables.

3. From the set of variables listed in item 2, identify all of the terms that need to be operationally defined. Operationally define any two of these terms.

4. Write one hypothesis for this research based on the problem statement. Write the hypothesis first in the null form, then in an alternative nondirectional form, and finally in an alternative directional form.

✎ **Exercise 1–19** Historically, the students in a high school have raised money to enable them to participate in field trips like the senior trip. The school board has continued to receive complaints from the community on what community members deem to be excessive fund-raising activities. As a result, the school board is considering passing a resolution that would curtail fund-raising activities, and students would finance their own field trips. However, the board is concerned that some students will be unable to finance their own senior trips and may not be able to participate. The board decides to study field trip financial data from other school districts of similar socioeconomic status. It will do a comparative study of districts that fully finance the field trips through fund-raising and those districts in which students finance their own senior trips to determine the percentage of students who participate in the senior class field trip. Districts in which field trips are funded by a combination of self-finance and fund-raising will be eliminated from the study.

1. Write a problem statement for this research.

2. Identify the relevant variables and label them as *independent, dependent, intervening, control, predictor,* or *criterion* variables.

3. From the set of variables listed in item 2, identify all of the terms that need to be operationally defined. Operationally define any two of these terms.

4. Write one hypothesis for this research based on the problem statement. Write the hypothesis first in the null form, then in an alternative nondirectional form, and finally in an alternative directional form.

Exercise 1–20   The university foundation is interested in increasing contributions of undergraduate students within the first five years after they graduate. It decides to do a comparative study of students in the College of Natural Sciences and Mathematics and the College of Education who gain employment within three months after they graduate. The foundation personnel believe that the dollar amount contribution is related to salary. Graduates in sciences and mathematics are employed at higher salaries than are teachers. They believe that a differentiated campaign for various majors is needed given the variability in beginning salaries. The male and female graduates from the five previous years will be studied. Through a career services survey, data for employment and starting salary of the graduates will be obtained. These data will be analyzed in relationship to the contributions to the university foundation.

1. Write a problem statement for this research.

2. Identify the relevant variables and label them as *independent, dependent, intervening, control, predictor,* or *criterion* variables.

3. From the set of variables listed in item 2, identify all of the terms that need to be operationally defined. Operationally define any two of these terms.

4. Write one hypothesis for this research based on the problem statement. Write the hypothesis first in the null form, then in an alternative nondirectional form, and finally in an alternative directional form.

ANSWERS TO RESEARCH PROBLEM EXERCISES

Answers to Exercises in Analyzing Research Situations

 *Exercise 1–1*

1. "A researcher is interested in determining whether or not there are differences in students' classroom participation as a result of the kind of feedback provided by the teacher."

2. a. Gender of teacher   Intervening variable
    b. Gender of student   Control variable
    c. Frequency of voluntary participation   Dependent variable
    d. Feedback group   Independent variable
    e. Age of Student   Intervening variable
    f. Student's enthusiasm for the subject   Intervening variable

3. Feedback, voluntary participation. Note: Some variables have a defin-
    ition that is obvious, and it is therefore not necessary to provide an
    operational definition for them. For example, "gender," "age," and
    "grade" require no operational definition because their meaning is
    clear without an operational definition. Definitions for such variables
    will not be provided in the answer section of this book.

4. a. Irrelevant
    b. Irrelevant
    c. Irrelevant
    d. Relevant   Null
    e. Relevant   Alternative, directional
    f. Irrelevant

✎ Exercise 1–2

1. "The transportation director plans to determine whether or not the
    computerized system results in fewer complaints."

2. a. Bus driver's experience   Intervening variable
    b. Bus driver's age   Intervening variable
    c. Student's educational level   Control variable
    d. Method of scheduling   Independent variable
    e. Number of complaints   Dependent variable
    f. Parents' income   Intervening variable

3. Complaints, method of scheduling

4. a. Relevant   Alternative, directional
    b. Irrelevant
    c. Irrelevant
    d. Irrelevant
    e. Relevant   Null
    f. Irrelevant

✎ Exercise 1–3

1. "The coordinator of university field experiences will conduct a
    research study to determine whether one program or the other leads
    to greater enthusiasm for teaching as a career. Of secondary interest is

whether or not there are differences in enthusiasm between elementary and secondary majors."

2. a. Gender of the student   Intervening variable
    b. Field experience group   Independent variable
    c. Student's age   Intervening variable
    d. Amount of prior experience   Intervening variable
        working with children
    e. Level of enthusiasm   Dependent variable
    f. Student's major   Control variable

3. Level of enthusiasm, field experience group

4. a. Irrelevant
    b. Relevant   Alternative, directional
    c. Relevant   Null
    d. Irrelevant
    e. Relevant   Alternative, nondirectional
    f. Irrelevant

✎ Exercise 1–4

1. ". . . a teacher hopes to determine if a 'hands-on' science process curriculum will produce higher achievement and more favorable attitudes toward science than a conventional 'text-based' curriculum."

2. a. Student's science achievement score   Dependent variable
    b. Student's IQ score   Intervening variable
    c. Science curriculum   Independent variable
    d. Teacher effectiveness   Intervening variable
    e. Student's attitude toward science   Dependent variable
    f. Student's gender   Control variable

3. Science achievement score, attitude toward science

4. a. Irrelevant
    b. Relevant   Alternative, nondirectional
    c. Irrelevant
    d. Irrelevant
    e. Irrelevant
    f. Relevant   Null

✎ Exercise 1–5

1. "A researcher is interested in studying the effects on student test performance of different types of preparation for the National Teachers Examination (Praxis Series) offered by a statewide commercial learning center."

2. a. Gender of student   Control variable
   b. Type of preparation   Independent variable
   c. Region of the state   Control variable
   d. Class designation   Control variable
   e. Student performance on the exam   Dependent variable
   f. Number of times the student took   Intervening variable
      the exam

3. Type of preparation, student performance, region of the state

4. a. Relevant   Null
   b. Irrelevant
   c. Irrelevant
   d. Relevant   Alternative, nondirectional
   e. Irrelevant
   f. Relevant   Alternative, directional

✎ Exercise 1–6

1. "A college of education is interested in determining whether or not the portfolio that students have to prepare is being used in the initial screening interviews."

2. a. Quality of the portfolio   Intervening variable
   b. Interaction of the dyad   Dependent variable
   c. Training of interviewer/researcher   Intervening variable
   d. Question that prompted use of   Independent variable
      the portfolio
   e. Gender of the interviewer   Intervening variable
   f. Gender of interviewee   Intervening variable

3. Interaction of the dyad, question that prompted use of the portfolio

4. a. Relevant   Alternative, directional
   b. Irrelevant
   c. Irrelevant
   d. Relevant   Alternative, nondirectional
   e. Relevant   Alternative, directional

✎ Exercise 1–7

1. "An elementary school principal is interested in assessing parent satisfaction with the flow of information from the school under two plans."

2. a. Flow of information   Independent variable
   b. Parent-teacher conferences   Control variable

      c.   Papers sent home as checked   Independent variable
      d.   Folio of papers sent home at the end   Independent variable
           of the week
      e.   Parent satisfaction   Dependent variable

3.   Flow of information: papers sent home when checked, folio of papers sent home at the end of the week, parent satisfaction

4.   a.   Relevant   Alternative, directional
      b.   Relevant   Null
      c.   Irrelevant
      d.   Irrelevant
      e.   Irrelevant

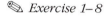 *Exercise 1–8*

1.   "The director of technology believes that a crucial issue in terms of whether teachers use the technology is in-service training."

2.   a.   School district   Control variable
      b.   Gender of the teacher   Intervening variable
      c.   Type of technology   Intervening variable
      d.   In-service training   Independent variable
      e.   Checkout of equipment   Dependent variable

3.   In-service training, checkout of equipment, type of technology

4.   a.   Relevant   Alternative, directional
      b.   Irrelevant
      c.   Irrelevant
      d.   Irrelevant
      e.   Relevant   Alternative, nondirectional

Exercise 1–9

1.   "A high school principal is interested in finding out whether or not there is any connection between the extent of students' participation in extracurricular activities and their academic grades."

2.   a.   Academic grades   Criterion variable
      b.   Students' IQ scores   Control variable
      c.   Gender of student   Control variable
      d.   Parents' income   Intervening variable
      e.   Type of extracurricular activity   Control variable
      f.   Number of hours of extracurricular   Predictor variable
           participation

3. Academic grades, hours of extracurricular participation, type of extracurricular activity

4. a. Relevant   Null
    b. Irrelevant
    c. Irrelevant
    d. Irrelevant
    e. Irrelevant
    f. Relevant   Alternative, directional

✎ *Exercise 1–10*

1. "The director of reading in a school district believes that knowledge of the alphabet and chronological age at entry into first grade are important factors in predicting success in reading."

2. a. Gender of the student   Control variable
    b. Socioeconomic status   Intervening variable
    c. Kindergarten experiences   Intervening variable
    d. Knowledge of the alphabet   Predictor variable
    e. Chronological age in September   Predictor variable
    f. Reading achievement score in May   Criterion variable

3. Knowledge of the alphabet, chronological age, reading achievement score

4. a. Relevant   Alternative, directional
    b. Relevant   Null
    c. Irrelevant
    d. Irrelevant
    e. Relevant   Alternative, nondirectional

Answers to Exercises in Writing Research Problems

✎ *Exercise 1–11*

1. The purpose of this research is to determine whether or not there are differences in comprehension and retention of information as a result of presenting that information pictorially rather than textually.

2. a. Mode of presentation (pictures or text)   Independent variable
    b. Comprehension   Dependent variable
    c. Retention   Dependent variable

    Note: Since the number of potential intervening, control, and moderator variables is virtually unlimited, there will be no attempt to list them unless the description of the research situation in the exercise explicitly mentions a variable, in which case it will be categorized appropriately.

3. Comprehension, retention

    Comprehension—the number of questions answered correctly on an instructor-made (or standardized) test pertaining to the information, administered right after the pictorial or textual presentation.

    Retention—the number of questions answered correctly on the same test, administered some specified time (e.g., one month) after the presentation.

    Note: Mode of presentation is already operationally defined, although there is probably a need for more specificity with regard to the characteristics of the pictorial and textual presentations. For example, a picture could be a photograph, a line drawing, or a cartoon.

4. Null hypothesis: There will be no difference in comprehension or retention between those learners who received a pictorial presentation of the information and those who received a textual presentation of the information.

    Alternative nondirectional hypothesis: There will be a significant difference in comprehension and retention between those learners who received pictorial presentation and those who received textual presentation of the information.

    Alternative directional hypothesis: Those learners who received a pictorial presentation of the information will have higher comprehension and retention scores than the learners who received a textual presentation of the information.

✎ *Exercise 1–12*

1. The purpose of this research is to find out if assigning, grading, and reviewing homework every day leads to greater mathematics learning, improved attitudes toward mathematics, or greater confidence in students.

2. a. Homework condition (daily or none)   Independent variable
    b. Mathematics learning   Dependent variable
    c. Attitude toward mathematics   Dependent variable
    d. Confidence   Dependent variable

3. Mathematics learning, attitude toward mathematics, confidence

    Mathematics learning—the student's score on a teacher-made or standardized mathematics achievement test.

Attitude toward mathematics—score on a rating scale attained by the teacher's (or an independent observer's) observations of students as they worked on mathematics.

Confidence—score on a rating scale score administered by the teacher following a unit of instruction.

There is probably no need to operationally define homework condition, since it is implicit in the problem statement as being either "daily" or "none."

4. Null hypothesis: There will be no difference between the mathematics grades of students who do no homework and the mathematics grades of students who are assigned daily homework assignments.

Alternative nondirectional hypothesis: There will be a significant difference between the mathematics grades of students who do no homework and the mathematics grades of students who are assigned daily homework assignments.

Alternative directional hypothesis: Students who are assigned daily homework will attain higher mathematics grades than will students who do not receive homework assignments.

✎ *Exercise 1–13*

1. The purpose of this research is to determine whether or not certain student factors (e.g., grades, extent of participation in extracurricular activities, popularity) are related to, and predictive of, being elected to the student council.

2. a. Grades   Predictor variable
    b. Election/nonelection to student council   Criterion variable
    c. Extent of participation in activities   Predictor variable
    d. Popularity   Predictor variable

3. Grades, extent of participation in activities, popularity

   Grades—the student's overall grade point average to date.

   Extent of participation—the average number of hours per week that a student spends in practice/rehearsal, meetings, or other form of participation in a school-sponsored extracurricular activity.

   Popularity—a "popularity" score from a researcher-designed peer rating scale. (Note: This scale should be tested for reliability and validity.)

4. Null hypothesis: There will be no relationship between whether or not a student is elected to the student council and any of the following variables: grades, extent of participation in activities, or popularity.

Alternative nondirectional hypothesis: There will be a correlation, either positive or negative, between a student's grades and whether or not he or she is elected to the student council.

Alternative directional hypothesis: There will be a positive correlation between a student's popularity and whether or not he or she is elected to the student council.

✎ Exercise 1–14

1. A district could save more money by buying from a local supplier rather than having school supply companies bid for the order.

2.   a. Cost of orders   Dependent variable
     b. Supplies to be ordered   Independent variable
     c. Dates of price lists   Intervening variable

3. Local supplier, school supplies

   Local supplier—a school supply company in the same county as the school district.

   School supplies—items found in a catalog of a company that sells school supplies, such as paper, pencils, markers, maps, computer software.

4. Null hypothesis: There will be no difference in the cost of bid and non-bid school supplies.

   Alternative, nondirectional hypothesis: There will be a significant difference in the cost of bid and non-bid supplies.

   Alternative, directional hypothesis: The cost of school supplies will be less when purchased locally through non-bid procedures as compared with bid procedures.

✎ Exercise 1–15

1. A high school band director believes that playing in the band influences interest in the type of music that the band plays.

2.   a. Type of music for leisure listening   Dependent variable
     b. Member/nonmember of the band   Independent variable
     c. Influence of the band director   Control variable

3. Type of music for leisure listening, member/nonmember of the band, influence of the band director

   Type of music for leisure listening—music for listening that is not required; source could be a tape, CD, radio, or TV.

Member/nonmember of the band—whether or not a student does or does not play an instrument in any school musical group.

Influence of the band director—the band director's effect on students in the band.

4. Null hypothesis: There will be no difference in the type of music chosen for leisure listening of the band members and nonmembers.

   Alternative, nondirectional hypothesis: There will be a significant difference in the type of music chosen for leisure listening of band members and nonmembers.

   Alternative, directional hypothesis: Band members who play jazz will choose jazz for leisure listening more often than band nonmembers.

✎ Exercise 1–16

1. The purpose of this study is to find out whether or not teachers' treatment of boys and girls differs, and whether or not any difference in treatment is the same in different subjects.

2. a. Gender of student   Independent variable
   b. Subject (i.e., math, science)   Independent variable
   c. Frequency of calling on a student   Dependent variable
   d. Frequency of providing feedback   Dependent variable
   e. Frequency of proximity   Dependent variable
   f. Frequency of offering individualized help   Dependent variable

3. Frequency of providing feedback, frequency of proximity

   Frequency of providing feedback—an instance of feedback will be counted whenever the teacher makes a comment or gesture that clearly indicates he or she heard the student's response and clearly indicates to the student that the response was correct or incorrect. Only one instance of feedback will be counted for each student response.

   Frequency of proximity—an instance of proximity will be counted whenever the teacher stops, for at least one second, within one arm's length of student. A teacher may provide proximity to several students at the same time, depending on the teacher's location when he or she stops.

4. Null hypothesis: There will be no differences between boys and girls in terms of the frequency with which they are called on, provided feedback, provided proximity, or offered individualized help.

   Alternative nondirectional hypothesis: The frequency with which they are called on, the amount of feedback given, the amount of proximity provided, and the amount of individual help offered will be significantly different for boys and girls.

Alternative directional hypothesis: On average, teachers will: call on, provide feedback to, provide proximity to, and offer individualized help to boys more frequently than girls.

✎ *Exercise 1–17*

1. The purpose of this investigation is to see if there is any relationship between the way lunchroom servers interact with students, the students' verbal behavior, and the amount of food that is wasted.

2. a. Server-initiated positive verbal comments   Predictor variable
    b. Student positive verbal comments   Criterion variable
    c. Amount of food wasted   Criterion variable

3. Server-initiated positive verbal comments, student positive verbal comments, amount of food wasted

    Server-initiated positive verbal comments—an instance will be counted every time a server makes a comment that is polite, friendly, helpful, and so on. Examples would include greetings, positive comments about appearance, and the use of overtly polite terms (e.g., please, thank you).

    Student positive verbal comments—an instance will be counted any time a student makes a polite, friendly, or similar comment to, or about, the server or about the food or lunchroom environment.

    Amount of food wasted—the estimated percentage of the total original serving that remains on the tray when it is returned to the kitchen.

4. Null hypothesis: There will be no correlation between server-initiated positive verbal comments to students and either student positive verbal comments or the amount of food wasted.

    Alternative nondirectional hypothesis: Student positive verbal comments and the amount of food wasted will be correlated to the number of server-initiated positive verbal comments to students.

    Alternative directional hypothesis: There will be a positive correlation between server-initiated positive verbal comments to students and student positive verbal comments to servers, and there will be a negative correlation between server-initiated positive verbal comments to students and the amount of food wasted.

✎ *Exercise 1–18*

1. The purpose of this research is to study universities that are similar in size to theirs where students own and operate the student store profitably.

2. a. Student economic status   Predictor variable
    b. Number of competing stores off-campus   Predictor variable
    c. Margin of profit   Criterion variable
    d. Size of the university   Control variable
    e. Types of items sold in the student store   Control variable

3. Student economic status, competing student stores off-campus, size of university, types of items sold in the student store

    Student economic status—annual income of family or self as indicated on student loan information

    Competing student stores off-campus—student stores within a one-mile radius of the campus

    Size of the university—student enrollment

    Types of items sold in the student store—books, school supplies, computers, and imprint items.

4. Null hypothesis: Student economic status and number of competing student stores off-campus will not predict the margin of profit of the student store.

    Alternative, nondirectional hypothesis: Student economic status and number of competing stores off-campus will predict whether the student store does or does not earn a profit.

    Alternative, directional hypothesis: Student economic status and number of competing student stores off-campus will predict the margin of profit of the student store.

✎ *Exercise 1–19*

1. The purpose of this research is to study field trip data to determine the feasibility of students' financing their own senior trip without the benefit of fund-raising activities.

2. a. Field trips financed by self-funding   Independent variable
    b. Field trips financed by fund-raising   Independent variable
    c. District socioeconomic status   Control variable
    d. Size of school district   Control variable
    e. Percent of students participating in trip   Dependent variable

3. Student self-funding, fund-raising, district socioeconomic status, size of the school district

   Student self-funding—students contribute 100 percent of the cost of the trip.

   Fund raising—school-sponsored fund-raising activities, such as bake sales, car washes, and candy sales

   District socioeconomic status—dollar reimbursement from the state

   Size of the school district—number of public school students at all levels

4. Null hypothesis: There will be no difference in the percentage of students who participate in the senior trip regardless of funding method.

   Alternative, nondirectional hypothesis: There will be a significant difference in the percentage of students who participate in the senior trip as determined by the method of funding.

   Alternative, directional hypothesis: A greater percentage of students who have opportunities for fund-raising activities to finance their senior field trip will participate in the trip as compared with students who self-fund the trip.

✎ Exercise 1–20

1. The purpose of this research is to study the relationship of contributions to the foundation from graduates of the College of Natural Sciences and Mathematics and the College of Education.

2.
a.	Contributions of undergraduate graduates	Dependent variable
b.	Beginning employment salaries	Independent variable
c.	Undergraduate colleges	Control variable
d.	Gender of the graduate	Control variable
e.	Graduates for the five previous years	Control variable
f.	Satisfaction with undergraduate education	Intervening variable

3. Contributions of undergraduate graduates, beginning employment salaries

   Contributions of undergraduate graduates—dollar amount contributed to the foundation.

   Beginning employment salaries—salary earned at the beginning of employment.

4. Null hypothesis: Contributions of graduates of the College of Natural Sciences and Mathematics and the College of Education to the university foundation will be the same.

Alternative, nondirectional hypothesis: Contributions of graduates of the College of Natural Sciences and Mathematics and the College of Education will differ significantly.

Alternative, directional hypothesis: Graduates of the College of Natural Sciences and Mathematics will contribute more to the university foundation than will graduates of the College of Education.

SUMMARY

This chapter addressed what, for many researchers, is the initial task in any research situation; that is, the identification of the research problem, including specifying the problem statement; identifying, categorizing, and defining the variables; and stating the hypotheses. Since many of the procedures used in a research study depend on the nature of the research problem, clearly understanding these elements of a research problem is an essential, but often overlooked, aspect of analyzing and/or designing research studies.

The exercises in this chapter were intended to provide practice in clarifying the essential aspects of the research problem. Chapter 2 will provide practice in choosing a research approach that is appropriate to the identified research problem.

2 SELECTING A RESEARCH APPROACH

INTRODUCTION

Research approaches can be classified in a variety of ways, for example, according to the nature of the data being collected or with respect to the nature of the question being asked.

NATURE OF THE DATA

When researchers distinguish research approaches according to the nature of the data being collected and analyzed, they often use the terms **quantitative** and **qualitative** (Bogdan & Bilken, 1992). According to Berg (1989, 1994), **quantitative** refers to research that involves measuring traits, characteristics, or attributes of things. **Qualitative** refers to research that involves the meanings, concepts, definitions, characteristics, metaphors, symbols, and description of things.

For example, if the researcher is collecting numerical data about individuals or groups, say height and weight, and expects to transform the numbers into mean (or average) scores for a group, then we usually refer to that research as quantitative. If, on the other hand, the researcher is planning to interview people to identify their health status and their exercise habits, and will transcribe the verbal responses of those interviews in order to characterize the habits of the group, we refer to that research as qualitative.

TYPES OF RESEARCH QUESTIONS

Another way of classifying research pertains to the nature of the question that the researcher is interested in answering. **Descriptive research** has as its goal "the careful mapping out of a situation or set of events in order to describe what is happening behaviorally" (Rosenthal & Rosnow, 1991, p. 10). If, for example, a researcher wants to identify the amount of time each week that typical American adults spend in various activities, including exercise, we would call that research descriptive.

Relational research has as its focus the identification of how changes in one characteristic or variable correspond (or do not correspond) to changes in another characteristic or variable. If, using an earlier example, a researcher is interested in finding out whether or not there is any relationship between exercise habits and health status (or between height and weight measurements) for a group of people, we would call that research relational.

Causal-comparative research has as its focus the identification of causes and effects. If, for example, a researcher wants to know if more exercise results in people being healthier, he or she might design a study where people were assigned to different groups, each of which was led in different amounts of exercise. By comparing the health status of the groups, after some time had passed, the researcher could infer the extent to which differences in exercise cause health status differences in people. Such a study would be considered causal-comparative.

Table 2–1 illustrates the relationship among the categories of research approaches just described and provides some examples of techniques classified according to these approaches.

COMPETENCIES

The exercises provided in this chapter will help you identify the various research approaches employed in studies and provide you with practice in choosing an approach that is appropriate to the purpose of proposed research. After completing the exercises in this chapter, you will be able to

- Define quantitative research
- Define qualitative research

TABLE 2–1 Classification of Research Approaches by Type of Data and Question

	Type of Research Question		
	Descriptive	**Relational**	**Causal-comparative**
Quantitative Data	Uses numerical data (e.g. mean, median) to describe a variable	Uses numerical data (e.g., correlation coefficient) to show a relationship among variables	Uses numerical data (e.g., critical ratio) to establish a cause and effect connection among variables
Qualitative Data	Uses verbal reports to describe a trait, characteristic, or phenomenon	Uses verbal reports to show how traits are related to each other	Uses verbal reports to establish a cause and effect connection among phenomena

- Identify a qualitative research approach in a study
- Identify a quantitative research approach in a study
- Describe how a researcher might choose to use a qualitative approach
- Describe how a researcher might choose to use a quantitative approach
- Define and explain the purpose of descriptive research
- Define and explain the purpose of correlational research
- Define and explain the purpose of causal-comparative research
- Identify a descriptive research approach in a study
- Identify a relational research approach in a study
- Identify a causal-comparative research approach in a study
- Analyze a given research problem for possible research approaches
- Recommend the appropriate research approach for a given research problem
- Classify research studies according to the type of question being studied and the nature of the data being collected

RESEARCH APPROACH EXERCISES

Two types of exercises are included in this chapter. The first is
intended to provide practice in identification and classification of a
research approach, given a description of a study. The second type
of exercise is intended to provide practice in analysis of research
problems and recommendations for choosing the research approach
most appropriate for the given situation.

   As you complete each exercise, use the following "blank" chart
to classify each exercise by placing the exercise number in the appropriate column and row on the chart.

Exercises in Identification and Classification of a Research Approach

For each research study described in the following section, identify
the type of research question as either descriptive, relational, or
causal-comparative; and further, decide whether the data used are
qualitative or quantitative. Give a rationale for your answer.

Chart for Classifying Research Approach Exercises

Place the exercise number for each exercise in the appropriate column and row.

	Type of Research Question		
	Descriptive	**Relational**	**Causal-comparative**
Quantitative Data			
Qualitative Data			

✎ **Exercise 2–1**   A school district director of staff development wants to identify the preferences of teachers in the district for staff development activities. The plan is to examine the enrollments in previous staff development programs and in-service workshops in order to identify trends or patterns among teachers of various backgrounds regarding their preferences for types of staff development activities.

> What type of research question is the director asking in this proposed study?
>
> What type of data would the director collect to answer the research question?
>
> Briefly describe how the study might be carried out.

✎ **Exercise 2–2**   A teacher is interested in determining whether there is a connection between how much television children watch and their performance in school.

> What type of research question is the teacher probably asking in this research?
>
> What type of data would the teacher collect to answer the research question?
>
> Briefly describe how the teacher is likely to employ the chosen research approach.

✎ **Exercise 2–3**   A science teacher has formed two groups of students for instruction in a unit on plants and has assigned different types of activities to each group. One group will conduct a series of "experiments" on plant growth, while the other group will observe and/or collect plant samples from around the school. The teacher wishes to examine the students' journals, reports, and notebooks to see which, if either, set of activities resulted in greater student progress.

> What type of research question is being asked by the teacher?
>
> What type of data will the teacher most likely collect in conducting this classroom "action research"?

✎ **Exercise 2–4**   The student congress on a large university campus is concerned about the delivery of health services. There are two health centers on campus, but students who are ill must sometimes wait two or three days to see a doctor, unless it is an emergency situation.

    The student congress commissions a researcher to determine if there is a significant difference in terms of how long students must wait to see a doctor at the two health centers. Students are randomly assigned to one of the health centers for health care when each new academic year begins, so no assignments to health centers need to be made. At both health centers, the researcher will keep a log of the "wait time" before seeing a doctor. At the North Health Center, students are permitted to walk in and sign a waiting list. They remain on-site until they meet with a doctor. At the South Health Center, students must call for appointments. At this center at peak times, such as during flu season, a student may need to wait for two to three days before seeing a doctor. Following collection of data for a full semester, the "wait times" will be statistically compared to see if there is a significant difference.

What type of research question is being asked?

What type of data will the researcher most likely collect in conducting this research?

✎ **Exercise 2–5** In a variation on the study of the health centers described in Exercise 2–4, no quantitative data will be collected. Instead, students who use health services will evaluate the quality of the service at the health centers through an exit questionnaire each time they visit the center. Carefully constructed open-ended questions will assess their perceived sense of whether the service was delivered quickly enough to meet their needs. Following collection of questionnaire data for a full semester, the students' perceptions of expediency of service at the two health centers will be compared. The results will be presented in narrative form.

What type of research question is being asked?

What type of data will the researcher most likely collect in conducting this research?

✎ **Exercise 2–6** An education department wants to assess the writing skills of students admitted to its program. During orientation, students will write an essay in which they are to explain why they want to be teachers. Essays will be evaluated by raters, who will use a checklist to note characteristics of writing, including such items as a well-developed theme, logical sequence, introduction, and conclusion or summary. The checklist will be used to write a brief narrative that characterizes the student's writing.

Evaluating these essays is time-consuming for departmental faculty. Therefore, they would like their graduate assistants to help with the evaluation of the essays. Both faculty and graduate assistants have been trained in scoring using the method described. Since this is the first time that graduate assistants have evaluated essays, the faculty would like to have two evaluations of each essay, one by a faculty member and one by a graduate assistant. They plan to compare the results of these evaluations.

What type of research question is being asked?

What type of data will the researcher most likely collect in conducting this research?

✎ **Exercise 2–7**   The Freshman Experience Committee is interested in comparing students' freshman year overall grade point averages with their grade point averages at the time of graduation from college to determine if a relationship exists between the two grade point averages.

What type of research question is being asked?

What type of data would be used to make the comparison?

Exercises in Analyzing and Recommending a Research Approach

In each of the following exercises you will be directed to collect either qualitative or quantitative data. Indicate whether the study is descriptive, relational, or causal-comparative, and briefly describe how this study might be carried out using the approach recommended.

✎ **Exercise 2–8**   A school superintendent would like to encourage more professional reading among the faculty in the school district. Before implementing a program to encourage professional reading, the superintendent realizes that there is no baseline information for determining the current practices of district faculty regarding professional reading and asks for your help in determining the "baseline."

Considering the purpose of the proposed staff development program and the probable use for the baseline information, what research approach would you recommend to the superintendent for identifying the "baseline"? Choose an approach that is quantitative.

Characterize the study according to the type of research question.

Describe briefly how the approach you recommend would be implemented.

✎ **Exercise 2–9**   For the same research question described in Exercise 2–8, choose an approach that is qualitative rather than quantitative.

Characterize the study according to the type of research question.

Describe briefly how the approach you recommend would be implemented.

✎ **Exercise 2–10**   Pizza is a popular choice for lunch and dinner at a university. However, a major complaint is about the inconsistency in the crust of the pizza. Students complain that sometimes the pizza crust has too much dough and at other times is too thin. Once the food service manager determines that pizza makers are being consistent in weighing the portion of dough for each pizza, she decides to determine if the dough is spread evenly across the pizza pan. As the pizza comes out of the oven, she rates the consistency of the pizza crust by observation, according to the following standard of preparation: (1) 76 to 100 percent consistent thickness, (2) 51 to 75 percent consistent thickness, (3) 26 to 50 percent consistent thickness, (4) 0 to 25 percent consistent thickness.

Characterize the study according to the type of research question.

Choose an approach for analyzing these data that is quantitative.

Describe briefly how the approach might be implemented to answer the research question.

✎ **Exercise 2–11**   A highway safety science program coordinator in a high school wants to focus on the effect of distractions on reaction time. The school has a laboratory where students have driving experiences through simulations. When engaged in the simulations, unexpected distractions, such as a dog crossing the highway or a light suddenly turning red, are randomly interspersed in the visual displays. The coordinator plans a quantitative study to collect reaction time to distractions data and reaction time to expected events data while students are engaged in simulated driving to emphasize the difference in the reaction times.

Characterize the study according to the type of research question.

Describe briefly how the approach might be implemented to answer the research question.

✎ **Exercise 2–12**   Student teachers in a college of education are attending IST (Instructional Support Team) training. They are required to keep a journal of their reactions to the training and its application to accommodating at-risk students. Using a qualitative approach, the trainers will analyze the journals over the period of one semester to determine if attitudes about support for at-risk students have changed as a result of participation in the program.

Characterize the study according to the type of research question.

Describe briefly how the approach might be implemented to answer the research question.

✎ **Exercise 2–13**   There are indications that a child in a third-grade class is being physically abused by someone outside of the school setting. Bruises are sometimes evident on the child's face and arms. The teacher needs more concrete evidence to report this suspicion to the home-school visitor. He decides to record the child's condition each day, using a qualitative approach.

Characterize the study according to the type of research question.

Describe briefly how the approach might be implemented to answer the research question.

✎ **Exercise 2–14**   It has been noted that teachers who volunteer to serve on curriculum committees seem to have a knowledge of current literature. A lead teacher who is interested in this topic decides to assess the relationship between the types of journals read for professional reading and volunteerism for committees. He designs a survey to send to teachers who vary in the extent to which they volunteer to serve on committees. Part of the survey in this qualitative study includes a question about the types of professional journals that are read.

Characterize the study according to the type of research question.

Describe briefly how the approach might be implemented to answer the research question.

✎ **Exercise 2–15**   The administration of a school district is concerned about the large number of student absences. One board member has suggested that there may be a relationship between the distance students travel by bus to school and the number of absences. The district is large, and the administration feels that a quantitative study of this issue would be worth pursuing.

Characterize the study according to the type of research question.

Describe briefly how the approach might be implemented to answer the research question.

✎ **Exercise 2–16**   The reading curriculum committee of a school district has decided, as its agenda for the academic year, to work on increasing students' abilities to answer higher-level questions. A consultant to the district has suggested a home reading program where students interact with parents about what they have read. The district implements a design that has as its focus a weekly plan in which a parent discusses a book with the child. Parents are to be trained in discussion techniques. The district administration wonders if the additional reading at home relates to answering higher-level questions at school and determines that a qualitative study of this program should be conducted.

Characterize the study according to the type of research question.

Describe briefly how the approach might be implemented to answer the research question.

✎ **Exercise 2–17**   The superintendent of a school district is interested in determining the attitudes and feelings of faculty and administrative staff in the district toward the school reform effort called Outcomes Based Education (OBE). Her plan is to conduct a qualitative study, using an open-ended (i.e., free-response) survey form to elicit attitudes, feelings, and opinions about various aspects of OBE.

Characterize the study according to the type of research question.

Describe briefly how the approach might be implemented to answer the research question.

ANSWERS TO RESEARCH APPROACH EXERCISES

The following is the completed chart for classifying the research approach exercises. This chart is followed by answers to the individual exercises.

Completed Chart for Classifying Research Approach Exercises

The number for each exercise has been placed in the appropriate column and row.

	Type of Research Question		
	Descriptive	**Relational**	**Causal-comparative**
Quantitative Data	2–1	2–2	2–4
	2–8	2–7	2–11
	2–10	2–15	
Qualitative Data	2–9	2–6	2–3
	2–13	2–16	2–5
	2–17	2–14	2–12

Answers to Exercises in Identification and Classification of a Research Approach

✎ *Exercise 2–1*   Since the purpose is to describe trends and patterns, the research approach most likely to be used is descriptive. Because enrollment information involves numerical data, the research approach would also be considered quantitative.

The director will probably look at the number of teachers who had enrolled in various staff development programs and then, for each activity (or type of activity), will probably compare the numbers of teachers from different backgrounds (e.g., elementary vs. secondary).

✎ *Exercise 2–2*   Since the teacher is looking for a possible connection, or relationship, between two variables (i.e., amount of television watched and school performance), the most likely research approach is relational. Since the data to be collected are most probably numerical, the study would also be considered quantitative.

The teacher will probably collect numerical data from a group of children that indicate the amount of television they watch; for the same children, the teacher will probably record some numerical measure of school performance.

✎ *Exercise 2–3*   Because the teacher is manipulating the group activity and is interested in determining whether or not those activities made a difference in student learning, the research approach would be categorized as causal-comparative. The data the teacher plans to use (i.e., journals, reports, and notebooks) are verbal. Therefore, the research approach would also be considered qualitative.

✎ *Exercise 2–4*   Because the researcher is interested in determining whether the method of admitting students to the health centers affects the "wait time," the type of research question is causal-comparative. Since numerical data will be analyzed to determine if there is a significant difference, the type of data collected would be classified as quantitative.

✎ *Exercise 2–5*   Since the researcher is interested in determining if the method of admitting students to the health centers produces differences in students' judgments of the expediency of care, the type of research question would be classified as causal-comparative. The research would further be classified as qualitative, because the narrative questionnaire data would be analyzed.

✎ *Exercise 2–6*   Because the purpose of the research is to determine the relationship between the ratings of two raters, the research would be categorized as relational. Since the data being collected are in narrative (i.e., verbal) form, this research would be classified as qualitative. The verbal evaluations of each rater's scoring of an essay will be compared to see if they are similar (i.e., to see if they are related). The nature and strength of this relationship would be described in narrative form to establish the degree of consistency among raters.

✎ *Exercise 2–7* Since these grade point averages will be correlated to determine the relationship, the research question would be classified as relational. Numerical data are being correlated, indicating that this is a quantitative study.

Answers to Exercises in Analyzing and Recommending a Research Approach

✎ *Exercise 2–8* Since the purpose of the baseline information is to describe the current status of professional reading activities of district faculty, the research question would be classified as descriptive. Since the superintendent can collect either numerical data (e.g., by surveying faculty regarding their professional reading) or verbal data (e.g., by interviewing or observing faculty with respect to professional reading), the superintendent could use either a quantitative or a qualitative approach.

Using a quantitative approach, the superintendent would choose or develop a survey questionnaire including items that would characterize teachers' attitudes, perceptions, behaviors, and so on with respect to professional reading. The questionnaire would probably use a Likert-type scale for teacher responses and would produce a numerical rating for each item or category of items. A Likert-type scale is one which assigns a numerical value to the response for each item. The score for the scale is the sum of the item values. An example of a Likert-type scale is a series of statements to which the respondent indicates degree of agreement by marking the appropriate number: 1-Strongly Disagree, 2-Disagree, 3-Undecided, 4-Agree, 5-Strongly Agree. Such a survey could be administered in a group setting, like a faculty meeting, and the data could be tabulated for later analysis.

✎ *Exercise 2–9* Using a qualitative approach, the superintendent would choose or develop a structured interview or observation form that would probably be used with individuals or small groups. The structured interview or observation would probe the teachers' attitudes, perceptions, behaviors, and so on and would elicit verbal responses, which would be recorded on the form. The verbal responses would then be classified and compared with the responses for all teachers interviewed or observed. The analysis would consist primarily of a search for patterns of attitudes, perceptions, behaviors, and so on.

✎ *Exercise 2–10* Using a quantitative approach, the researcher would tabulate the ratings of pizza crusts. Having completed the tabulation, she would use a descriptive approach and present the results in narrative form.

✎ *Exercise 2–11* Using a quantitative approach, the coordinator would compare the reaction times of the drivers during the two conditions—unexpected distractions and expected events—to see if there is a significant difference. Since the researcher is interested in determining whether or not the type of event (i.e., expected or unexpected) causes differences in reaction times, the research would be classified as a causal-comparative study.

✎ *Exercise 2–12* Using a qualitative approach, the trainers would analyze patterns in these journal data and summarize the patterns of change in attitudes from the beginning of the training to the conclusion of the training. Because participation in the training program is presumed to cause a change in attitudes, this research would be classified as a causal-comparative study.

✎ *Exercise 2–13* Using a qualitative approach, anecdotal notes of the child's physical condition would be recorded each day. Results would be shared in narrative form, using the anecdotal records as supporting documentation. Since the teacher's purpose for collecting the data is to provide a more complete description of the child, this study would be classified as descriptive research.

✎ *Exercise 2–14* In this qualitative study, the lead teacher would collect survey data from teachers regarding their degree of volunteering and their professional reading patterns. Since the researcher's goal is to find out whether or not the type of professional reading and the extent of volunteering are related, the research would be classified as relational. The researcher would describe the nature of any pattern indicating a relationship between the responses about volunteering and the responses about the types of professional journals read.

✎ *Exercise 2–15* In this quantitative study, data would be collected on the bus riders in terms of the miles they travel and their number of absences from school. Since the purpose is to determine whether or not the two variables (i.e., miles traveled and number of absences) are related, the study would be classified as relational. These data would be correlated using appropriate statistical methods.

✎ *Exercise 2–16* In this qualitative study, data from classroom observations about the nature of students' responses to higher-level questions would be compared with the parents' reports of the extent of "at-home" reading and discussion. These data would be examined to determine whether or not a relational pattern exists. Since the purpose is to identify any possible relationships, the research would be classified as a relational study. The report, describing the nature of any patterns identified, would be presented in narrative form.

✎ *Exercise 2–17*   In this qualitative study, the superintendent would administer a written survey to faculty and administrative staff. The results of this survey would be compiled into a narrative that characterizes the attitudes, feelings, and opinions regarding Outcomes Based Education. This research would be classified as a descriptive study.

SUMMARY

In this chapter we have tried to organize the common research approaches into a systematic framework. It should be kept in mind that there are many research techniques that are not addressed here. The examples used in the discussion and exercises are not intended to be exhaustive, but rather illustrative, of the various ways that research questions and problems can be approached.

The exercises in this chapter dealt mainly with the general approach to addressing a research problem, but not with the specific details of designing a research study. The next chapter of this workbook will address those details more directly and will provide practice in designing specific research studies.

3 | RESEARCH DESIGNS

INTRODUCTION

The fundamental goal of a research design is to develop a set of methods and procedures that will answer the research question or test the research hypothesis with a high degree of confidence. In other words, the researcher will "attempt to design a study so that it will yield the strongest possible evidence to support or refute a knowledge claim" (Borg & Gall, 1989, p. 324).

In order to accomplish this, researchers must develop procedures that will allow them to conclude confidently that the results they obtained were due to the factors they were studying and not to extraneous or irrelevant factors. For example, if a researcher wants to know whether or not a particular innovative teaching technique will improve student attitudes toward the subject matter, it is not sufficient merely to have one class learn using the innovative technique and another class learn using a traditional technique. Even if the "innovative" class expresses more positive attitudes, the researcher cannot know if those attitudes are a result of the technique or a result of many other factors. The students in the "innovative" class may have had more positive attitudes to begin with, or the teacher of the "innovative" class may have been more enthusiastic or more concerned with teaching to affective objectives. A good research design will help the researcher believe the results of the study so that any conclusions about the effectiveness of the new technique can be made with confidence.

We shall use the term **research design** to refer to the procedural details of a study by which a researcher collects data, and which offer some level of control over the research situation. As a result of that control, the research design provides a corresponding level of confidence in the results of the study. The elements of research design are important aspects for increasing the internal validity of a research study, a topic that will be treated more comprehensively in Chapter 4.

The idea of control, and planning a series of procedures to maximize control, is a very common aspect of most quantitative research studies, but it may be less common for qualitative research. One of the distinguishing features, and strengths, of qualitative research is that it tends to be more open than quantitative approaches. This means that the qualitative researcher is less likely to have a highly structured plan, or design, in mind at the outset of the study, preferring instead to let the initial observations of the research situation help form the research questions. In contrast, the quantitative researcher is likely to specify each step in the research process in much greater detail. This does not mean, of course, that the qualitative researcher has no plan, or that the quantitative researcher rigidly adheres to a flawed design.

Good researchers, both qualitative and quantitative, have carefully considered plans, or designs, and good researchers, both qualitative and quantitative, are responsive to conditions in the research situation that might justify altering the plan. The qualitative/quantitative distinction, with respect to research designs, is one of emphasis. For a more complete discussion of research designs, we suggest referring to a comprehensive research text that addresses research designs from a qualitative perspective (e.g., Berg, 1994) and a quantitative perspective (e.g., Tuckman, 1994).

Although some specific design considerations may depend on the kind of data the researcher plans to collect, many of the aspects of research design discussed in this chapter are relevant irrespective of the nature of the data being collected. In other words, many of the aspects of research design are appropriate for qualitative as well as quantitative research studies.

Perhaps the most basic way of establishing confidence in a result is through the use of comparisons. Campbell and Stanley (1966) suggest that in order to obtain the minimum of useful scientific information a researcher must make at least one formal comparison. In the following section, various commonly used designs are described. Formal comparisons are important elements of some of these designs. In fact, it is often the lack of a formal comparison that weakens a design and, as a consequence, lessens the confidence of the researcher in making any claims based on the research findings.

RESEARCH DESIGN SYMBOLS

Researchers commonly use certain symbols to depict specific research designs. This system, which is used in the next section, may require some explanation. The symbol O is used to indicate an observation. This could refer to the administration of a test, the use of a survey, an interview, or any other technique for collecting data. Sometimes there will be a subscript following the O (e.g., O_2) to indicate that this particular observation is different from other observations with different subscripts. The symbol X is used to indicate some intervention or treatment on the part of the researcher or some other event that will occur. The X can also have a subscript, to distinguish it from other interventions, treatments, or events. The X is typically used to represent the different levels of the independent variable(s) or control variable(s).

The relative position of the X and O symbols indicates the time sequence. Thus, the depiction:

$$O_1 \rightarrow X \rightarrow O_2$$

means that an observation (O_1) was followed by an event (X), which in turn was followed by a different observation (O_2).

In the following sections, various approaches to designing research studies are described. The advantages and disadvantages of the various approaches are also discussed. In the explanation for each design we will use, as an example research topic, a situation where a researcher is interested in determining the usefulness of teacher feedback to students after the student makes a classroom response. The researcher has reason to believe that providing feedback during mathematics instruction might enhance student performance on a mathematics unit test, and the researcher is interested in collecting some data to support this belief. Feedback, then, is the independent variable, and performance on the math test is the dependent variable.

This example will be used to illustrate how a researcher would use each of the following approaches to design a study to address this research topic.

PREEXPERIMENTAL DESIGNS

In the following designs, significant weaknesses seriously undermine the credibility of any results that might be obtained. In these cases, results could be attributable to many extraneous factors that were not adequately controlled, or accounted for, in the research design. These designs are included here because they illustrate the need for relevant formal comparisons as the basis for controlling extraneous influences on the research findings.

One-Shot Case Study

$$X \rightarrow O$$

In this design, a treatment is implemented, following which an observation is conducted. The implied assumption is that whatever happened in the treatment influenced what was found in the observation. However, since there is nothing with which to compare the observation, there is no way to ascertain with confidence whether the treatment had any influence at all on the findings.

Using our feedback example for this design, we would expect to see the researcher implement a plan of providing feedback to students during math instruction (X). The researcher would then look at student performance on the math test following the instruction (O). Since the researcher has no other data, there is no way to tell whether the test performance was higher or lower than it would have been without the feedback.

One-Group Pretest-Posttest Design

$$O_1 \rightarrow X \rightarrow O_2$$

This design uses a pretreatment observation as an attempt to provide some basis for comparison for the posttreatment observation. Presumably, the difference between the posttreatment observation and the pretreatment observation is a consequence of the intervening treatment, but again the researcher's confidence in the findings must be low. There is no way of knowing what the difference between the two observations would have been without any intervening treatment.

Applying our feedback example to this design, we see that the researcher has measured student math performance (O_1) prior to the instruction with feedback (X) and measures math performance again following the instruction (O_2). The comparison of O_2 to O_1 will show whether or not there was a gain (or loss) in math performance. Since the reason for the research was to investigate the effect of providing feedback, and since there is no way of being sure that the difference between O_2 and O_1 was due to the feedback, the instruction, or something else, the researcher still cannot answer the question about the usefulness of feedback.

Intact-Group Comparison

$$X \rightarrow O_1$$
$$\rightarrow O_2$$

Here the researcher used a comparison group that received no treatment (often referred to as a **control group**). Now there is some element of control through the use of a comparison between the two groups, one of which received the treatment and the other of which did not. This comparison is only useful if the two groups were equivalent to begin with, but in this design, unfortunately, there is no basis for thinking that they were.

In this situation the researcher gave the students in the first group instruction with feedback (X) and the students in the second group instruction, with no feedback. Following the instruction, the math test scores from both groups (O_1 and O_2) were compared. As was mentioned earlier, the comparison of the math scores of the two groups is useful if we can be confident that the groups were equivalent prior to instruction.

In all of the designs described in this section, there are serious flaws that render the results of studies using these designs virtually useless. In order to obtain data that allows meaningful and useful comparisons, a researcher must use more rigorous designs, some of which are described in the following sections.

TRUE EXPERIMENTAL DESIGNS

One of the main flaws in several of the preexperimental designs discussed previously is that the equivalence of the groups being compared cannot be established. This flaw is addressed in true experimental designs. The **random assignment** of subjects to different treatment groups is the essential ingredient of a true experimental design (Fraenkel & Wallen, 1993). Random assignment enables the researcher to control the characteristics of subjects that might threaten the validity of the research study. Random assignment of subjects is intended to distribute evenly among the groups the non-relevant characteristics of subjects, which may alter the outcome of the study. For example, if differences in the motivation of the participants could alter the outcome in a study, random assignment will increase the likelihood that the average motivation of all groups is approximately the same.

Many designs can be classified as true experimental designs. Two of the more common true experimental designs are described in the following. Note that the symbol R indicates that the participants have been randomly assigned to the different groups.

Posttest-Only Control Group Design

$$R \left\{ \begin{array}{l} X \rightarrow O_1 \\ \rightarrow O_2 \end{array} \right.$$

In this design, two groups are formed by random assignment. One group, the experimental group, receives the experimental treatment (X), while the other, the control group, does not. Both groups are observed at the same time (O_1 and O_2) following the experimental treatment. Following the feedback example introduced in the previous section, in this design we would find the researcher selecting a sample of students to participate in the study. Then the researcher would randomly assign the students to either the experimental or the control group. This should result in two groups that are equivalent in all ways except with regard to the method of mathematics instruction (feedback or no feedback). Now when the researcher compares the math test scores for the two groups (O_1 and O_2) there is reason to believe that any observed differences are due to the difference in treatment, since that is the only way in which the two groups were different.

A variation of this design, often used in educational research, is one where there is no actual control group (i.e., a group that receives no treatment whatsoever), but rather where one group receives a standard or conventional treatment while the other group receives the experimental treatment. Sometimes the group receiving the conventional treatment is called a "quasi-control" or "pseudocontrol" group. This variation is symbolically depicted as follows:

$$R \left\{ \begin{array}{l} X_1 \rightarrow O_1 \\ \\ X_2 \rightarrow O_2 \end{array} \right.$$

For the feedback example, this might mean that it is actually unreasonable, and perhaps unethical, to provide instruction with no feedback whatsoever. Instead, the researcher provides special instruction in providing "quality" feedback to the instructor of the experimental group (X_1), while the instructor in the quasi-control group (X_2) provides whatever feedback he or she normally provides.

Pretest-Posttest Control Group Design

$$R \left\{ \begin{array}{l} O_1 \rightarrow X \rightarrow O_2 \\ \\ O_3 \;\;\;\;\;\; \rightarrow \;\;\;\;\;\; O_4 \end{array} \right.$$

The only difference between this design and the posttest-only control group design is the use of a pretreatment observation (sometimes referred to as a pretest). Again, two groups are formed by random assignment. The math performance of both groups is assessed prior to receiving math instruction (O_1 and O_3); the experimental group then receives math instruction with quality feedback (X), while the control group receives no feedback or "conventional" feedback. Finally, the math performance of both groups is measured again (O_2 and O_4) after the completion of the unit of math instruction.

The purpose of the pretreatment observations is to allow the researcher to check whether or not the two groups are really similar. In other words, the researcher can find out if the random assignment did its job of making the groups equivalent. If a comparison of the groups on the initial observation reveals that they were not, in fact, equivalent, the researcher can use a matching technique or a statistical procedure to compensate for the inequality.

Variations of both the posttest-only control group design and the pretest-posttest control group design can be arranged simply by adding additional groups, each receiving a different treatment. In all cases the common elements are the formation of the groups by random assignment and comparison of the groups following the treatments.

One common variation is actually a combination of both designs called the **Solomon four-group design.**

$$
R
\begin{cases}
O_1 \rightarrow X \rightarrow O_2 \\
O_3 \quad \rightarrow \quad O_4 \\
\quad X \rightarrow O_5 \\
\quad \rightarrow \quad O_6
\end{cases}
$$

This design uses two control groups and two experimental groups. One control group and one experimental group receive the pretest and the other control group and experimental group receive the posttest only. (Note that since there is only one experimental manipulation the "X" has no subscript.) The main advantage of the Solomon four-group design is that it permits the researcher to find out whether or not there were any effects due to pretesting.

Referring to the feedback example, since pretesting is not a common occurrence in most classrooms, it is possible that pretesting could alert the participants to the fact that they were being studied, and therefore their performance on the posttest might be different than it would have been had no pretesting occurred. Or it is possible that the pretesting affects the influence of the feedback, and that any differences observed between groups on the posttest might be due to the interaction of the pretest and the treatment, and not due to the treatment alone. The Solomon four-group design allows us to compare the performance of students who received feedback, with and without a pretest, to the performance of students who received no feedback, with and without a pretest.

FACTORIAL ARRANGEMENTS

In all of the designs described so far, only one relationship has been examined. That is, the relationship between one independent variable and a dependent variable. Factorial arrangements expand the number of relationships that can be examined. For example, in the factorial arrangement below, there are two independent variables (indicated by the symbols X and Y).

$$R \begin{cases} Y_1 \rightarrow X_1 \rightarrow O_1 \\ Y_1 \rightarrow X_2 \rightarrow O_2 \\ Y_2 \rightarrow X_1 \rightarrow O_3 \\ Y_2 \rightarrow X_2 \rightarrow O_4 \end{cases}$$

This arrangement is basically a posttest-only control group design (discussed in the preceding section) with the addition of a second independent (or control) variable denoted by the symbol Y. For each level of the variable Y there are two groups, one of which receives the experimental treatment X and the other of which is a control group and receives no treatment.

Another common way of illustrating this arrangement is shown in Table 3–1.

Using our feedback example to illustrate this arrangement, we would expect a sample of students to be randomly assigned to two groups, one receiving feedback and the second receiving no feedback (or conventional feedback.) Perhaps the researcher feels that boys and girls may respond differently to feedback, so gender is used as a control variable. The Y variable then represents student's gender, and the X variable represents the feedback group, as shown in Table 3–2.

TABLE 3–1 Factorial Arrangement of Variable X and Variable Y

	Variable X	
	X_1	X_2
Y_1	O_1	O_2
Y_2	O_3	O_4

Variable Y

TABLE 3–2   Factorial Arrangement of Feedback Group and Gender

Feedback Group

	Feedback	No Feedback
Male	O_1	O_2
Female	O_3	O_4

(Gender)

This arrangement allows the comparison of those in the experimental group (feedback) with those in the control group (no feedback) and the comparison of males with females. In addition, it also permits analysis of any possible interaction between the two variables (group and gender), that is, whether or not feedback is more or less effective for boys than for girls. A variation on this factorial arrangement is shown in the following:

$$R \begin{cases} O_1 Y_1 \rightarrow X_1 \rightarrow O_2 \\ O_3 Y_1 \rightarrow X_2 \rightarrow O_4 \\ O_5 Y_2 \rightarrow X_1 \rightarrow O_6 \\ O_7 Y_2 \rightarrow X_2 \rightarrow O_8 \end{cases}$$

This arrangement is basically a pretest-posttest control group design (discussed in the preceding section) with the addition of a second independent (or control) variable in the same way as the factorial arrangement described earlier.

Using the feedback example, this arrangement shows how the pretest-posttest control group design, described earlier, can be expanded to include the additional variable, gender, as shown in Table 3–3.

The factorial arrangement described in this section has two independent or control variables. This arrangement, when depicted in a table, results in a 2 × 2 matrix. The number of integers indi-

TABLE 3–3 Factorial Arrangement of Feedback Group and Gender with Pretest and Posttest Observations

		Feedback Group	
		Feedback	**No Feedback**
Gender	**Male**	O_1 O_2	O_3 O_4
	Female	O_5 O_6	O_7 O_8

cates the number of independent or control variables, and the value of each integer indicates the number of groups there are for that variable. For example, if there had been three feedback groups (i.e., no feedback, moderate feedback, extensive feedback), with gender as a control variable, the arrangement would result in a 3×2 matrix. There are two integers (3 and 2), so there are two independent or control variables. The "3" indicates that there are three groups of one variable (no feedback, moderate feedback, extensive feedback), and the "2" indicates that there are two groups of the other variable (male and female).

Factorial arrangements can be expanded to include additional independent and control variables. If, for example, we designed this study so that data were collected at grades 2, 5, 8, and 11, grade level would be a new variable and the arrangement would result in a $3 \times 2 \times 4$ matrix. There are now three integers (3, 2, and 4), indicating three independent or control variables (feedback group, gender, grade level). The "3" again indicates the three feedback groups, the "2" again indicates the two genders, and the "4" indicates the four different grades.

QUASI-EXPERIMENTAL DESIGNS

Random assignment of participants to experimental groups is a very important aspect of experimental design. Nevertheless, random assignment is often not practical. For example, in the feedback study that we have been using as an example in this chapter, it would be ideal if the researcher could randomly assign students to either the experimental (feedback) group or the control (no feedback) group. School personnel, however, might reasonably object to the disruption to scheduling that this might cause. The researcher is then left with the choice of either abandoning the research project or using less than ideal methods. If the researcher chooses to continue the research in spite of the inability to assign participants randomly, the use of one of the following quasi-experimental designs might be appropriate. It is essential however, for the researcher using these methods to be cautious in drawing conclusions and making generalizations based on the results obtained using these designs.

Pretest-Posttest Nonequivalent Control Group Design

In an earlier section of this chapter, where several preexperimental designs were discussed, the intact-group comparison was described. This design is illustrated again:

$$X \rightarrow O_1$$
$$\rightarrow O_2$$

Some researchers refer to this as a posttest-only nonequivalent control group design and classify it as quasi-experimental. We prefer, however, to consider it pre-experimental. Since this design is preexperimental (i.e., the intact-group comparison), it is appropriate to recall that in this design the comparison between the two groups is only useful if the two groups were equivalent to begin with, but in this design there is no basis for thinking that they were. This problem can be addressed in the following design, called the **pretest-posttest nonequivalent control group design:**

$$\text{Group 1:} \quad O_1 \rightarrow X \rightarrow O_2$$
$$\text{Group 2:} \quad O_3 \quad \rightarrow \quad O_4$$

This design is very similar to the pretest-posttest control group design except that intact groups of participants are used, rather than randomly assigning participants to groups. The intact groups are measured twice: once before the experimental treatment takes place and again following the experimental treatment.

A variation of this design uses systematically assigned participants instead of intact groups. This design can be modified to contain as many different groups as there are experimental treatments, plus a control group.

Using the feedback example, the math performance of both groups is assessed prior to receiving math instruction (O_1 and O_3); the experimental group then receives math instruction with quality feedback (X), while the control group receives no feedback or "conventional" feedback. Finally, the math performance of both groups is measured again (O_2 and O_4) after the completion of the unit of math instruction. The comparison of the groups on the pretreatment observations allows the researcher to determine whether or not the two groups are similar. If this comparison reveals that they were not equivalent, the researcher can use a matching technique or a statistical procedure to compensate for the inequality.

Time-Series Designs

Time-series designs involve the repeated measurement of one or more groups of intact groups. When only one group is involved, we refer to the design as a **single-group time-series design.**

$$O_1 \rightarrow O_2 \rightarrow O_3 \rightarrow O_4 \rightarrow X \rightarrow O_5 \rightarrow O_6 \rightarrow O_7 \rightarrow O_8$$

When two or more groups are involved, we call the design a **multiple-group time-series design.**

$$O_1 \rightarrow O_2 \rightarrow O_3 \rightarrow O_4 \rightarrow X \rightarrow O_5 \rightarrow O_6 \rightarrow O_7 \rightarrow O_8$$
$$O_1 \rightarrow O_2 \rightarrow O_3 \rightarrow O_4 \quad \rightarrow \quad O_5 \rightarrow O_6 \rightarrow O_7 \rightarrow O_8$$

For the feedback example, in the single-group design the group would be observed on several occasions prior to the implementation of the feedback treatment and again on several occasions following the feedback. The same procedure would occur in the case of the multiple-group time-series design, with the addition of a second group, that would not receive any feedback.

It should be noted that the single-group time-series design is basically a variation of the one-group pretest-posttest design (a preexperimental design) and that the multiple-group time-series design is basically a variation of the pretest-posttest nonequivalent control group design (a quasi-experimental design). The defining characteristic of the time-series designs is the use of multiple pretreatment and posttreatment observations.

Equivalent Time-Samples Design

When there is only one group available for study, the researcher may construct a design that, in effect, uses the group as its own control group. This is done by systematically introducing, removing, and reintroducing the treatment. As in the time-series designs described earlier, the participants are observed repeatedly at different times, but where the times-series designs introduce the treatment only once, this design alternates the treatment with another experience several times.

$$X_1 \rightarrow O_1 \rightarrow X_0 \rightarrow O_2 \rightarrow X_1 \rightarrow O_3 \rightarrow X_0 \rightarrow O_4$$

In the feedback example, X_1 would represent the use of feedback and X_0 would represent the control treatment, which in this case would be similar instruction without the use of feedback.

The choice of a research design is often a compromise between what is desired and what is possible. With the exception of the pre-experimental designs, all of the research designs described here have strengths and weaknesses. The researcher should be aware of these strengths and weaknesses when considering a design and the consequences of that choice.

COMPETENCIES

The exercises provided in this chapter will provide practice in identifying, classifying, analyzing, and selecting appropriate research designs to test research hypotheses and answer research questions. After completing the exercises in this chapter, you will be able to

- Distinguish among preexperimental, true experimental, and quasi-experimental research designs
- Identify the type of research design given a description of a study

- Express various research designs using symbolic conventions
- Develop appropriate true experimental designs for a given research situation
- Develop appropriate factorial arrangements for research situations
- Develop appropriate quasi-experimental designs for a given research situation

RESEARCH DESIGN EXERCISES

Two types of exercises are included in this chapter. The first type of exercise is intended to provide practice in identification and classification of research designs. The second is intended to provide practice in analysis of research problems and in designing studies appropriate to the research problem.

Exercises in Identification and Classification of a Research Design

Classify the design of each of the following studies according to the broad category (i.e., preexperimental, true experimental, factorial, or quasi-experimental) and according to the specific type (e.g., one-shot case study, one-group pretest-posttest design, intact-group comparison.) Express each design symbolically.

✎ **Exercise 3–1**   A social studies teacher is interested in determining the effects of a new textbook series, which has a multicultural thematic approach. The teacher will teach a unit on colonization in America. After the unit, a multicultural attitude scale will be administered to students.

✎ **Exercise 3–2**   A school administration wants to field-test an AIDS curriculum in the health course that is offered in the summer. Two health classes are to be offered during the summer session. Students in both classes will be given a pretest to measure their knowledge of AIDS. One health class will study AIDS using traditional textbook materials with a mostly lecture-style of delivery. Another class, an experimental health class, will study AIDS using films and contemporary materials along with presentations by guest speakers. The final exam for the course, a parallel form of the pretest, will be given to both groups.

✎ **Exercise 3–3**   A publishing company president is interested in determining the effect of the company's presentation on teachers' knowledge of the features of textbooks. Prior to presenting its science texts to teachers, the company gives the teachers a checklist of ten characteristics of a textbook and asks them to rank them according to importance. After a presentation of the qualities inherent in their textbooks and an opportunity to review the textbooks, the company representatives ask the teachers to once again rank order the ten characteristics of a textbook.

✎ **Exercise 3–4**   A guidance counselor wants to assess the effects of structured-play recess and free-play recess on the attention spans of students who are and who are not on medication for hyperactivity. Within a grade level of four classes of twenty-five students each, she randomly selects and assigns students to four groups: structured play, medicated; structured play, nonmedicated; free play, medicated; and, free play, nonmedicated.

✎ **Exercise 3–5**   A football coach is interested in assessing the effects of structured study sessions on the grades of the players. Football players begin study sessions with tutors in September; grades are issued in October; study sessions continue but without tutors; grades are issued in December; study sessions with tutors are resumed; grades are issued in February; study sessions continue without tutors; grades are issued in April.

✎ **Exercise 3–6**   Community service is one emphasis of the student activities board at a university. The dean for student affairs has been curious about the meaning of current community service as it affects future community service and requests a study of the situation. Students who volunteer for community service are randomly assigned to two groups. One group will receive intensive training in various needs of communities and how best to serve those needs throughout the semester prior to registering for community service. The other group will not receive training. During two semesters, the students in both groups will be tracked in terms of the number of hours that they spend in community service.

✎ **Exercise 3–7**   At a university, there are two tracks for students majoring in elementary education. Students can take courses in the urban track or the general track. The coordinator of the programs is interested in determining why students enroll in the urban track. Until the time of the junior field experience, both the urban and general tracks are identical, except the urban-track students are required to take a three-credit seminar in urban education and two required general education social sciences—one in contemporary urban social problems and one in sociology of the urban family. When these courses have been completed, but prior to the field experiences, all students will be interviewed to determine their reasons for interest or noninterest in the urban track.

✎ **Exercise 3–8**   A high school counselor is interested in the effect of mentors on students' postsecondary plans. All freshmen will be given a written survey at orientation to assess their interest in postsecondary education. The freshman class will be randomly assigned to mentor and nonmentor programs. The mentor program will involve mentoring of freshmen by college-bound seniors who have been trained in academic mentoring. At the end of the year, all freshmen will be surveyed with a parallel form of the interest in postsecondary education instrument.

✎ **Exercise 3–9**   A school district has contracted for an on-line service that will connect it with other school districts across the country. Initially, the service is going to be used by fourth-grade students who will communicate with pen pals. The principals and teachers believe that students who write on-line will produce longer letters and be willing to continue the exchange of letters longer than fourth-grade students who handwrite and mail letters. The students who will be on-line and those who will handwrite letters are in different buildings in the district. Letter writing will commence in September and end in May of the academic year.

✎ **Exercise 3–10**   A physical education teacher wants to determine if he can influence interest in watching the Olympics on television. Two of his junior high groups will be selected for the study. One group will be presented with oral and written guidelines each week for viewing the Olympics. The other group will receive no guidelines. On Monday, each student in the classes will be required to submit the total number of hours spent viewing the Olympic games for the previous week.

Exercises in Analyzing and Designing a Research Study

These exercises present a research question and suggested design. For each exercise, specify how the sample will be selected, describe the treatment, indicate how subjects will be assigned to the treatment groups, and identify relevant variables (dependent, independent, control). Do not include variables in the design that are not mentioned. Depict each research design symbolically.

✎ **Exercise 3–11**   A school district has budgeted some funds for satellite television reception of educational broadcasts. The social studies teachers are interested in assessing the results of news broadcasts on the students' awareness of international news events in weekly news quizzes in college preparation classes. Students discuss international news events at the beginning of each social studies class. Describe this study using a quasi-experimental, pretest-posttest nonequivalent control group design.

Exercise 3–12   Some male and female athletes who compete in the high jump event in a high school have been complaining about the limited hours that the conditioning laboratory is open. They feel sure that they could jump higher if the lab were open additional hours prior to the beginning of school so they could spend more time conditioning. The track and field coach would like to explore the question. He proposes that the lab be opened from 6:00 to 7:00 A.M. Monday, Wednesday, and Friday for the athletes from one of the district's two high schools. To establish a pretest height jump, each student in the control and experimental groups will jump five times. Describe this study using a quasi-experimental, pretest-posttest nonequivalent control group design.

Exercise 3–13   An academic principal for curriculum is exploring the results of "pushing in" an additional teacher during mathematics class to support "at-risk" students in the primary grades. She would like to run a pilot study to determine the effectiveness of this procedure because the board of education will need to be convinced that the additional expense of a teacher's salary will be worth the outcome. She determines that the best design for this situation would be to introduce and reintroduce the "push-in" tutoring. For one month the "push-in" teacher will come into class three class periods a week to support students by tutoring them during the math lesson. Then a test developed and validated by the school district will be given to students. The second month no "push-in" tutoring will be available to the "at-risk" students. This sequence will be implemented two additional times during the third and fourth months. Describe this study using a quasi-experimental, equivalent time-samples design.

Exercise 3–14   The English faculty of a large school district is interested in studying three instructional treatments for writing. They will initiate a Friday morning instructional program in writing for fourth-, fifth-, and sixth-grade students. Three instructional treatments are planned with varied writing instruction (process writing, published writing, and no instruction) and length of writing period (thirty minutes and sixty minutes). Students will be randomly assigned to one of three treatments. One group of each instructional group will be assigned to a thirty-minute period and another to a sixty-minute period. Each group will initially write a pretest sample, which will be scored holistically. Following treatment, a posttest writing sample will be taken and scored holistically. Describe this study using a factorial arrangement.

✎ **Exercise 3–15** With the current emphasis on parental involvement in children's academic endeavors, a researcher is interested in assessing the confidence level of parents who will read orally to children in schools. He also wants to know if there is a difference in the confidence level of parents of different educational levels. From a list of volunteers who are interested in reading orally to students, parents will be randomly selected and assigned to one of two conditions—training or no training. Following training of parents in the experimental condition, all parent volunteers will complete a confidence scale. Describe this study using a true experimental posttest-only control group design.

✎ **Exercise 3–16** The director of admissions at a university would like to study the effect of a new recruitment procedure on the number of male and female, traditional and nontraditional students who accept the invitation to attend the university. This procedure departs from the traditional recruitment procedures at the university in that selected prospective students will be invited to campus for a weekend to engage in typical college activities. Some of the activities will include attending an athletic event, participating at a dance at the student union, and staying two nights in a residence hall. Describe this study using a true experimental posttest-only control group design.

✎ **Exercise 3–17** A company that sells toys for young children wants to conduct a research study to collect data for advertisement purposes. The marketing director believes that the company's computer software enhances the ability of children in early childhood settings to learn to count. The company decides to place computers and counting software in four of eight prekindergarten and kindergarten classrooms in a district. The study will occur during the fall semester, and no other counting activities will occur during the study. Students in the experimental condition will be assigned to work on the computer for a specified length of time each day for two weeks. Students in the control group will not use counting software. Prior to the implementation of the treatment, a researcher will interview each child in both conditions twice a week for two weeks to assess counting ability. Following the treatment, the researcher will again interview each child in both conditions twice a week for two weeks to assess counting ability. Describe this study using a quasi-experimental, multigroup time-series design.

✎ **Exercise 3–18** The dean of a college of education is interested in determining if the education majors who take an optional course in working with students with disabilities are using the strategies learned in the course. He decides to study this issue. Fifty education majors will be randomly assigned to take the course when they enter as freshmen. The control group of fifty education majors will be assigned a multicultural education course. The junior field experience will occur prior to the courses, thus allowing monitoring for strategies prior to taking the course. Students will again be monitored for use of strategies during student teaching. In both the precourse and postcourse field experiences, students will each teach ten lessons in their classrooms. These lessons will be videotaped. A researcher will view the videotapes and observe the lessons to determine which strategies are used. Describe this study using a true experimental, pretest-posttest control group design.

Exercise 3–19 A reading researcher is interested in determining which, if any, of three instructional strategies would be best for improving students' reading comprehension. The three instructional strategies are as follows:

1. *Questioning:* Teaching students to independently generate inferential questions related to what they have read.

2. *Imagery:* Teaching students to construct and describe vivid mental images of what they have read.

3. *Mapping:* Teaching children to construct concept maps of what they have read.

The researcher is also aware of much research that suggests that gender may be a factor that influences the way different strategies may affect reading comprehension.

Describe this study using a factorial arrangement. Be sure to compare the three strategies, as well as taking into account the possible effects of gender.

Exercise 3–20 The mathematics curriculum in a large school district is undergoing a comprehensive review. Some teachers are advocating a new curriculum that is "concept-based" (i.e., it focuses on students' comprehending mathematics concepts and processes rather than computations). A second group of teachers is advocating an approach that is based on the memorization of various algorithms and formulas for computing the solution to mathematics problems. Finally, there are those in the middle, who are in favor of a "balanced" approach that would use a blend of methods from both other points of view. The central administration decides to test each of these approaches for one year with a sample of students in the third, fourth, and fifth grades.

Because of the logistical problems that would be associated with randomly assigning students to different treatment groups, the curriculum coordinator in charge of this project decides to use several different schools as the sample, each of which would use a different curriculum. Describe this study using a pretest-posttest nonequivalent control group design.

ANSWERS TO RESEARCH DESIGN EXERCISES

Answers to Exercises in Identification and Classification of a Research Design

✎ *Exercise 3–1* Preexperimental, one-shot case study

$$X_{unit} \rightarrow O$$

✎ *Exercise 3–2* Quasi-experimental, nonequivalent control group design

$$\text{Group 1:} \quad O_1 \rightarrow X_{contemporary} \rightarrow O_2$$
$$\text{Group 2:} \quad O_3 \qquad \rightarrow \qquad O_4$$

✎ *Exercise 3–3* Preexperimental, one-group pretest-posttest design

$$O_1 \rightarrow X_{presentation} \rightarrow O_2$$

✎ *Exercise 3–4* Factorial arrangement

$$R \begin{cases} Y_{structured\ play} \rightarrow X_{medicated} \rightarrow O_1 \\ Y_{structured\ play} \rightarrow X_{nonmedicated} \rightarrow O_2 \\ Y_{nonstructured\ play} \rightarrow X_{medicated} \rightarrow O_3 \\ Y_{nonstructured\ play} \rightarrow X_{nonmedicated} \rightarrow O_4 \end{cases}$$

	Medication	
	Medicated	**Nonmedicated**
Structured Play	O_1	O_2
Nonstructured Play	O_3	O_4

Type of Play

✎ *Exercise 3–5*   Quasi-experimental, equivalent time-samples design

$$X_{tutors} \rightarrow O_1 \rightarrow X_{no\ tutors} \rightarrow O_2 \rightarrow X_{tutors} \rightarrow O_3 \rightarrow X_{no\ tutors} \rightarrow O_4$$

✎ *Exercise 3–6*   True experimental, posttest-only control group design

$$R \left\{ \begin{array}{l} X_{training} \rightarrow O_1 \\[2ex] \quad\quad\ \rightarrow O_2 \end{array} \right.$$

✎ *Exercise 3–7*   Preexperimental, intact-group comparison

$$X_{courses} \rightarrow O_1$$
$$\rightarrow O_2$$

✎ *Exercise 3–8*   True experimental, pretest-posttest control group design

$$R \left\{ \begin{array}{l} O_1 \rightarrow X_{mentors} \rightarrow O_2 \\[2ex] O_3 \quad\quad \rightarrow \quad\quad O_4 \end{array} \right.$$

✎ *Exercise 3–9*   Quasi-experimental, pretest-posttest nonequivalent control group design

$$\text{Group 1:} \quad O_1 \rightarrow X_{on\text{-}line} \rightarrow O_2$$
$$\text{Group 2:} \quad O_3 \quad\quad \rightarrow \quad\quad O_4$$

✎ *Exercise 3–10*   Preexperimental, intact-group comparison

$$X_{guidelines} \rightarrow O_1$$
$$\rightarrow O_2$$

Answers to Exercises in Analyzing and Designing a Research Study

✎ *Exercise 3–11*   Quasi-experimental, pretest-posttest nonequivalent control group design

The sample will be selected from intact groups. The experimental group will watch international news broadcasts on television, in addition to discussing the news in class. The control group will discuss news in class. Intact classes will be randomly assigned to treatments. Relevant variables are independent variable (TV news broadcasts), dependent variable (weekly news quizzes), control variable (type of preparation—college preparation/noncollege preparation).

$$\text{Group 1:} \quad O_1 \rightarrow X_{\text{broadcasts}} \rightarrow O_2$$
$$\text{Group 2:} \quad O_3 \qquad\quad \rightarrow \qquad\quad O_4$$

✎ *Exercise 3–12* Quasi-experimental, pretest-posttest nonequivalent control group design

The sample will be selected from intact groups (able/not able to use the weight room before school begins). The experimental group will condition on Monday, Wednesday, and Friday before school. The control group will not condition during these times. Relevant variables are independent variable (conditioning Monday, Wednesday, and Friday before school), dependent variable (averaged height jumped), and a control variable (gender).

$$\text{Group 1:} \quad O_1 \rightarrow X_{\text{conditioning}} \rightarrow O_2$$
$$\text{Group 2:} \quad O_3 \qquad\quad \rightarrow \qquad\quad O_4$$

✎ *Exercise 3–13* Quasi-experimental, equivalent time-samples design

The sample will be selected from intact primary classes. The teacher will "push in" for math tutoring three class periods a week for the first and the third months. During the second and fourth months no math tutoring by the "push-in" teacher will occur. At the end of each month, a math test will be given. Relevant variables are independent variable (math tutoring), dependent variable (math tests), and control variable (grade level).

$$X_{\text{push-in}} \rightarrow O_1 \rightarrow X_{\text{no push-in}} \rightarrow O_2 \rightarrow X_{\text{push-in}} \rightarrow O_3 \rightarrow X_{\text{no push-in}} \rightarrow O_4$$

✎ *Exercise 3–14* Factorial arrangement

Subjects will be selected from students in grades four, five, and six, and will be randomly assigned to one of three treatment groups. Each type of treatment group will be randomly assigned to one of two periods of instruction (thirty or sixty minutes). Relevant variables are independent variables (type of writing instruction, period of instruction), dependent variable (writing sample), and control variables (grade in school and period of instruction).

$$R \begin{cases} Y_{\text{process writing}} & \rightarrow X_{30 \text{ minutes}} \rightarrow O_1 \\ Y_{\text{process writing}} & \rightarrow X_{60 \text{ minutes}} \rightarrow O_2 \\ Y_{\text{published writing}} & \rightarrow X_{30 \text{ minutes}} \rightarrow O_3 \\ Y_{\text{published writing}} & \rightarrow X_{60 \text{ minutes}} \rightarrow O_4 \\ Y_{\text{no instruction}} & \rightarrow X_{30 \text{ minutes}} \rightarrow O_5 \\ Y_{\text{no instruction}} & \rightarrow X_{60 \text{ minutes}} \rightarrow O_6 \end{cases}$$

	Length of Period	
	30 Minutes	**60 Minutes**
Process	O_1	O_2
Published	O_3	O_4
No Instruction	O_5	O_6

(Type of Writing)

✎ *Exercise 3–15* True experimental posttest-only control group design

The sample will be selected from a list of volunteers who are interested in reading orally to students. The experimental group will undergo training in reading stories orally. The control group will receive no training. Relevant variables are independent variable (oral reading training), dependent variable (confidence level assessment), and control variable (parental level of education).

$$R \begin{cases} X_{\text{training}} \rightarrow O_1 \\ \phantom{X_{\text{training}}} \rightarrow O_2 \end{cases}$$

✎ *Exercise 3–16* True experimental post-test only control group design

The sample will be randomly selected from students who apply to and are accepted to the university. This prospective group of students will be randomly assigned to one of two treatments, a weekend on campus/no weekend on campus. Variables are independent variable (weekend on campus), dependent variable (acceptance of admission), and control variables (gender and classification according to traditional age of university students).

$$R \begin{cases} X_{\text{weekend}} \rightarrow O_1 \\ \\ \quad\quad\quad \rightarrow O_2 \end{cases}$$

✎ *Exercise 3–17* Quasi-experimental, multigroup time-series design

The sample will be selected from intact kindergarten classrooms. The classrooms will be randomly assigned to treatments. The experimental group will be assigned to work on the computer utilizing counting software during weeks 1 and 3. The control group will not use counting software. The variables are independent variable (work with counting software), dependent variable (counting task), and control variable (grade in school).

$$O_1 \rightarrow O_2 \rightarrow O_3 \rightarrow O_4 \rightarrow X_{\text{software}} \rightarrow O_5 \rightarrow O_6 \rightarrow O_7 \rightarrow O_8$$
$$O_1 \rightarrow O_2 \rightarrow O_3 \rightarrow O_4 \quad\quad\quad \rightarrow \quad\quad\quad O_5 \rightarrow O_6 \rightarrow O_7 \rightarrow O_8$$

✎ *Exercise 3–18* True-experimental, pretest/posttest control group design

The sample will be randomly selected from an incoming freshman class and randomly assigned to one of two conditions, learning disabilities class or multicultural class. The variables are independent variable (type of class), dependent variable (use of strategies), and control variable (type of major).

$$R \begin{cases} O_1 \rightarrow X_{\text{disabilities class}} \rightarrow O_2 \\ \\ O_3 \rightarrow X_{\text{multicultural class (control)}} \rightarrow O_4 \end{cases}$$

✎ *Exercise 3–19* In this factorial arrangement (3×2), a sample would be randomly selected from the target population. Separately, the males and the females in the sample will be randomly assigned to one of the three "strategy" groups. Following the administration of the pretest, reading instruction would take place using the various strategies in each group. Following the instruction, the researcher would administer a posttest of reading comprehension and compare the scores among the three strategy groups and between male and female students. The interaction between strategy group and gender would also be examined. The variables are independent variables (strategy group and gender) and dependent variable (reading comprehension score).

The factorial arrangement is shown in the following using both conventions used in Chapter 3.

Note: A pretest of reading comprehension may be administered to determine whether the random assignment procedure resulted in equivalent groups with regard to reading comprehension. In that case, the depictions would reflect the additional observations.

$$R \begin{cases} \text{Males} & \rightarrow X_{\text{questioning}} \rightarrow O_1 \\ \text{Males} & \rightarrow X_{\text{imagery}} \rightarrow O_2 \\ \text{Males} & \rightarrow X_{\text{mapping}} \rightarrow O_3 \\ \text{Females} & \rightarrow X_{\text{questioning}} \rightarrow O_4 \\ \text{Females} & \rightarrow X_{\text{imagery}} \rightarrow O_5 \\ \text{Females} & \rightarrow X_{\text{mapping}} \rightarrow O_6 \end{cases}$$

| | Strategy Group | | |
	Questioning	Imagery	Mapping
Male	O_1	O_2	O_3
Female	O_4	O_5	O_6

Gender

Exercise 3–20   After the curricula for the three "new" mathematics programs had been identified, the researcher would identify four schools to participate in the study. The schools would be randomly assigned to the curricula: one school would receive the "concept-based" curriculum, another school would receive the "algorithm" curriculum, the third school would receive the "balanced" curriculum, and the fourth school would continue to use the current mathematics curriculum and would serve as a control group. The third-, fourth-, and fifth-grade students in all participating schools would be pretested using the same standardized mathematics achievement test to determine the extent to which they were equivalent (or not) at the outset. At the end of the school year the students would be tested again and the scores for the four groups would be compared. If pretesting had revealed significant differences among the groups initially, the researcher would choose an appropriate statistical analysis procedure to adjust for those differences in making the posttest comparisons.

The variables are independent variables (type of curriculum), dependent variables (mathematics achievement posttest), and possible control variable (mathematics achievement pretest).

The symbolic depiction of this design is shown in the following:

$$School\ 1: \quad O_1 \rightarrow X_{concept\text{-}based} \rightarrow O_2$$

$$School\ 2: \quad O_3 \rightarrow X_{algorithm} \quad \rightarrow O_4$$

$$School\ 3: \quad O_5 \rightarrow X_{balanced} \quad \rightarrow O_6$$

$$School\ 4: \quad O_7 \rightarrow X_{current} \quad \rightarrow O_8$$

SUMMARY

This chapter has presented examples of several common research designs, a commonly used way of categorizing those designs, and symbolic conventions commonly used in depicting those designs. There are many other possible ways of designing research studies and virtually countless variations on those designs. Those described in this chapter are among the most commonly used in educational research studies.

The exercises in this chapter have provided practice in identifying and evaluating various research designs. Chapter 4 extends the process of evaluating research designs by examining the various factors that compromise the internal and external validity of research studies.

4 THREATS TO INTERNAL AND EXTERNAL VALIDITY

INTRODUCTION

The results of a research study are only useful to the extent that they can be accurately and confidently interpreted. The issue of accurate and confident interpretation of results is at the center of any discussion of validity. **Validity,** which is derived from the Latin word *validus,* meaning "strong," refers to the degree with which correct inferences can be made from the results of a research study. The idea of validity in a research study involves two concepts at the same time. A researcher wants to have confidence that the outcomes observed in a research study are a function of the conditions observed, measured, and/or manipulated in the study and not due to some other factors that were not addressed in the study. Such confidence reflects the **internal validity** of a study. Usually researchers want to use the results of a research study to make a claim not just about the participants in a study but also about a larger population of which the participants are a sample. The ability to make such claims, or generalizations, depends on the **external validity** of the study. These two aspects of research validity as well as factors that threaten research validity will be discussed separately in the following sections.

INTERNAL VALIDITY

As just described, internal validity refers to the extent to which the results obtained in a research study are a function of the variables that were systematically manipulated, measured, and/or observed in the study. Suppose, for example, that a researcher is interested in determining which of two instructional methods is superior for teaching a history concept. Suppose further that the researcher asked two teachers to each use one of the methods of instruction and then the researcher compared the mean test scores of each class following the instruction. It is apparent that the researcher is interested in test score differences that are attributable to the different instructional methods. However, because there are so many other ways in which the classes differed, the researcher cannot confidently conclude that any test score differences that were observed between the groups are due to the methods of instruction. The teachers may have been different in terms of their teaching effectiveness or enthusiasm, the classes may not be equivalent with respect to interest or preparation, or there may have been interruptions (such as fire drills or assemblies) in one class and not the other. The list of possible conditions that could have produced test score differences between the two classes is almost endless. Each of those possible conditions constitutes a potential threat to the internal validity of the research study. Several common threats to internal validity are explained in the following sections.

Potential Threats to Internal Validity

History refers to the occurrence of events that could alter the outcome or the results of a study. These events could occur before the study, in which case we refer to *previous history*, or during the study, in which case we refer to *concurrent history*. For example, in a study of the effectiveness of a new method for teaching a unit on the biology of a cell, suppose we realize that many of the students had recently watched a television documentary entitled "The Cell." This would be an example of previous history influencing the results of a study. In another situation, suppose we are interested in examining the effectiveness of using musical activities to teach mathematics concepts. If we have one teacher use the standard curriculum and another teacher use the musical activities curriculum, it is impossible for us to determine whether the outcome we observe is attributable to differences in the curricula or differences between the teachers. The different effects of the teacher are an example of concurrent history as a possible threat to the internal validity of the study.

    Maturation pertains to any changes that occur in the subjects during the course of the study that are not part of the study and that might affect the results of the study. Such changes could be biological, that is, growth processes during the study that may affect the results, or they may be psychological, that is, learning or development that occurs during the study may affect the results. If we were to examine the weight gain and increase in height of second graders from September to May as a function of the school breakfast and lunch program, we would have to consider that normal growth would account for some of the change in those variables during that period. Biological maturation is a possible source of invalidity in this case. On the other hand, if we were examining the effects of certain instructional techniques on concept learning of sixth graders from September to May, we would have to consider the attainment of formal operational thought during that period by some of the students as a possible reason for what we observe. In this example, psychological maturation is a potential threat to internal validity.

Testing relates to the possible effects of a pretest on the performance of participants in a study on the posttest. For example, the effect may be sensitizing in that a pretest may alert subjects to the fact that they are being studied, leading them to react in a manner that may affect the results. Another possibility is that of multiple testing effects, where performance on a pretest may affect performance on later administrations of the test or other tests. In either case, the posttest may not be measuring just the influence of the treatment but also the effects of the earlier pretesting.

Instrumentation is concerned with the effects on the outcome of a study of the inconsistent use of a measurement instrument. In other words, what the instrument is measuring changes during the duration of the study. For example, suppose a researcher is trying to ascertain the effect of a new instructional technique on achievement. The achievement test may be initially valid, but if the students become fatigued during the period of data collection because of the length of the achievement test, and that fatigue affects their scores on the test, the validity of the test would deteriorate. Toward the end of the testing period, the test would be measuring fatigue as well as achievement. As a result, the results of the study may be due to the deterioration of the testing instrument rather than to the variables being studied.

Statistical regression is the term applied to the tendency of extreme scores to move (or regress) toward the mean score on subsequent retesting. For example, a group of students is given an IQ test, and those scoring in the lowest 25 percent are selected to participate in the study. After the treatment, the students are given another IQ test. Since the students were in the lowest extreme to begin with, we would expect the scores on the posttest to be higher, simply due to statistical regression. We could not confidently attribute the results of the study to the treatment, since statistical regression is a possible threat to the internal validity of our study.

Mortality refers to the loss of subjects from a study due to their initial nonavailability or subsequent withdrawal from the study. Mortality can occur when potential participants agree to take part in a study in a nonrandom way. In other words, the participants are different from those who chose not to participate. Mortality can also affect the outcome of a study when participants drop out in a nonrandom fashion from different groups being compared in a study. For example, if more high-scoring people drop out from the experimental group than from the control group, the outcome of the study may be invalid due to mortality.

Selection pertains to the possibility that groups in a study may possess different characteristics and that those differences may affect the results. For example, one group might differ from another in age, ability, gender or racial/ethnic composition, or any of an almost unlimited number of ways. To the extent that such differences in group characteristics could affect the outcome of the study, they constitute a potential threat to internal validity due to selection.

In the following section, techniques are suggested for minimizing these threats and thereby maximizing the internal validity of a research study.

Procedures for Maximizing Internal Validity

A researcher can maximize internal validity by taking steps to minimize the potential threats to internal validity. Fraenkel and Wallen (1993) suggest four general ways in which these threats can be minimized:

1. Standardization of the conditions under which the research study is carried out will help minimize threats to internal validity from history and instrumentation.

2. Obtaining as much information as possible about the participants in the research study aids in minimizing threats to internal validity from mortality and selection.

3. Obtaining as much information as possible about the procedural details of the research study, for example, where and when the study occurs, minimizes threats to internal validity from history and instrumentation.

4. Choosing an appropriate research design can help control most other threats to internal validity.

The following are some specific suggestions for minimizing the potential threat to internal validity from each of the sources mentioned earlier.

History: The use of a control group, selected from the same population as the experimental group(s) and which experiences the same concurrent history as the experimental group(s), can help eliminate most of the effects of history. Also, the shorter the duration of an experiment, the less likely history will be a threat.

Maturation: The effects of maturation, like the effects of history, can be minimized by the use of a control group, selected from the same population as the experimental group(s). Also, like the effects of history, the effects of maturation tend to be minimized in studies of short duration.

Testing: The use of a research design that does not include a pretest can eliminate testing as a potential threat to internal validity. If baseline or pretreatment data are needed, the use of unobtrusive measures (data collection techniques about which the experimental participant is unaware) may minimize the effects of testing. It also may help for a researcher to use different equivalent forms of a test for pretesting and posttesting.

Instrumentation: Careful specification and control of the measurement procedures can eliminate most instrumentation threats. Standardized instruments, administration or data collection procedures, and the training of observers are among the procedures that help control the instrumentation threat.

Statistical regression: Avoiding the use of extreme scorers, when average scorers are excluded, will minimize the threat due to statistical regression.

Mortality: Choosing large groups and ensuring that they are representative of the population from which they were selected can minimize mortality threats. The use of follow-up procedures with a portion of those who leave the study or who were initially unavailable can further minimize mortality as a threat.

Selection: Random selection and random assignment of subjects minimize selection as a threat to internal validity. If random selection and assignment are not possible, the use of certain statistical techniques, used as part of a careful quasi-experimental design, can adjust for group differences and thereby minimize selection as a threat.

EXTERNAL VALIDITY

Rarely is a researcher interested in drawing conclusions only about the participants in a study. Usually, the researcher would like to claim that the results that were obtained for the participants are also applicable, or generalizable, to a larger population (or a larger set of settings and contexts). External validity, as described earlier, refers to the extent to which the results of a research study are able to be generalized confidently to a group larger than the group that participated in the study (Bracht & Glass, 1968.)

Using the example from the discussion of internal validity, suppose that the researcher is interested in generalizing the results of the comparison of the two instructional methods to a larger population of students, teachers, and settings. In order for the results to be generalized with confidence, the researcher must have reason to believe that the students, teachers, and settings (and other aspects of the study) in the study are similar to those aspects as they exist in the larger population.

Threats to the external validity of research findings may be related to the **population,** that is, the extent to which a sample is representative (or not representative) of the population from which it was selected, or to the **ecology,** that is, the extent to which characteristics of the setting or context of the research study are representative (or not representative) of the setting and context to which the results are to be generalized. The following section describes some of the common threats to external validity.

Potential Threats to External Validity

Effect of testing refers to the fact that the administration of a test (for example, a pretest) may affect the responses or the performance of the participants in a research study. If this happens, it means that the performance of the people being studied may be different from what it might have been if they had not been pretested. Therefore, the results may not be generalizable to situations where pretesting will not occur.

Multiple-treatment interference pertains to the situation in which participants in a study receive more than one treatment. In such a case, the effects of the multiple treatments may interact. For example, suppose a study is using students to test the effectiveness of a "new" method of instruction in mathematics. These students are also receiving many other "treatments" during the normal course of the school program, and those other "treatments" may have some impact on the effect of the new mathematics technique. The results of this study can be validly generalized only to similar situations.

Selection-treatment interaction is concerned with the possibility that some characteristic of the participants selected for the study interacts with some aspect of the treatment. Examples of such characteristics could include prior experiences, learning, personality factors, or any traits that might interact with the effect of the treatment. For the results to be validly generalizable to a larger population, that population must possess the same traits, characteristics, experiences, and so on as the sample.

Effects of experimental arrangements pertain to situations where participants become aware that they are involved in a study, and, as a result of that awareness, their response or performance is different from what it would have been otherwise. The effect on performance may be due to the "newness" of the experimental treatment (sometimes called the "novelty effect"), to the belief on the part of participants that they are receiving some "special" treatment (sometimes referred to as the "Hawthorne effect"; Roethlisberger & Dickson, 1939), or to the participant's belief in the effectiveness of the treatment (sometimes called the "placebo effect").

Experimenter effects refer to the possibility that an experimenter may sometimes unintentionally influence the performance of participants in a study. Rosenthal (1966, p. 40) classified these effects as "passive" (e.g., the gender, race, or personal attributes of the researcher or observer affect participants' performance) or "active" (e.g., the expectations of the researcher or observer are communicated to the participant in a manner that affects performance.)

Specificity of variables is concerned with the extent to which the variables in a study are adequately described and operationally defined. Variables can be defined too specifically. For example, if a researcher defines intelligence as the IQ score obtained from the Stanford-Binet test, any results may not be validly generalizable for other definitions of intelligence. Minimally, all variables must be described in sufficient detail to allow another researcher to replicate the study. In addition, the description and definition of variables must employ measurement instruments or observational devices that are themselves reliable and valid. To the extent that the variables included in a study are not adequately described and carefully defined, the ability validly to generalize the results of the study is threatened.

Procedures for Maximizing External Validity

In general, threats to the external validity of a study can be minimized when the researcher has taken steps to ensure that the sample, the setting, and the context are representative of the population, setting, and context to which the results are intended to be generalized.

Effect of testing: The use of research designs that do not include pretests (see Chapter 3) can help eliminate this potential threat. Research designs such as the Solomon four-group design are especially useful in determining the extent to which pretesting may have influenced the results of a study.

Multiple-treatment interference: When there is reason to believe that there will be interference of multiple treatments, the researcher should try to choose a design in which only one treatment is assigned to each subject. If such a design is practical, the researcher should try to control and/or measure the effects of all relevant treatments and incorporate them into a multiple-treatment design.

Selection-treatment interaction: This threat is similar to the internal validity threat of selection, and the remedy is also similar. Random selection and assignment of participants can minimize much of the threat to external validity due to selection-treatment interaction. When random selection or random assignment is not practical, statistical techniques such as analysis of covariance, used in conjunction with a careful quasi-experimental design, can take into account differences due to measurable attributes of the individual, thus minimizing selection-treatment interaction as a threat.

Effects of experimental arrangements: The most effective way to minimize the reactive effects of various experimental arrangements is to have a control group (i.e., a group that receives no treatment whatsoever) and a "placebo" group (i.e., one that receives a "placebo" or nonexperimental treatment.) In educational settings, it is often impossible to have "true" control groups, but we can usually arrange for a "placebo" group. An example would be a case in which an experimental group receives the "new" method of instruction and the "placebo" group (sometimes called the quasi-control group) receives the "traditional" method of instruction. It is important that both groups be treated the same in all respects, except in regard to the treatment itself, and it is important that all of the participants believe they are being treated comparably.

Experimenter effects: The use of "blind" data collection procedures can be an effective means of minimizing threats to external validity due to experimenter effects. This means that the researcher does not collect data or make observations but instead trains a "naive" observer to do so. The person collecting the data or making the observations should be unaware of the purpose of the study and should be unaware of which participants are receiving the experimental treatment.

Specificity of variables: Careful definition of variables is the key to minimizing this threat to external validity. In order to ensure generalizability, the researcher must operationally define variables in a way that is meaningful in settings beyond that in which the study is being conducted. The use of widely agreed upon definitions or multiple competing definitions should be considered.

COMPETENCIES

The exercises in this chapter will provide practice in identifying potential threats to the internal validity and external validity of research studies, and in describing specific procedures for minimizing those potential threats to validity. After completing the exercises in this chapter, you will be able to

- Define internal validity

- Define external validity

- List the major potential threats to the internal validity of research studies

- List the major potential threats to the external validity of research studies

- Identify the potential threats to internal validity in a specific research study

- Identify the potential threats to external validity in a specific research study

- Describe specific procedures that will minimize the potential threat to internal validity in a particular research study

- Describe specific procedures that will minimize the potential threat to external validity in a particular research study

VALIDITY EXERCISES

Two types of exercises are included in this chapter. The first set of exercises will require identification of threats to internal and external validity. The second will require suggestions for minimizing the threats to internal and external validity.

Exercises in Identification of Threats to Internal and External Validity

Identify specific potential threats to internal validity in Exercises 4–1 to 4–7 and specific potential threats to external validity in Exercises 4–8 to 4–13. Indicate the specific threat (e.g., mortality, history). Identify only obvious threats.

Potential Threats to Internal Validity

✎ **Exercise 4–1**   The instructor of a marriage and family issues class plans to use a pretest and posttest to assess attitudes concerning family living arrangements and their effects on children. She uses several current sources of information to construct an attitude scale about this topic. The instructor takes the total number of questions from an instructor's manual and some that she has constructed and assigns them to one of the two tests. One test becomes the pretest; the other is the posttest.

✎ **Exercise 4–2**   During a six-week classroom unit in which cooperative learning is being studied, several of the students in the class are severely injured on a field trip in a bus accident and are hospitalized for a brief time. Following their release from the hospital, they continue as participants in the study.

✎ **Exercise 4–3**   Students in a gifted class are the participants in a study in which the dependent variable consists of the results of an achievement test. The students have been pretested as part of the research procedures.

✎ **Exercise 4–4**   A researcher begins a study of the effects of an individualized spelling program on intact groups in fifth grade. An experimental group receives individualized spelling instruction that focuses on peer tutoring. The control group receives traditional spelling instruction. Before the study concludes, some of the students in the control group are moved to their home school, where renovations have been completed. This move was anticipated but occurs earlier than expected and before the collection of data for the research study had been completed.

✎ **Exercise 4–5**   The governing body of a national fraternity is interested in assessing the commitment of brothers to local service projects. The representative of the governing body asks for volunteers from fraternities on campus to participate in specific charity drives, such as A Walk for Children's Hospital.

✎ **Exercise 4–6**   A researcher is interested in studying the impact of international films on students' understanding of specific pieces of literature. Due to scheduling and time constraints on the college campus, the nine films must be shown on three Saturdays. Students in the study will view three films consecutively from 9:00 A.M. until 3:00 P.M. on each scheduled Saturday, with short breaks between films.

✎ **Exercise 4–7**   A posttest for a study on the use of the database for library periodicals on a university campus was scheduled for a Thursday afternoon at 1:00 P.M. and 2:00 P.M. for the control and experimental groups, respectively. It was necessary to schedule the posttest sessions sequentially rather than concurrently because of the number of available terminals. The posttest for the control group was completed and the posttest for the experimental group was ready to begin when a partial power failure occured resulting in the loss of about half of the terminals. As a result, data collection for the experimental group took nearly twice as long as for the control group.

Potential Threats to External Validity

✎ **Exercise 4–8**   A study of the effects of computer-assisted instruction has been conducted in a high school in which computers have been used for limited applications. After collecting data from two groups, one which received traditional instruction and the other which received computer-assisted instruction, the results indicated a significant benefit ($p < .001$) for those students in the computer instruction group.

✎ **Exercise 4–9**   A researcher conducting a study of process writing introduces the session in which the initial sample will be written by saying, "The sample that you are going to write is very important to your future. The quality of the text will be assessed to determine your placement in groups. Some groups will be writing every day, while others will write once a week."

✎ **Exercise 4–10**   Two researchers are conducting a study on drug and alcohol awareness. The researcher working with the experimental group is using print materials that he wrote.

✎ **Exercise 4–11**   An elementary guidance counselor is assessing the effects of a new career awareness program. The only time he is able to meet with students is during their recess period. He is concerned that assignment of students to this program during their recess will bias the results, so he asks for volunteers to participate in the program.

✎ **Exercise 4–12**   A middle school health teacher is interested in studying the "comfort level" of seventh-grade students in a coed sex education class. All of the topics that are generally covered in sex education classes at this level will be covered in the coed class. "Comfort level" is to be assessed by observation of body language. Body language is defined as positive or negative nonverbal reactions.

✎ **Exercise 4–13**   A principal of a school wants to study the effects on achievement scores of the inclusion in general education classrooms of students normally assigned to a resource room. She feels that the students assigned to the resource room can be successful in the general education classroom. Concurrent with assignment to the general education classroom, a high-tech CD-ROM tutorial program is being installed in the resource room. Time is planned for students to return to their resource room to use the new program.

Exercises in Minimizing Threats to Internal and External Validity

You are assisting a researcher in planning each study described in Exercises 4–14 to 4–24. Suggest procedures to minimize the specific threats to internal and external validity that are mentioned.

Exercise 4–14   The director of a campus theater is interested in studying the cultural attitude index of freshmen who are required to attend productions as compared with those who attend productions voluntarily. In planning this study for him, how would you control for the following internal validity threat: mortality? external validity threat: selection-treatment interaction?

Exercise 4–15   A basketball coach wants to study the effects of a unique way of coaching players to shoot from the foul line. She plans to pretest the players using a foul-shooting activity before instructing them on foul shooting. In planning this study for her, how would you control for the following internal validity threat: statistical regression? external validity threat: experimenter effects?

Exercise 4–16   At a recent conference, preschool teachers across the state heard of an environmental procedure that is claimed to reduce the number of colds in young children in school settings. However, the teachers aren't convinced the procedure will reduce colds and would like to study its effect before contracting with the company for purchase. Recently, the school district installed an air-filtering system to reduce bacteria in the air, but the teachers are not convinced that this alone will help the cold situation. In planning this study for them, how would you control for the following internal validity threat: maturation? external validity threat: multiple-treatment interference?

Exercise 4–17   A university college of education is trying to determine if it should continue its accreditation by a national accrediting agency. The accreditation review is very expensive both in administrative and faculty time and cost. The university decides to join efforts with other universities in rural, suburban, and urban settings to study the effects of accreditation on recruitment of students. The question is, Does accreditation influence the student's choice when making a decision about which university to attend? In planning this study for the university, how would you control for the following internal validity threat: history? external validity threat: multiple-treatment interference?

✎ **Exercise 4–18**   A university is considering closing its campus school, which currently includes kindergarten through twelfth grade. A proposal has been submitted to close the school and put the money budgeted for it into transportation of university students to public school sites. The administration decides to study other campus schools, some which have closed and others which have remained open, to determine the cost-effectiveness of the move. In planning this study for the administration, how would you control for the following internal validity threat: statistical regression? external validity threat: selection-treatment interaction?

✎ **Exercise 4–19**   Parking on campus is a major problem. Commuters have been complaining about the lack of available parking space. The parking committee that proposed the new lots decides to study the impact of new lots away from campus. Some commuters will be assigned to these new lots, which will be serviced by shuttle buses. Other commuters will park on the fringe areas of campus with no shuttle service. These fringe areas have parking lots that students have been using for five years. Satisfaction with the parking situation will be assessed by pretest and posttest interviews of commuters who have and do not have the shuttle service. In planning this study for the committee, how would you control for the following internal validity threat: testing? external validity threat: effects of experimental arrangements?

✎ **Exercise 4–20**   The state system has entered into a contract with a specific soda vendor, which has offered funding to the university for an outdoor track and field facility. This contract will not take effect until next year. When the contract goes into effect, there will be fewer brands of soda offered at the university. The dining service plans to compare soda sales this year and next year. In planning this study for the university, how would you control for the following internal validity threat: selection? external validity threat: effects of testing?

✎ **Exercise 4–21**   A university internship office has one placement for a White House internship program each year. This is a prime internship, traditionally awarded to a political science major. Other universities place majors other than political science in the White House internship. The internship office would like to assess the competence of other majors in this position. Standardized test data on one aspect of competence of the White

House interns are available. In planning this study for the internship office, how would you control for the following internal validity threat: instrumentation? external validity threat: selection-treatment interaction?

✎ **Exercise 4–22**   A reading supervisor in a school district believes that reading high-quality literature can be encouraged through ownership of books. He decides to conduct a study in two of the district's four elementary schools. The two schools are approximately equal in student population and economic status. In one school the students will be able to buy inexpensive paperback books of selected titles classified as high-quality literature. These books will be sold by the librarian. In the other school, titles of those same books will be available in the library and mentioned in library sessions as they always have been. At the end of each grading period, students will check off the books on the list that they have read. These lists will be verified by a teacher. In planning this study for the reading supervisor, how would you control for the following internal validity threat: mortality? external validity threat: specificity of variables?

✎ **Exercise 4–23**   The faculty at an elementary school received a grant to purchase electronic homework helpers. These homework helpers are new on the market and claim to increase the homework completion rate even for students who are generally lax in completing assignments. The premise behind the homework helper is that if the student goes home with the assignments written and the necessary materials, chances are better that the assignment will be completed. The homework helper enables the students to record assignments orally. The helper suggests materials and books that might be needed to complete the assignments. The faculty plans to study the rate of homework completion with the homework helper as compared with the traditional way of recording homework on an assignment pad. In planning this study for them, how would you control for the following internal validity threat: maturation? external validity threat: effects of experimental arrangements?

✎ **Exercise 4–24**   A band committee in charge of purchasing uniforms is interested in determining the best buy of three gradations of uniforms: perdurable, durable, and wearable. There is a considerable difference in price of the three grades of uniforms. The committee decides to survey schools that have purchased the uniforms to determine how long the uniforms were able to be used. The questions asked will include gradation of the uniform purchased, the number of years of use, and the reason for purchase of new uniforms to determine why uniforms were replaced. In planning this study for the committee, how would you control for the following internal validity threat: selection? external validity threat: specificity of variables?

ANSWERS TO VALIDITY EXERCISES

Answers to Exercises in Identification of Threats to Internal and External Validity

Potential Threats to Internal Validity

✎ *Exercise 4–1* Internal validity—testing. The instructor has not validated the pre- and posttest items to ensure that the forms are parallel.

✎ *Exercise 4–2* Internal validity—history. Students who were members of cooperative learning groups were severely injured and hospitalized, thus potentially affecting the experiences of the groups differently.

✎ *Exercise 4–3* Internal validity—statistical regression. It is assumed that gifted students will score at a high level on an achievement test. On a second test or posttest, they are subject to statistical regression. Chances are their scores will not be as high as the scores on the pretest, indicating regression to the mean.

✎ *Exercise 4–4* Internal validity—mortality. Subjects from one group dropped out of the experiment.

✎ *Exercise 4–5* Internal validity—selection. Volunteers are a biased sample.

✎ *Exercise 4–6* Internal validity—maturation. Students viewing the films will possibly grow weary and be less attentive as the film viewing progresses.

✎ *Exercise 4–7* Internal validity—instrumentation. The administration of the posttest for both groups was inconsistent, since the posttest took longer for the experimental group.

Potential Threats to External Validity

✎ *Exercise 4–8* External validity—effects of experimental arrangements. It is possible that the experimental group using computer-assisted instruction benefited solely from the novelty of the treatment.

✎ *Exercise 4–9* External validity—effects of testing. The statement may affect the subjects' responses on the writing sample.

✎ *Exercise 4–10*   External validity—experimenter effects. The researcher has a vested interest in the materials being used and may inadvertently communicate his expectations to the experimental group.

✎ *Exercise 4–11*   External validity—selection-treatment interaction. The sample of volunteers is not representative of the population that it is supposed to represent. Volunteers in this situation may be students who are trying to avoid outdoor activity.

✎ *Exercise 4–12*   External validity—specificity of variables. "Comfort level" is ambiguously defined. This condition should be more clearly distinguishable during observations.

✎ *Exercise 4–13*   External validity—multiple-treatment interference. Students in the resource room are provided additional tutoring through a CD-ROM program. In addition to support strategies in the inclusive classroom, this computer program might affect their performance.

Answers to Exercises in Minimizing Threats to Internal and External Validity

✎ *Exercise 4–14*   Internal validity—mortality. Select a large sample of freshmen so that if students drop out of the study the sample remains adequate in size. Another way to minimize this threat would be to include measurements of relevant background variables on the pretest. If there is substantial mortality, the remaining sample could be compared with the initial sample on those variables to determine whether the mortality affected the characteristics of the final sample.

External validity—selection-treatment interaction. Since random selection and assignment of participants are not possible due to the nature of the sample (required to attend/volunteers), analysis of covariance can be used in analysis to control for the possible initial differences. For example, SAT scores could be used as a covariate.

✎ *Exercise 4–15*   Internal validity—statistical regression. Omit subjects from the study who score extremely high or extremely low on the pretest foul-shooting activity.

External validity—experimenter effects. She should include a control group in her study. All data should be collected by someone who is unaware of the training in foul shooting that is occurring.

✎ *Exercise 4–16*   Internal validity—maturation. Include a control group for the study of colds and/or minimize the length of time for the research.

External validity—multiple-treatment interference. Since an air-filtration system has been installed, it may contribute to the reduction of colds, as might the environmental procedure under consideration. A control group in another similar setting without the air filtration system could also be subjected to the environmental procedure.

✎ *Exercise 4–17*   Internal validity—history. Include control groups from universities that do not have accredited programs and that have a similar concurrent history (e.g., have not revised their programs) as the experimental groups. Also, minimize the length of time for the research.

External validity—multiple-treatment interference. Make sure that other enticements to enroll in the universities are comparable.

✎ *Exercise 4–18*   Internal validity—statistical regression. Exclude from the study any campus schools that had extremely high or low budgets.

External validity—selection-treatment interaction. Randomly select campus schools from among all closed-or open-campus schools.

✎ *Exercise 4–19*   Internal validity—testing. Omit the pretest interviews of commuters or choose two different random samples of the population for the pretest and posttest.

External validity—effects of experimental arrangements. These effects will be minimized because of the inclusion of a control group, the group parking on the fringe area of campus.

✎ *Exercise 4–20*   Internal validity—selection. Randomly select students to be pretested and posttested.

External validity—effects of testing. Avoid the use of a pretest in the study or choose two different random samples of the population for the pretest and posttest.

✎ *Exercise 4–21*   Internal validity—instrumentation. Use a standardized test to collect data and administer the test under carefully controlled circumstances. Any other data-collection procedures should be carefully controlled.

External validity—selection-treatment interaction. Since groups, political science and other majors, are already established, use a statistical analysis like analysis of covariance to adjust for possible differences between groups. One covariate could be grade point average.

✎ *Exercise 4–22*   Internal validity—mortality. Select a large sample of students so that if students drop out of the study the sample remains adequate in size.

External validity—specificity of variables. Books that "have been read" is ambiguous. Establish a criterion for reading a book, such as being able to answer five comprehension questions about the book.

✎ *Exercise 4–23*   Internal validity—maturation. Include a control group for the study of the homework helper and/or minimize the length of time for the research.

External validity—effects of experimental arrangements. Establish a control group that uses the traditional method of recording homework on an assignment pad. Make sure that conditions for the experimental and control groups are as similar as possible.

✎ *Exercise 4–24*   Internal validity—selection. Randomly select schools in each of the three categories of uniform type.

External validity—specificity of variables. Be sure that gradation of uniform, years of use, and reason for purchase of new uniforms are carefully defined before conducting the survey.

SUMMARY

This chapter has described the most common threats to the internal validity and external validity of research studies and has described specific procedures that could be followed to minimize these threats to validity. Chapter 5 continues the discussion of the process of designing high-quality research studies by an examination of various strategies and techniques for selecting samples to participate in research studies.

5 | SAMPLING

INTRODUCTION

Sampling essentially refers to choosing a portion of the target population for your research, rather than studying the entire target population. For example, a researcher may want to study the impact of compensatory reading programs on students. The entire population of students in compensatory reading programs is not accessible or is too large to study. Therefore, a subgroup or sample of that population is selected for the research. The primary advantages of sampling, rather than studying the entire population, are feasibility and convenience. In cases where the target population is sufficiently small and also accessible, it may be preferable to conduct your research using the entire population.

There are many approaches to selecting a research sample, and they are described in detail in most research textbooks. Among the most common types of sampling are **random sampling, stratified random sampling, cluster sampling,** and **systematic sampling.** Check your research text for descriptions of these, and perhaps other, sampling approaches.

The selection of a research sample has important consequences for the validity of your research findings (Saslow, 1982). Remember that the major purpose of conducting the research is to be able to make some claim about a larger population. Therefore, it is essential to choose a sample that will enable you confidently to generalize your findings to that larger population. Your goal should be to avoid, as much as possible, any biases in the selection of your sample.

TYPES OF SAMPLING

Researchers identify various types of sampling. The four most common types of sampling are defined in this section. **Random sampling** involves selecting a sample from a population using a table of random numbers or a computer program so that each member of the population has an equal chance of being selected. **Stratified random sampling** involves selecting a sample from specified strata or subpopulations. The number chosen from each stratum may be equal or proportional to the number in each stratum. This is done to make sure that the sample "looks like" the population. **Cluster sampling** involves choosing a sample from intact mutually exclusive groups, such as school classes. The clusters may be randomly selected from a set of available clusters. All members of the cluster can be included in the sample. **Systematic sampling** involves choosing every nth (e.g., 4th, 10th) name or number associated with a name on a list. The first name or number is chosen by randomly selecting a name or number from the beginning of the list.

One other type of sampling needs to be mentioned, although a researcher would not plan for this type of sampling. It is a **biased sample** or **sample of convenience.** A biased sample is a sample that is not representative of the population to which the results will be generalized. Individuals who volunteer to participate in a study would constitute a biased sample.

Sometimes various types of sampling can be used in combination with each other to help make the sample more representative of the targeted population.

COMPETENCIES

After completing the exercises in this chapter, you will be able to

- Explain the advantages and disadvantages of the various types of research samples

- Describe the steps involved in selecting a random sample for a research study

- Describe the steps involved in selecting a stratified random sample for a research study

- Describe the steps involved in selecting a systematic sample for a research study

- Describe the steps involved in selecting a cluster sample for a research study

- Describe the steps involved in randomly assigning a sample for a research study

- Identify a biased sample, sometimes called a sample of convenience

- Explain the impact of selection as an internal validity issue

- Explain the impact of generalizing from the sample to the targeted population as an external validity issue

- Evaluate the adequacy of the sampling procedures for a research study

SAMPLING EXERCISES

Three types of sampling exercises are included in this chapter. The first type is an abbreviated exercise and gives practice in sampling when the sampling type has been designated. The second provides practice in sampling requiring a more detailed response. The third requires analysis of sampling scenarios.

Practice in Sampling with the Sampling Type Designated

The following exercises ask you to briefly describe how the samples would be chosen. Later exercises will ask for detailed information on sampling.

Exercise 5–1   Random sampling exercise: A school district produces educational television programming for its residents. This is a costly venture. Since budget cuts need to be made, the administration wants to survey district residents as to the value of the programming. It plans to do this by randomly selecting families and conducting telephone interviews. Briefly, describe how the sample would be chosen.

Exercise 5–2   Stratified random sampling exercise: A local university department of professional studies wants to design a doctoral program in educational administration, but the doctoral committee is not sure of the market for this type of program. Specific program details are fully described in a one-page bulletin. The committee plans to mail this description with a survey assessing interest. They want to target three groups: principals, superintendents, and teachers, so they decide to use stratified random sampling. Briefly, describe how the sample would be selected.

✎ **Exercise 5–3**   Cluster sampling exercise: A medium-sized metropolitan area has ten shelters for the homeless. The mayor of the city has asked you to provide assistance in assessing the health status of individuals in the shelter on a given day by interviewing some individuals who come for dinner and stay overnight. Each shelter can accommodate approximately thirty individuals for overnight stay. Because the groups are intact, you decide to use cluster sampling to identify the individuals to be surveyed. Briefly, describe how the sample would be selected.

✎ **Exercise 5–4**   Systematic sampling exercise: You have been asked to survey university faculty to assess the need for child care. Plans call for systematically sampling 10 percent of the twelve hundred faculty and mailing a questionnaire about child care to them. Briefly, describe how the sample would be selected.

Practice in Sampling Requiring More Detail

These exercises require you to include more detail when describing your sampling procedures. For example, give the exact steps that you would use when entering and using a table of random numbers.

✎ **Exercise 5–5**   You have been asked to conduct a staff development "needs assessment" for the teachers in your district. Your district, which is in a city of about three hundred thousand people, is composed of eight senior high schools, fourteen junior high schools, and twenty-five elementary schools. There is a total of 2,150 teachers in the district.

Realizing that it is impractical to survey every teacher in the district, you decided to survey a randomly selected sample of 10 percent of the teachers.

1.   Describe in detail how you would select the sample to be surveyed.

2.   Explain how your sampling procedures would minimize selection as a threat to internal validity.

✎ **Exercise 5–6**   As a member of your teachers' union bargaining committee, you have been asked to conduct a survey of teachers with respect to their priorities in upcoming contract negotiations. Since there are about 1,800 teachers in the district, you decide that it would be more practical to survey only a sample of the teachers. You decide to select a sample of 10 percent, or 180 teachers.

You have reason to believe there may be differences in priorities between elementary and secondary teachers, as well as differences among teachers with different levels of education (bachelor's degree, master's degree or master's equivalent, and master's degree plus at least thirty graduate credits). Therefore, you decide that you should select a stratified random sample. For the purpose of making comparisons, assume there is the same number of elementary and secondary teachers. Also, assume that an equal number of teachers falls into each of the categories regarding levels of education. Describe in detail how you would select the sample to be surveyed.

Exercise 5–7   As a curriculum specialist, you have been asked to design a study intended to compare the relative effectiveness of three approaches to reading instruction: language experience approach, basal/phonics approach, whole language approach. The county schools to be studied include twelve school districts with the following characteristics: one large urban district with forty-seven elementary schools, six suburban districts with four to eight elementary schools in each district, and five rural districts with two to four elementary schools each. All of the elementary schools throughout the county typically have three classes at each grade, kindergarten through fifth grade. You have permission to implement the research study within budgetary constraints that will permit you to use all of the classes in a total of twelve elementary schools.

1.   Describe in detail how you would select and assign the sample of schools and classes to be used in this study.

2.   How would the sampling procedures described in this study limit the external validity of the results in regard to generalizing from the sample to the targeted population?

Exercise 5–8   After a recent strike, a teachers' union in a suburban school district of three hundred teachers wants to try to turn around its negative image in the community. The union leadership decides to do a study of the amount of community volunteerism by its members. In this community there are five elementary schools and two secondary schools.

1.   Use stratified random sampling to identify a sample. Begin by identifying possible strata.

2.   Suppose you chose the age of teachers as your stratum of interest. You decide to group teachers by ages in ten-year intervals, 21 to 30

years old, 31 to 40 years old, 41 to 50 years old, and over 50 years old. Approximately the same number of teachers is in all age ranges, except the 41- to 50-year-old teachers. There are twice as many teachers in the 41- to 50-year-old range as in the other groups. Using stratified random selection, choose teachers for the study.

✎ **Exercise 5–9** A state university wants to determine the relationship between attendance in large lecture-type classes in a liberal studies fine arts course and grades in the course. One-half of the freshmen takes the fine arts course. The researcher decides to identify four specific days during each of three months of a fall semester when attendance will be taken. Students in the course have assigned seats.

1. Use random sampling to select the months.

2. Use stratified random sampling to identify the days each month that attendance will be taken.

3. Use systematic sampling to identify the individuals whose attendance will be tracked.

✎ **Exercise 5–10** Career Services on campus holds an annual recruiting fair in which prospective employers are invited to interview students. Career Services wants to survey students who have been interviewed to assess the impact of the recruiting fairs on campus. As you look at the list of interviewees, you note a pattern among the names. Even-numbered entries on the list seem to include more females, while odd-numbered entries seem to include more males.

1. You have been instructed to choose every second name on the list and mail a questionnaire to those individuals. Explain how selection as a threat to internal validity is affected by this procedure.

2. What should be your first step before doing any sampling?

3. Use systematic sampling to identify a sample to be surveyed.

✎ **Exercise 5–11** A middle school principal is interested in assessing the effects of mathematics tutoring on seventh-grade students who are at-risk. These students will be tutored for ten minutes, three times a week by the math teacher during math class using a special technique called Tutoring in Class (TIC). There are eight sections of seventh-grade mathematics with two at-risk students in each class.

1. Using random sampling, determine which four sections (clusters) will be involved in the study.

2. Then, randomly assign the clusters to treatment (TIC) or no treatment (no TIC).

✎ **Exercise 5–12**   As a result of a significant educational reform initiative, the new governor of your state has been convinced that it is worth studying the effect of class size on student achievement. You have been asked to design a study to examine whether or not there would be any differences in student achievement among students who had been instructed in classes of different sizes and adult-student ratios. The three classroom configurations are one teacher alone with 25 students, one teacher and one full-time instructional aide with 25 students, and one teacher alone with 15 students.

Assume that you have adequate resources to conduct this full-blown study across the state, and that you have (or will have) the cooperation of all necessary individuals and organizations.

1. Describe how you would select and assign your sample of subjects for this study.

2. Discuss how the sample-to-population match threat related to external validity could be minimized.

Sampling Exercises Requiring Analysis

These exercises require you to analyze specific sampling situations. Critically examine each sampling plan.

✎ **Exercise 5–13**   Prior to fully adopting a new substance abuse prevention curriculum for the district's schools, the superintendent asked the elementary supervisor to evaluate the effectiveness of the new curriculum by comparing it to the curriculum that had been in place for about ten years. The district is in a predominately white, middle-class, suburban community near a large city. In the district there are four elementary buildings, each with four classes of each grade (kindergarten through sixth grade), and there is one building that serves as the junior and senior high school. The substance abuse program is used in the fourth through twelfth grades.

The supervisor randomly assigned the new curriculum to two of the elementary buildings, while the other two elementary buildings continued to use the old curriculum. The district's elementary guidance counselor (there is only one) taught the substance abuse curriculum (both the old program and the new) in all four schools over the course of one academic year.

1. What was the population, and what kind of sample was used in this study?

2. Discuss the advantages and disadvantages of the sampling procedures used in this study and recommend an alternative that would reduce the disadvantages identified.

✎ **Exercise 5–14**   A researcher is interested in surveying elementary teachers with respect to their attitudes about the "whole language" approach to language instruction. Through personal contacts, the researcher obtains permission to interview teachers from nine nearby school districts. Of the nine school districts, one is in a medium-sized city, four are suburban districts near a large city, and four are rural.

The researcher contacted the central office for each school district and was given the name of a building principal to contact. After contacting the principals and obtaining their consent, the researcher solicited teachers to volunteer for the study by taking a "sign-up" sheet to building-level faculty meetings. A total of one hundred teachers volunteered to be interviewed, with an approximately equal number of teachers from each building/district.

1.   Describe the population for this study and describe the sampling approach used by the researcher.

2.   Discuss the advantages and disadvantages of the sampling procedures used in this study and recommend an alternative that would reduce the disadvantages identified.

✎ **Exercise 5–15**   An intermediate-grade teacher wants to assess the effectiveness of computer software on problem-solving. She decides to compare the problem solving skills of fifteen students in an after-school computer club with those of fifteen students who do not belong to the computer club.

1.   How might the selection of this sample influence the results of the comparison of problem-solving skills.

2.   What are the potential biases of the sample?

✎ **Exercise 5–16**   A third-grade teacher wants to study the effect of the use of the author's chair on revision of student writing. The use of the author's chair involves a student sitting on the chair and sharing his or her writing with the class. The class responds to the writing by first praising it, then asking questions for clarification, and finally making suggestions for improvement of the piece of writing. No other suggestions for revision will be made by the teacher or the student's peers. Each child will have the opportunity to sit in the author's chair two times during the writing of a piece. The teacher has asked his colleagues on the third-grade team to randomly select two of four classes for this study.

1.   What sampling methods were used?

2.   One of the third-grade teachers will participate in the study as a senior researcher working with the experimental group. Another third-

grade teacher will work with the control group. Explain how this arrangement can be a threat to internal validity.

✎ **Exercise 5–17** A publishing company has published a new social studies text series in the format of interactive video for use in junior high school courses. A large urban school district has adopted the text series and will begin using it when the new academic year begins in September.

The publishing company is interested in assessing the effectiveness of the interactive video format on student achievement. The district had funds for putting the new series in one-half of the junior high schools. The other schools will receive the series in time for the next academic year. This situation enables the publishing company randomly to select particular schools to participate in this study.

1. Discuss biases inherent in this sampling technique.

2. Suppose the results of this study indicate that the students who learn by interactive video as compared with those students who learn by traditional textbook methods achieve at a significantly higher level. In interpreting these results, to what population can researchers generalize these results?

✎ **Exercise 5–18** A candidate for mayor in a city with a population of one hundred thousand wants to compare the overall academic achievement of homeless students with students with permanent addresses. Her interest in this information is to build a case for improving the plight of the homeless through federally subsidized housing. She is successful in petitioning the school to release information about these students in grades kindergarten through twelve. The information for one thousand students, five hundred elementary and five hundred secondary, is without names. The information has the student's current grade level, gender, and total battery achievement test score from the most recently administered achievement test three months ago. Twenty-five of the students have been identified as homeless. The mayoral candidate decides to randomly select students for this study.

1. What are the biases inherent in this sampling plan?

2. Suppose the mayoral candidate found that the students who have permanent addresses are achieving at a significantly higher level than those students who are homeless. Suggest further considerations.

✎ **Exercise 5–19** A college of education wants to assess the value of the additional information that the National Teachers Exam (Praxis Series) gives, such as student knowledge of his or her major. An administrator feels that grade point average at the time of graduation is as good an indicator of knowledge as the NTE specialty exam score. A researcher gets the names, grade point averages, and NTE scores of five hundred students who have graduated in the last three years. He randomly selects one hundred graduates and correlates their final grade point average and NTE specialty exam scores.

1. What has the researcher overlooked?

2. What changes could you make to improve the sampling design?

✎ **Exercise 5–20**   A principal in a school district wants to assess the effects of mock interviews for a teaching position given to student teachers in the building. Her plan is to offer the opportunity to participate in a mock interview to all first-quarter student teachers who volunteer. During the second quarter of the semester, a principal from another building will interview those student teachers who volunteered using identical questions. The principal interviewing during the second quarter will also interview student teachers from another building, so the principals can compare the value of an initial interview with no initial interview.

1. What kind of sampling procedure will be used in this study?

2. Discuss selection as an internal validity issue.

3. Suppose the student teachers who participated in the initial interview performed at a significantly higher level in the second interview than the student teachers who had only participated in one interview. What inferences could be made?

4. Recommend an alternative to this sampling procedure.

✎ **Exercise 5–21**   A entire teaching staff of a school district was trained in the use of a new approach to classroom management. In order to assess the extent to which that approach was being implemented, the staff development coordinator decided to conduct a series of classroom observations on a sample of the teaching staff. Since there was reason to believe there would be differences in the degree of implementation as a function of the level of teaching (i.e., elementary school, middle school, senior high school), the designer of the study employed the following sampling procedures.

First, the entire teaching staff of 2,402 teachers was classified according to teaching level. There were 1,512 elementary school teachers (63 percent), 504 middle school teachers (21 percent), and 386 senior high school teachers (16 percent). The sample size was then set at 240 teachers (or 10 percent of the population). Using a table of random numbers, the researcher then selected 151 elementary school teachers, 50 middle school teachers, and 39 senior high school teachers to participate in the assessment study.

1. What kind of sample was used in this study?

2. Describe some of the advantages and disadvantages of the approach described here.

3. Suppose that the district needed to obtain the information very quickly, and/or less expensively. What modifications could be made to these sampling procedures?

✎ **Exercise 5–22**   A university department needs to justify its programs since there is a budget crunch. One criterion that has been identified to explore is the number of graduates who are employed. Lists of graduates for the past three years are available. The lists are merged in sequential order, with graduates from the earliest year being first and the most recent graduates being at the end of the list. The researcher who has been assigned to organize the phonathon to survey the graduates about their employment status selects the graduates to be called. He uses systematic sampling and selects the first name on the list and every fourth name until he reaches the end of the list.

1. Is his method of systematic sampling correct? Why or why not?

2. One of the researcher's colleagues suggests that stratified random sampling would have been a better sampling method. Do you agree with the researcher's colleague? Why or why not?

ANSWERS TO SAMPLING EXERCISES

Answers to Sampling Exercises with the Sampling Type Designated

✎ *Exercise 5–1*   Random sampling exercise

1. Obtain a list of families in the school district.

2. Assign a number to each family.

3. Randomly enter a table of random numbers.

4. Identify the families to be surveyed by using the table of random numbers.

✎ *Exercise 5–2*   Stratified random sampling exercise

1. Obtain a list of superintendents, principals, and teachers in the local area.

2. Randomly select a sample from each of the strata: superintendents, principals, and teachers. Since the populations of these groups will not be equal, decide the proportion to be selected from each group. Mail the bulletin and survey to those selected.

✎ *Exercise 5–3* Cluster sampling exercise

1. List all of the possible shelters from which the sample will be drawn.

2. Randomly select the shelters where interviewing is to occur.

3. Interview all individuals at the selected shelters or randomly select a specified number of individuals at the selected shelters.

✎ *Exercise 5–4* Systematic sampling exercise

1. Obtain a current list of faculty.

2. Randomly select a name near the beginning of the list.

3. Beginning with that name on the list, take every twelfth name on the list until 120 faculty have been chosen. Mail the questionnaire to them.

Answers to Sampling Exercises Requiring More Detail

✎ *Exercise 5–5*

1. Selection of the sample
    a. Having already identified the population (the 2,150 teachers in the district) and the sample size (10 percent, or 215 teachers), the first step is to list the names (or other identifying label such as social security numbers) of all the teachers in the district.
    b. Assign each individual on the list a number, beginning with "1" and continuing consecutively to "*n*" (however many names are on the list.)
    c. Select an arbitrary number from a table of random numbers. (Point to a number from the table with eyes closed.)
    d. Since the population is 2,150, use only the last four digits of the random number chosen from the table. Compare the selected random number with the numbers assigned in step c. If the random number selected corresponds to the number assigned to one of the teachers on the list, that teacher will be included in the sample. For example, if you pointed to random number 11693, you would find that the last four digits (1693) correspond to a teacher

on the list (since there are 2,150 teachers on the list.) The teacher with number 1693 will be included in the sample. If you chose random number 24319, the last four digits (4319) would not correspond to a teacher on the list (since there are only 2,150 teachers on the list) and you would ignore that number.

e. Go to the next random number on the list and repeat the procedure described in step d. Continue selecting teachers for the sample until 215 teachers have been selected.

2. Random selection minimizes selection as a threat to internal validity. Random selection enables the researcher to feel reasonably confident that the group of individuals chosen to be surveyed is equivalent to the group of individuals not chosen to be surveyed.

✎ *Exercise 5–6*

1. Having already identified the population (the 1,800 teachers in the district), the sample size (10 percent, or 180 teachers), and the relevant subgroups (elementary vs. secondary, and bachelor's degree [BA], master's degree or master's equivalent [MA], and master's degree plus at least thirty credits [MA+]), the first step is to classify all members of the total population according to the identified subgroups. First list the names (or other identifying label such as social security number) of all teachers in the district, along with their grade level (elementary or secondary) and educational level (BA, MA, or MA+).

2. Next make six subgroup lists, one for each intended subgroup (i.e., BA-elementary, BA-secondary, MA-elementary, MA-secondary, MA+-elementary, and MA+-secondary). Since the total sample is to be 180 teachers, and since you want each of the six subgroups to be equal in size, the number of teachers in each sample subgroup will be thirty.

3. Within each list, assign each individual on the list a number, beginning with "1" and continuing consecutively to "n" (however many names are on the subgroup list).

4. Select an arbitrary number from a table of random numbers. (Point to a number from the table with eyes closed.) Begin the sample selection with the BA-elementary subgroup (although you can begin with any of the subgroups).

5. Since the population is eighteen hundred, you would need to use only the last three digits of the random number chosen from the table (since there will be fewer than one thousand people in each subgroup.) Compare the selected random number with the numbers assigned in step 3. If the random number selected corresponds to the number assigned to one of the teachers on the list, that teacher will

be included in the sample. For example, if you pointed to random number 14073, and find that the last three digits (073) correspond to a teacher on the list, than the teacher with number 73 will be included in the sample. If you chose random number 68974, the last three digits (974) probably would not correspond to a teacher on the list and you would ignore that number.

6. Go to the next random number on the list and repeat the procedure described in step 5. Continue selecting teachers for the sample from this subgroup until thirty teachers have been selected.

7. Repeat steps 4 through 6 for each of the remaining subgroups until each has thirty teachers selected.

✎ *Exercise 5–7*

1. Selection and assignment of sample
   a. Since it is highly probable that the characteristics of the district (urban, suburban, or rural) might affect the results, it would be wise to choose schools from each of those settings. One sampling choice would be to choose a stratified random sample of schools. You would select such a sample by choosing, at random, four elementary schools from each type of district. To do this you would list all of the schools in each category, and within each category you would assign each school a number from "1" to "*n*."
   b. Select an arbitrary number from a table of random numbers.
   c. Since no category contains more than ninety-nine schools, you would use only the last two digits of the random number. Compare the selected random number with the numbers assigned in step b. If the random number selected corresponds to the number assigned to one of the schools on the list, that school will be included in the sample. For example, if you pointed to random number 80637, and found that the last two digits (37) correspond to a school on the list, then the school with number 37 will be included in the sample. If you chose random number 05396, the last two digits (96) probably would not correspond to a school on the list and you would ignore that number.
   d. Go to the next random number on the list and repeat the procedure described in step c. Continue selecting schools for the sample from this subgroup until four schools have been selected.
   e. Repeat steps b through d for each of the remaining subgroups until each has four schools selected.
   f. Within each school you would randomly assign one of the three classes at each grade level to each of the three instructional approaches.

2. Validity of results. External validity is limited to schools in the county. There might be characteristics of schools in the participating region that influence results. Other counties might not have those characteristics, so there is limited generalization. For example, the county might be economically depressed, so the results could not be generalized to a more prosperous county.

✎ *Exercise 5–8*

1. Possible strata include gender, elementary/secondary teachers, union/nonunion membership, age of teachers, length of service in the district, and level of education.

2. Sort teachers' names into age groups. Randomly select names from within those groups. Select twice as many names from the 41- to 50-year-old group. Determine their volunteerism activities.

✎ *Exercise 5–9*

1. Identify the three months in which attendance will be taken using a table of random numbers.

2. Divide the month into four parts. From each of the parts, randomly select one day in which attendance will be taken.

3. Determine the sample size. Using the class lists from each section of the course, assign a number to each student. Randomly enter the table of random numbers near the top. Select every "*n*th" student to be tracked.

✎ *Exercise 5–10*

1. Even-numbered entries on the list seem to include more females, while odd-numbered entries seem to include more males. When you choose every second name, you may have a sample of mostly males or females. The group chosen would not be equivalent to the group that is not chosen, thus causing a threat to internal validity.

2. Before choosing every second name on the list, reorder the list in some logical way, such as by alphabetical order, to ensure an approximately equal number of males and females being chosen.

3. Randomly enter the list near the beginning. Then select every second name on the list and mail the survey to individuals who have been chosen.

✎ *Exercise 5–11*

1. Randomly select four sections (clusters) to be involved in the study.

2. Randomly assign two clusters to serve as the treatment groups. The other two groups will serve as the control groups (no treatment).

✎ *Exercise 5–12*

1. Randomly select school districts for participation. Of the approximately 500 districts, choose about 50. Then randomly assign districts to one of three groups. Assume that all teachers in a given district will have the same class size/staffing arrangement.

2. School districts should be representative of all areas in the state—urban, suburban, and rural. The results can be generalized to the state in which the study was conducted.

Answers to Sampling Exercises Requiring Analysis

✎ *Exercise 5–13*

1. The population for this study consists of the students in the district in grades four through twelve. The sample was a cluster sample of elementary students.

2. The primary advantage in this study was economy/convenience. By limiting the study to elementary students, the researcher was able to use a single teacher, the guidance counselor. The disadvantages are mainly related to the external validity of the results. The researcher cannot know whether the results obtained are generalizable to the junior/senior high school students. The researcher could have selected classes from all grade levels, fourth through twelfth. (This probably would have meant that the school counselor could not have done all of the teaching.)

✎ *Exercise 5–14*

1. Although the researcher may be interested in generalizing to all elementary teachers, the actual population for this study is probably the elementary teachers in the nine school districts. The sample is best described as a biased sample or sample of convenience, since it is not truly random, nor is there any assurance that it is representative of the population.

2. The most serious problem with this sample is the fact that it is not necessarily representative of the population. The fact that the districts were chosen through personal contacts may bias the sample in many ways, as can the fact that buildings within the district were chosen not at random but by a central office administrator. Finally, the fact that the participants were volunteers is a possible source of sample bias. There is a question whether the results would be the same if different teachers had been interviewed.

    A sample with greater potential external validity could be chosen by various procedures, depending on whether the intended population was all elementary teachers, elementary teachers in this region, or elementary teachers in the nine districts studied. If the intended population was elementary teachers in the region, a representative sample of regional districts must first be selected. Then from within those districts teachers should be selected, using either random sampling techniques or stratified random sampling techniques. The results from such a sample could more confidently be generalized to the population.

✎ *Exercise 5–15*

1. The computer club is a self-selected group with interest in computers. They may be students who are better at problem solving.

2. Potential biases exist because of dubious representation in the sample. There is no consideration of such variables related to the sample, for example, grade level, gender, interest, attitude, and the opportunity to participate because of the availability of transportation home after school.

✎ *Exercise 5–16*

1. Cluster sampling was used since the classes are intact.

2. Two of the teachers will conduct research—one for the experimental group and one for the control group. Either one of these researchers, because of his or her investment in the project, may unintentionally affect the subjects' behaviors through nonverbal or verbal cues.

✎ *Exercise 5–17*

1. There is no guarantee of equal representation on such criteria as ability, gender, and socioeconomic status.

2. The results can be generalized to an urban setting of similar characteristics.

✎ *Exercise 5–18*

1. The sample is limited and may not be representative of homeless students. For example, some homeless students may not be in school, or some homeless families may have reported permanent addresses and are not identified as homeless. In situations like these, not all homeless students have an equal opportunity to be chosen during sampling and therefore may not be included in the sample.

2. The sample is small. There needs to be further exploration as to why students with a permanent address are achieving at a significantly higher level. The achievement may be based on additional factors other than being homeless, such as regularity of attendance in school.

✎ *Exercise 5–19*

1. The researcher has not accounted for major, gender, or year of graduation, all of which might reveal different patterns in relationships.

2. The researcher might use stratified random sampling with major, gender, and year of graduation as variables for stratification.

✎ *Exercise 5–20*

1. Volunteers are a biased sample.

2. There is at least one threat to internal validity because volunteers are a biased sample.

3. The tentative conclusion might be that practicing for the interview enhances interviewing skills. However, this conclusion is unwarranted until the study can be replicated with a larger sample of subjects who are not volunteers.

4. One alternate procedure would be to randomly select interviewees from a larger population.

✎ *Exercise 5–21*

1. The sample described here is a proportional stratified random sample.

2. The advantage of using a stratified random sample in this study is that the sample is more likely to be representative of the population, with respect to the level of teaching (which was believed to be important). The disadvantages are primarily practical. It would probably take more time and be more expensive to require observers to travel to several schools throughout the district to make their observations, and any particular school might have only one or two teachers in the sample.

3. A cluster sample could be selected by randomly choosing elementary, middle, and senior high schools, rather than individuals. Then, having chosen the schools, teachers within each chosen school would be randomly selected for inclusion in the sample.

✎ *Exercise 5–22*

1. The researcher's systematic sampling method is faulty. He should have randomly chosen a name with which to begin his count, rather than starting with the first name on the list.

2. Stratified random selection would offer more representative groups to be surveyed. Strata might include males/females; majors, if the department offers more than one program; regional areas of employment; and number of years of employment.

SUMMARY

This chapter has focused on the more common sampling designs. Certain sampling designs are preferred over others. The researcher should use random sampling or stratified random sampling, whenever possible. These sampling designs strengthen internal validity more so than cluster sampling or systematic sampling. An alternative may be to use combinations of the sampling designs, as suggested in some solutions to the problems in this chapter. Bias sampling or sampling for convenience should be avoided because this type of sample is not representative of the population to which the results will be generalized.

6 CHOOSING STATISTICAL TECHNIQUES

INTRODUCTION

Once the data have been collected in a research study, the next step usually involves the analysis of those data. The choice of the analytical procedures depends on several factors, including the type of research question that was asked originally and the characteristics of the data that were collected (Sowell & Casey, 1982). These factors are discussed in the following sections, and a procedure is provided that will assist in the systematic selection of an appropriate statistical analysis technique.

TYPE OF RESEARCH QUESTION

In Chapter 2 the different types of research questions were described. The type of research question is an important consideration in choosing the appropriate statistical procedure. Each type of research question, **descriptive, relational,** or **causal-comparative,** is associated with a kind of statistical procedure, namely, **descriptive, correlational,** and **inferential.** The statistics are described in the following.

Descriptive Statistics

In some descriptive studies there may be no need for statistical analysis of the data collected. It may be sufficient merely to present the number or percentage of people who answered a question in a certain way, or who behaved in a particular manner. If there is a need to simplify those data in some way, descriptive statistics may be appropriate. **Descriptive statistics** include the **arithmetic mean** (or **mean**), the **median,** the **mode** (these are often collectively referred to as **measures of central tendency**), the **range,** and the **standard deviation** (these are often referred to as **measures of variability** or **measures of dispersion**).

The **measures of central tendency** are so named because they represent a kind of center to the set of scores we are examining. This "center" is often a score around which the other scores tend to be clustered. The **mean** is the average of a set (or distribution) of scores and is calculated by adding up all of the individual scores and dividing the total by the number of scores in the set. The **median** is the "middle" score in a distribution of scores and is determined by finding the point above which, and below which, half of the scores fall. The **mode** is the score, or range of scores, that occurs most frequently in a distribution of scores. It is determined simply by comparing the frequency with which each score or range of scores occurs and identifying the most frequently occurring value.

If we look at the distribution of scores in Table 6–1, we can calculate or determine the three measures of central tendency. If we add all of the individual scores, we obtain a sum of 820. Since there are ten scores, if we divide 820 by 10, we obtain an average, or mean, score of 82.

TABLE 6–1   *Example of Student Scores*

Student	Score	Student	Score
Alan	75	Fredina	88
Becky	83	Greg	77
Carlos	86	Herb	82
Devonna	84	Indira	79
Eduardo	79	Jiening	87

By rearranging the scores from highest to lowest (or lowest to highest) as follows,

88   87   86   84   83   82   79   79   77   75

we see that the middle of the distribution is between the score of 83 and the score of 82. Half of the scores are above that point, and half of the scores are below that point. The "midpoint" between 83 and 82 is 82.5, so we would call 82.5 the median score for this distribution.

Finally, we see that the score of 79 occurs twice, which is more frequent than any other score. The mode (or modal score) for this distribution is 79. Note that a distribution can have more than one mode or no mode at all.

The mean is the most commonly used measure of central tendency, probably since most people are familiar with the concept of an average. The median is used, instead of the mean, to represent the center of a distribution that has no limit on one or both of its ends, and which can therefore have extreme scores in a distribution. Using the previous example, suppose we add an extremely low score to this distribution, say a score of 0. The sum is still 820, but it is now divided by 11, yielding a mean for the distribution of 74.5. The midpoint of this new distribution is obtained by finding the midpoint of the following rearranged scores:

88   87   86   84   83   82   79   79   77   75   0

The midpoint of this distribution is 82, with five scores above 82 and five scores below 82. The median score is 82. Notice that the addition of an extreme score caused the mean score to drop 8.5 points, while the median dropped only 0.5 points. It is clear by looking at the distribution that 82 is more accurately the "center" of the new distribution than is 74.5.

The mode is used when the research intends to identify a preference or a common response.

The **measures of variability** are so named because they provide an indication of how "spread out" (or "variable" or "dispersed") a distribution of scores tends to be. The **range** is the difference between the maximum score achieved and the minimum score achieved. The **standard deviation** is a kind of average of the amount by which the typical score in the distribution differs (or deviates) from the mean score. The range for the first distribution of scores above is 13, and the range for the second distribution of scores is 88.

The standard deviation is obtained by first calculating the mean score and then calculating the amount by which each individual score differs, or deviates, from the mean. Then the individual deviation score is squared and the squared deviation scores are totaled. Table 6–2 summarizes these steps.

TABLE 6–2   *Computation of Standard Deviation*

Mean = 82

Student	Score	Deviation Score	Deviation Score Squared
Alan	75	−7	49
Becky	83	+1	1
Carlos	86	+4	16
Devonna	84	+2	4
Eduardo	79	−3	9
Fredina	88	+6	36
Greg	77	−5	25
Herb	82	0	0
Indira	79	−3	9
Jiening	87	+5	+ 25
			174

We now divide the total of the squared deviation scores either by the number of scores (if we are calculating for a population) or by the number of scores minus 1 (if we are calculating for a sample). If we assume that these students represent the entire population, we divide 174 by 10 and get a result of 17.4. This quantity is called the variance, and its square root is the standard deviation. The square root of 17.4 is 4.17. We can use this quantity to say that the mean score for this group is 82, and the typical score deviates from the mean by 4.17 points. The larger the standard deviation is, the more spread out or dispersed are the scores in the distribution.

Descriptive statistics are usually presented in a table or in a histogram or bar chart to summarize the data for the attribute, trait, or characteristic under consideration.

Correlational Statistics

As discussed in Chapter 2, **relational research** has as its focus the identification of how changes in one characteristic or variable correspond (or do not correspond) to changes in another characteristic or variable. If, to use the example mentioned in Chapter 2, a researcher is interested in finding out whether or not there is any association or relationship between exercise habits and health status (or between height and weight measurements) for a group of people, we would call that research relational, and we would choose a procedure to calculate a coefficient of correlation.

The coefficient of correlation is a number that varies between −1.0 and +1.0 and that indicates the strength of the relationship between two variables. A correlation coefficient of +1.0 indicates that there is a perfect positive relationship between the two variables. That is, for every increase (or decrease) in one variable, there is a corresponding increase (or decrease) in the other variable. A correlation coefficient of −1.0 indicates a perfect negative relationship between two variables. That is, for every increase in one variable there is a corresponding decrease in the other, and for every decrease in the first variable, there is a corresponding increase in the second.

Table 6–3 provides three measurements for the group of students used in the earlier examples. Note that for each student there are three different scores.

We can visually illustrate the relation between two variables by plotting a scattergram (or scatterplot). In a scattergram, one variable is represented on the vertical axis and the other variable is represented on the horizontal axis. The scattergram in Figure 6–1 shows the relationship between scores on test 1 and scores on test 2 from Table 6–3.

By examining closely the data in the table, we can see that for every increase in the score on test 1, there is a corresponding increase in the score on test 2. This is a perfect positive correlation, and, as the scattergram in Figure 6–1 shows, is indicated by a straight line from the lower left to the upper right of the graph.

The scattergram in Figure 6–2 shows the relationship between scores on test 2 and scores on test 3.

By examining closely the data in the table, we can see that for every increase in the score on test 2, there is a corresponding

TABLE 6–3   *Example of Three Scores for Students*

Student	Test 1	Test 2	Test 3
Alan	75	43	87
Becky	83	51	79
Carlos	86	54	76
Devonna	84	52	78
Eduardo	79	47	83
Fredina	88	56	74
Greg	77	45	85
Herb	82	50	80
Indira	79	47	83
Jiening	87	55	75

FIGURE 6–1

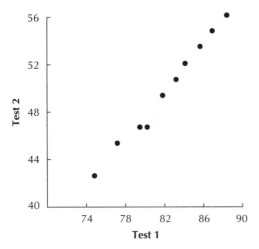

decrease in the score on test 3. This is a perfect negative correlation, and, as the scattergram in Figure 6–2 shows, is indicated by a straight line from the upper left to the lower right of the graph.

The idea of the null hypothesis was discussed in Chapter 1. For correlational research questions, the null hypothesis would be that there is no relationship between the two variables. Another way of stating this null hypothesis is that there is no statistically significant coefficient of correlation between the two variables. There are several statistical procedures for calculating the coefficient of correlation.

FIGURE 6–2

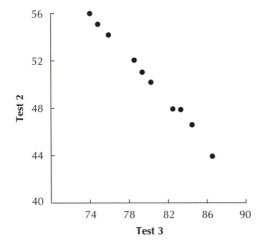

The process of choosing the appropriate procedure will be discussed later in this chapter.

Inferential Statistics

The third category of research questions described in Chapter 2 was causal-comparative research, which has as its focus the identification of causes and effects. Using the example from Chapter 2, if a researcher wants to know if more exercise results in people being healthier, he or she might design a study where people are assigned to different groups, each of which was led in different amounts of exercise. By comparing the health status of the groups, after some time has passed, the researcher can infer the extent to which differences in exercise cause health status differences in people. The statistical procedures for analyzing the data would use the values on the posttreatment measurement of health status. The mean "scores" on that measure for each exercise group would be compared to determine whether any differences were statistically significant. The null hypothesis is that the mean scores for all groups would be the same. Another way of stating this null hypothesis is that there is no statistically significant difference between (or among) the mean scores for the different groups. There are various statistical procedures for deciding whether statistically significant differences exist between (or among) the groups. The process of choosing the appropriate procedure will be discussed in a following section.

PARAMETRIC OR NONPARAMETRIC TECHNIQUES

The choice of a specific statistical procedure depends on several factors. First, the nature of the research question must be determined. Once that has been identified, the researcher must decide whether parametric or nonparametric techniques are most appropriate.

Parametric statistics are those that make certain assumptions about the nature of the data that have been collected and about the nature of the distribution of those data. If any of the assumptions can not confidently be supported, the researcher should consider nonparametric statistics, which are based on less rigid assumptions.

The assumptions underlying the use of parametric statistics pertain to the *measurement scale* of the data being collected, the extent to which the data are *normally distributed,* and the extent to which the data distributions for all groups have *equal variances.* Each of these assumptions is discussed briefly in the following.

Measurement Scales

A **nominal** scale is one where numbers are used to label or categorize the various groups formed by a variable. For example, for the variable "undergraduate major" we might use a "1" to represent education majors, a "2" to represent science majors, a "3" to represent arts majors, and so on. The numbers do not represent any quantity of anything, but are merely numerical labels for purposes of identification.

An **ordinal** scale is one on which the numbers are used to indicate the rank or order for the value of some trait. For example, a data-collection instrument may ask respondents to indicate the extent to which they agree with a series of statements. If "1" indicates disagreement, "2" indicates neutrality, and "3" indicates agreement, we can think of the number as indicating the degree of agreement, with "3" representing more agreement than "2" and "2" indicating more agreement than "1." We know that a person responding with a "3" to a statement agrees more to that statement than another person who responds with a "2," but we do not know how much more that person agrees.

An **interval** scale not only provides ranking information but also represents an amount or quantity of the trait being measured. It is called an interval scale, because an interval between any points on the scale represents the same quantity, regardless of where on the scale it occurs. For example, we often measure temperature using the Fahrenheit or Celsius scales. In either case, 1° represents the same amount regardless of where on the scale it is. In other words, the difference between 17° and 24° represents the same amount of "temperature" as the difference between 82° and 89°.

A **ratio** scale is one that has all the properties of an interval scale but also has an "anchor point," which is often indicated by a value of zero, which represents an absence or "not any" of the trait being measured. For example, on a linear scale with units of inches, a length of zero inches means no length at all. This property allows us to express different quantities as ratios or multiples of each other. A line that is four inches long is twice as long as a line two inches long. (Note that we cannot validly make these kinds of comparisons for interval data such as temperature, since a temperature of 0°F does not represent zero average heat because there are temperatures below 0° on both the Fahrenheit and Celsius scales).

In order to use parametric statistical procedures, the data for the dependent variable must be from an interval or ratio scale. Since ratio scales are uncommon in educational data (Gay, 1992; Tuckman, 1994; Wiersma, 1991); and, since for purposes of statistical analysis, there is no need to distinguish between ratio and interval data, interval data will be considered to include ratio data. If the dependent variable consists of ordinal or nominal data, the researcher should consider nonparametric procedures.

Normal Distributions

A normal distribution is a frequency polygon (i.e., a graph on which the height of the curve indicates the frequency with which the score at that point is obtained) that has certain characteristics. The mean, median, and mode all occur at the same point, and, when plotted and smoothed, the graphed data appear as the familiar symmetrical bell-shaped curve shown in Figure 6–3. In addition, the normal curve has certain proportions of scores in each identified region, as shown in Figure 6–3.

When the distribution is substantially skewed, or unbalanced, like the distributions shown in Figure 6–4, the curve is not "normal."

When the frequency distribution is badly skewed, the use of parametric statistics may not be appropriate. This is generally not a problem when the number of scores is greater than thirty (Wiersma, 1991). For smaller samples, you can quickly plot the scores to get an idea of whether or not the distribution is skewed. For example,

FIGURE 6–3

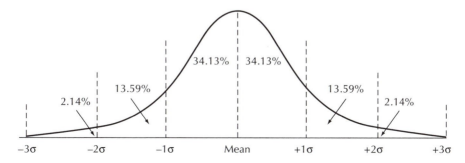

FIGURE 6–4

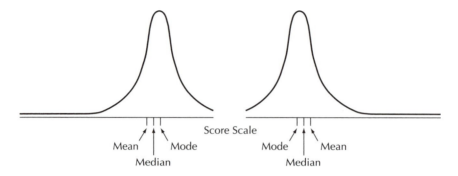

if we use the data for the students shown in Table 6–4, we could plot the frequency histogram shown in Figure 6–5.

The data plotted in Figure 6–5 seem to be symmetrical, with the mean, median, and mode all falling on the same point. It is probably safe to conclude that the distribution is normal, or at least not significantly "non-normal." By contrast, if we plot the data for the scores shown in Table 6–5, we see a very different distribution.

The data from Table 6–5 can be plotted to form the graph shown in Figure 6–6. It is clear that the data in this graph are definitely skewed and therefore the distribution is "non-normal."

TABLE 6–4   Example of Normally Distributed Student Scores

Student	Score	Student	Score
Alan	45	Fredina	45
Becky	35	Greg	55
Carlos	65	Herb	55
Devonna	75	Indira	65
Eduardo	55	Jiening	55

FIGURE 6–5

```
                        X

                        X

              X    X    X

         X    X    X    X    X

        35   45   55   65   75
```

TABLE 6–5   *Example of Non-Normally Distributed Student Scores*

Student	Score	Student	Score
Alan	95	Fredina	85
Becky	85	Greg	75
Carlos	85	Herb	65
Devonna	75	Indira	55
Eduardo	95	Jiening	85

FIGURE 6–6

```
                         X

                         X

                 X       X       X

         X       X       X       X       X

        55      65      75      85      95
```

Equality of Variance

The final assumption underlying those parametric statistical tests used for comparing groups is that the variance in all groups to be compared should be equal. An easy way to check this assumption is merely to examine the standard deviations for the groups to be compared. If the standard deviations are about equal, the assumption is probably satisfied.

Suppose that for a group of boys and girls we obtain the results shown in Table 6–6. The standard deviations for the two groups (i.e., males and females) is nearly the same. We could confidently conclude that the equality of variance assumption for these groups is satisfied. If, on the other hand, the standard deviation for the females was 11.94 instead of 6.71, we would probably question the validity of the equality of variance assumption.

TABLE 6–6   *Midterm Mathematics Examination Scores*

	Mean	Number	Standard Deviation
Males	75.4	34	6.58
Females	78.9	38	6.71

Some computerized programs for statistical analysis (e.g., the t-test in Statistical Package for the Social Sciences) automatically test whether or not this assumption is supported, and many such programs offer an alternate test that does not assume equal variances in all groups being compared.

Choosing Parametric or Nonparametric Methods

When trying to choose between parametric and nonparametric tests, a researcher will typically ask the following questions:

1. Are the data for the dependent variable on an interval or ratio scale? If the answer is no, then consider a nonparametric test.

2. Are the data for the dependent variable normally distributed? If the answer is no, then consider a nonparametric test.

3. Are the standard deviations approximately equal for all groups being compared? If the answer is no, then consider a nonparametric test.

Although many research texts stress the assumptions that underlie the use of parametric tests, there are some who point out that these assumptions are often not critical. Scheffé (1959) noted that "among the underlying assumptions made in deriving statistical methods are usually some that are apt to be violated in applications and are introduced only to ease the mathematics of the derivation" (p. 360).

Similarly, Kerlinger (1986) argued that "parametric methods are robust in the sense that they perform well even when the assumptions behind them are violated—unless, of course, the violations are gross or multiple. Nonparametric methods, then, are highly useful secondary or complementary techniques that can often be valuable in behavioral research" (p. 275).

STATISTICAL PROCEDURES

Having decided on parametric or nonparametric statistical tests, the next step for the researcher is to choose the appropriate specific statistical procedure. The first question that the researcher asks here is whether the research question points to a possible relationship or a possible difference.

Relate or Compare

Using the example of health habits and health status introduced earlier, the research question was framed in a manner that suggests a relationship or association between the two variables. In this example, there is one group of participants, and for each participant there are two measurements, one for health habits and another for health status. The researcher is interested in finding out whether or not there is a pattern in the way these two measurements vary together. When the researcher is looking for a relationship or an association between variables, correlational statistics are in order.

On the other hand, suppose a researcher was interested in comparing males and females in regard to their health habits. The research question in this case points toward a comparison of the two groups, and the researcher will test to see if there is a significant difference between the two groups.

Independent or Dependent Samples

The next thing to look for is whether the data for any of the groups to be compared are independent of each other or whether they are somehow dependent on each other (i.e., related or linked). For example, when comparing males and females, the data are taken from two separate and therefore independent samples, but when using a single group and comparing their pretreatment scores with their posttreatment scores, the scores are dependent on each other since they come from the same individuals.

Number of Groups

Finally, after the researcher has decided whether the test should relate or compare (i.e., look for an association or a difference) and whether the samples are independent or dependent (related), the next step in choosing a specific statistical procedure involves identifying the number of dependent variables and/or the number of groups to be compared. For example, if the researcher is looking for a difference between two groups, the appropriate statistic might be a t-test, but if there are three or more groups, an analysis of variance

(ANOVA) might be appropriate. Similarly, if a researcher is trying to predict health status based on a measurement of health habits, a simple correlation might be appropriate, but if the researcher is using several predictors (e.g., exercise habits, dietary habits, other lifestyle factors) to try to predict health status, a multiple regression might be appropriate.

Applying the Decision-making Process

In order to try to put the entire process of choosing a specific statistical procedure into a systematic framework, the following **statistical procedure decision chart** shown in Figure 6–7 has been devised. Each intersection on the chart represents a decision point that corresponds to one of the questions addressed in this section or the preceding section on parametric versus nonparametric tests. After making each of the indicated decisions, a path is chosen which leads to the next decision, and ultimately to a specific statistical test. Please keep in mind that not every possible statistical procedure is depicted on this chart, but that it does include many of the most widely and frequently used procedures. You may want to refer to a text that provides a more thorough discussion of various statistical procedures.

To illustrate the use of this chart, let us, as an example, use the situation referred to earlier. Suppose a researcher was interested in comparing males and females in regard to their health habits and, in particular, the number of hours of vigorous exercise males and females get, on average, each week. We would start by identifying the dependent variable (hours of exercise per week) and deciding on the nature of the measurement scale for that dependent variable. Time (i.e., hours per week) is scaled on a ratio scale. (Note that ratio and interval data are treated in exactly the same way here. Therefore, all references will be to interval data, which include ratio data as well.)

The next step on the chart pertains to the research question, whether we are looking for an association (relationship) or a difference (comparison). In our example we are comparing males to females. Now we must decide if the distributions are normal and if the variances (standard deviations) are equal in the two groups. Next, we ask if the samples are independent or dependent (they are independent in our example). Finally, we ask if there are two groups or more than two groups (there are two groups).

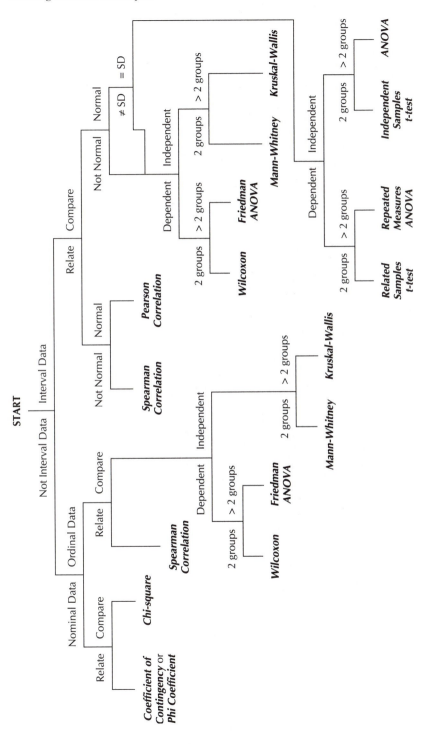

FIGURE 6–7 Statistical Procedure Decision Chart

Depending on whether we judged the distributions to be normal or not, and the standard deviations to be equal or not, we end up choosing either a **Mann-Whitney test** or an **independent samples t-test.** Since no information was provided about the nature of the distribution or the magnitude of the variance in the groups, we are unable to choose between these two tests. However, the comments of Scheffé and Kerlinger, quoted earlier, suggest that both tests would result in the same decision about rejecting or not rejecting the null hypothesis.

STATISTICAL SIGNIFICANCE

The purpose of conducting a statistical analysis of the data is to make a decision regarding the null hypothesis. From Chapter 1, you should recall that there are two basic decisions regarding the null hypothesis: the researcher could decide to reject the null hypothesis, or the researcher could decide not to reject the null hypothesis.

Since these decisions are based on probabilities, not certainties, there is a chance that the researcher will make an incorrect decision. The researcher should decide, before analyzing the data, how much of a risk of being wrong he or she is willing to take. Much educational and social sciences research uses a risk level of 5 percent. That is, the researcher is willing to accept a 5 percent probability of being wrong if a decision is made to reject the null hypothesis. This risk level is often referred to as alpha (α). The choice of α is somewhat arbitrary. There are situations where more or less risk is acceptable, depending on the consequences of making a wrong decision. In any case, α represents the maximum risk of being wrong that a researcher is willing to assume in making a decision to reject the null hypothesis.

The results of most statistical analyses include an indication of the actual probability of being wrong in deciding to reject the null hypothesis. This indication is usually referred to as p, or the statistical significance level. It represents the actual probability that the researcher made an error if he or she decided to reject the null hypothesis.

The decision to reject or not reject the null hypothesis is based on a comparison of p with α. If, for example, a researcher decided that a risk of 5 percent ($\alpha = .05$) was acceptable, and conducted a statistical analysis that resulted in a statistical significance of $p = .03$, we can see that the actual likelihood of being wrong is less than the risk that was acceptable. That is, $p < \alpha$. In this case, the researcher would decide to reject the null hypothesis. If, on the other hand, the researcher found $p > \alpha$, the decision would be not to reject the null hypothesis, since the likelihood of making an error is greater than the allowable risk.

In summary:

if $p \leq \alpha$, reject the null hypothesis

if $p > \alpha$, do not reject the null hypothesis

When we say that a result was significant at the $p < .05$ level, we are saying that these results would occur by chance only 5 times (or fewer) out of 100. Since there is only a 5 in 100 probability that the results occurred by chance, there is only a 5 (or fewer) in 100 probability that the researcher made an incorrect decision if the null hypothesis was rejected.

POST HOC ANALYSES

For some situations it is necessary to conduct additional statistical analyses after completing the initial analysis. For example, suppose a researcher has collected data to compare the achievement scores of two groups of students, each of which had been taught using a different instructional method. Suppose further that the researcher had used Figure 6–7 to select a t-test as the appropriate analysis procedure, and that the t-test indicated that the null hypothesis should be rejected. The null hypothesis for this situation is that there is no difference in the mean achievement scores of the two groups. In other words:

$$\text{mean achievement}_{\text{group 1}} = \text{mean achievement}_{\text{group 2}}$$

The alternative hypotheses are:

$$\text{mean achievement}_{\text{group 1}} > \text{mean achievement}_{\text{group 2}}$$

$$\text{mean achievement}_{\text{group 1}} < \text{mean achievement}_{\text{group 2}}$$

Since the t-test indicated that there was a significant difference between the two groups, the researcher would simply look at the means and see which of the two means was larger.

Suppose that instead of two groups, there were three groups. Now the researcher, using Figure 6–7, would select an analysis of variance (ANOVA) as the appropriate analysis procedure. Assume that the ANOVA indicated that the null hypothesis should be rejected. The null hypothesis for this situation is that there is no difference in the mean achievement scores of the three groups. In other words:

mean achievement$_{\text{group 1}}$ = mean achievement$_{\text{group 2}}$ = mean achievement$_{\text{group 3}}$

Unlike the first case, with two groups, there are now many alternative hypotheses such as the following:

mean achievement$_{\text{group 1}}$ = mean achievement$_{\text{group 2}}$ > mean achievement$_{\text{group 3}}$

mean achievement$_{\text{group 1}}$ = mean achievement$_{\text{group 2}}$ < mean achievement$_{\text{group 3}}$

mean achievement$_{\text{group 1}}$ > mean achievement$_{\text{group 2}}$ = mean achievement$_{\text{group 3}}$

mean achievement$_{\text{group 1}}$ < mean achievement$_{\text{group 2}}$ = mean achievement $_{\text{group 3}}$

mean achievement$_{\text{group 1}}$ > mean achievement$_{\text{group 2}}$ > mean achievement$_{\text{group 3}}$

mean achievement$_{\text{group 1}}$ < mean achievement$_{\text{group 2}}$ < mean achievement$_{\text{group 3}}$

A possible set of means is shown in the following:

	Group 1	Group 2	Group 3
Achievement Score	73	67	75

Even if the ANOVA indicates a significant difference among the groups, the researcher cannot know which group is significantly different from which other group(s). Is the achievement of group 1 significantly different from that of group 2? Is it different from that of group 3? What about the difference between group 2 and group 3? Which of the alternative hypotheses explains why the null hypothesis should be rejected?

The researcher could conduct separate t-tests for each pair. That is, group 1 could be compared with group 2, then group 1 could be compared with group 3, and finally group 2 could be compared with group 3. For reasons that are not relevant here, such a plan, while logical, is not statistically appropriate. Fortunately, there is a set of analysis procedures that makes all of these comparisons, and that is statistically appropriate. These techniques are called **post hoc tests.** (They are sometimes also referred to as **a posteriori** tests or tests of multiple comparisons.) There are numerous post hoc tests, including the **Scheffé, Duncan's,** and **Newman Keul's** tests, as well as many others. Consult a statistics textbook or a statistical program manual (e.g., SPSS) for a more complete listing and criteria for choosing one test over another.

When to Use a Post Hoc Test

A post hoc test should be used when two conditions are met:

1. When more than two groups are being compared

2. When the ANOVA indicates that the null hypothesis should be rejected

Although post hoc tests are parametric techniques, and there are no nonparametric post hoc tests, Huck, Cormier, and Bounds (1974) suggest that the **Wilcoxon** or the **Mann-Whitney** tests could be used for multiple comparisons if the nonparametric ANOVA (i.e., Kruskal-Wallis or Friedman) results in a decision to reject the null hypothesis.

The results of post hoc tests or other follow-up tests of multiple comparisons give us a clearer picture of why the null hypothesis was rejected. By indicating which mean scores were significantly different from which other mean scores, they provide us with a better idea of which alternative hypothesis was the reason for rejecting the null hypothesis.

COMPETENCIES

The exercises in this chapter will provide practice in choosing the appropriate statistical procedure to analyze the data from a research study. After completing the exercises in this chapter, you will be able to

- Describe relevant descriptive statistics and their appropriate uses

- Choose appropriately between correlational and inferential statistical procedures

- Describe the relevant characteristics of the different measurement scales: nominal, ordinal, interval, ratio

- Identify the nature of the measurement scale (i.e., nominal, ordinal, interval, ratio) for the data collected in a research study

- Identify the extent to which data satisfy the assumptions for parametric statistical procedures

- Make decisions regarding the choice of parametric or non-parametric statistical procedures

- Make appropriate choices of statistical procedures for data analysis given a research situation

- Defend the choice of a statistical procedure for data analysis

STATISTICAL ANALYSIS EXERCISES

Read each research situation and answer the questions. Base your response to each question only on the information given in the description. If data are provided, plot the distribution and calculate the standard deviation. If data are not given, assume they are normally distributed, unless otherwise noted. Use Figure 6–7 as a reference.

✎ **Exercise 6–1**   A school guidance counselor was interested in determining if instruction and practice in participating in a more formal setting in kindergarten would affect the ability to attend to formal instructional tasks in first grade. The null hypothesis stated, "There is no difference in time-on-task as a function of instruction." The time-on-task data shown below were collected from twenty kindergarten students, ten in each group. One kindergarten group had no instruction on time-on-task behavior; the other kindergarten group had instruction on time-on-task behavior. The study was conducted during the second semester of the academic year. Data were gathered using an observation instrument that measured time-on-task during the first month of first grade.

Data: Time on task in minutes—instruction (12, 15, 24, 21, 15, 18, 21, 18, 18, 18); no instruction (9, 12, 21, 18, 12, 15, 18, 15, 15, 15)

Note: Plot frequency histograms of the data for each group to determine if the distributions appear normal. Calculate the means and standard deviations.

1. Were the data to be related or compared?

2. How many groups were studied? Are these groups dependent or independent?

3. Decide whether or not to use parametric statistics.
   a. What is the dependent variable?
   b. What kind of measurement scale is used?
   If the scale is interval, answer parts c and d.
   c. Are the data normally distributed in all groups?
   d. Are there equal variances in all groups?

4. Identify one statistical test that would be appropriate for analysis. Indicate whether this is a parametric or a nonparametric test.

5. Specify whether there is a need to use follow-up procedures (a post hoc test).

✎ **Exercise 6–2**   A college of education requires students to take an exam to demonstrate competence in working with special needs students. Since many of the education majors were not passing the competency exam, the department administering the exam decided to determine if the students would be more successful with additional study sessions. Eighty students registered for the exam. Forty of these students were assigned to ten study sessions; the other forty students attended two study sessions. The null hypothesis stated, "There is no difference in the number of students who pass or fail the exam as a function of the number of study sessions." When students completed the study sessions, they took a competency exam that was scored pass (P) or fail (F).

1. Were the data to be related or compared?

2. How many groups were studied? Are these groups dependent or independent?

3. Decide whether or not to use parametric statistics.
   a. What is the dependent variable?
   b. What kind of measurement scale is used?
   If the scale is interval, answer parts c and d.
   c. Are the data normally distributed in all groups?
   d. Are there equal variances in all groups?

4. Identify one statistical test that would be appropriate for analysis. Indicate whether this is a parametric or a nonparametric test.

5. Specify whether there is a need to use follow-up procedures (a post hoc test).

✎ **Exercise 6–3** A college of education dean was interested in determining if an urban junior field experience made a difference in student teachers' choice of an urban location for their student teaching. The null hypothesis stated, "There is no difference in the choices of student teaching location as a function of junior field experience location." The sample was fifty students, twenty-five in each group, from the college of education at the dean's university. Data analysis consisted of calculating the mean rank of the urban student teaching choices of students who had and did not have an urban junior field experience.

1. Were the data to be related or compared?

2. How many groups were studied? Are these groups dependent or independent?

3. Decide whether or not to use parametric statistics.
    a. What is the dependent variable?
    b. What kind of measurement scale is used?
    If the scale is interval, answer parts c and d.
    c. Are the data normally distributed in all groups?
    d. Are there equal variances in all groups?

4. Identify one statistical test that would be appropriate for analysis. Indicate whether this is a parametric or a nonparametric test.

5. Specify whether there is a need to use follow-up procedures (a post hoc test).

✎ **Exercise 6–4** College admission officers were interested in determining if there was a relationship between rank in high school graduating class and success in college as indicated by rank in overall grade point average. The null hypothesis stated, "There is no relationship between rank in high school graduating class and rank in overall grade point average earned in college." The sample was one thousand students randomly selected from community colleges across the northeastern United States.

1. Were the data to be related or compared?

2. How many groups were studied? Are these groups dependent or independent?

3. Decide whether or not to use parametric statistics.
    a. What is the dependent variable?
    b. What kind of measurement scale is used?
    If the scale is interval, answer parts c and d.
    c. Are the data normally distributed in all groups?
    d. Are there equal variances in all groups?

4. Identify one statistical test that would be appropriate for analysis. Indicate whether this is a parametric or a nonparametric test.

5. Specify whether there is a need to use follow-up procedures (a post hoc test).

✎ **Exercise 6–5**   A state department of education wanted to consider allowing school districts to determine their own regulations regarding curriculum. The officials decided to try this plan on a pilot basis and gather some data prior to having the state board recommend a "curriculum regulation–free" system. The null hypothesis stated, "There is no difference in scores on the assessment of educational progress as a function of state regulation on curriculum." All of the school districts in the state were randomly selected and assigned to one of three curriculum conditions: no regulations, modified regulations, or full regulations. At the end of four academic years, a state assessment of educational progress was administered to assess achievement levels.

Note: No regulations—mean = 75; SD = 8.75
Modified regulations—mean = 90; SD = 8.25
Full regulations—mean = 60; SD = 8.35

Data are normally distributed.

1. Were the data to be related or compared?

2. How many groups were studied? Are these groups dependent or independent?

3. Decide whether or not to use parametric statistics.
    a. What is the dependent variable?
    b. What kind of measurement scale is used?
    If the scale is interval, answer parts c and d.
    c. Are the data normally distributed in all groups?
    d. Are there equal variances in all groups?

4. Identify one statistical test that would be appropriate for analysis. Indicate whether this is a parametric or a nonparametric test.

5. Specify whether there is a need to use follow-up procedures (a post hoc test).

✎ **Exercise 6–6**   A university department has established an internship abroad. The 100 students going abroad were required to complete a multicultural values assessment. The department was interested in determining the relationship between scores on the multicultural values scale (scores vary from 0 to 100) and grade point average in the major. The null hypothesis stated, "There is no relationship between multicultural values and grade point average in the major."

1. Were the data to be related or compared?

2. How many groups were studied? Are these groups dependent or independent?

3. Decide whether or not to use parametric statistics.
   a. What is the dependent variable?
   b. What kind of measurement scale is used?
   If the scale is interval, answer parts c and d.
   c. Are the data normally distributed in all groups?
   d. Are there equal variances in all groups?

4. Identify one statistical test that would be appropriate for analysis. Indicate whether this is a parametric or a nonparametric test.

5. Specify whether there is a need to use follow-up procedures (a post hoc test).

✎ **Exercise 6–7**   The administration of a large urban school district with thirteen high schools was interested in determining if wearing school uniforms decreased the incidence of violence in school. The administration decided randomly to assign the schools to one of three groups. One group would wear school-determined uniforms, a second group would wear their own "formal dress" (shirts/ties for boys; dresses for girls), and a third group would wear what adolescents generally wear to school. At the end of the period of the study, all thirteen schools were ranked according to the incidents of violence that occurred within the period of the study. The null hypothesis stated, "There will be no significant difference in mean rank of incidents of violence as a function of school dress style."

1. Were the data to be related or compared?

2. How many groups were studied? Are these groups dependent or independent?

3. Decide whether or not to use parametric statistics.
   a. What is the dependent variable?
   b. What kind of measurement scale is used?
   If the scale is interval, answer parts c and d.
   c. Are the data normally distributed in all groups?
   d. Are there equal variances in all groups?

4. Identify one statistical test that would be appropriate for analysis. Indicate whether this is a parametric or a nonparametric test.

5. Specify whether there is a need to use follow-up procedures (a post hoc test).

✎ **Exercise 6–8**   The attendance officer in a high school was concerned about the high rate of absenteeism, especially with male students. He explored his concern by comparing the attendance records of 9 pairs of brothers and sisters who were randomly selected from the high school. The null hypothesis stated, "There is no difference in the number of days of absence between brothers and sisters." Attendance was monitored during the first semester of the academic year.

Data: Number of days of absence—brothers (12, 12, 15, 18, 18, 18, 18, 21, 21); sisters (3, 3, 3, 6, 6, 9, 9, 12, 12)

Note: Plot frequency histograms of the data for each group to determine if distributions appear to be normal. Calculate the means and standard deviations.

1. Were the data to be related or compared?

2. How many groups were studied? Are these groups dependent or independent?

3. Decide whether or not to use parametric statistics.
   a. What is the dependent variable?
   b. What kind of measurement scale is used?
   If the scale is interval, answer parts c and d.
   c. Are the data normally distributed in all groups?
   d. Are there equal variances in all groups?

4. Identify one statistical test that would be appropriate for analysis. Indicate whether this is a parametric or a nonparametric test.

5. Specify whether there is a need to use follow-up procedures (a post hoc test).

✎ **Exercise 6–9**   A team of teachers at the elementary level was interested in determining which of three methods of teaching basic math facts was more successful. Sixty students were placed into groups of three, matched on the basis of mathematics achievement scores, thus forming matched triads. Members of each triad were randomly assigned to one of three methods of learning basic math facts: memorizing the facts, singing fact songs, or working on fact computer software. The null hypothesis was, "There is no difference in the number of correct answers on the math facts test as a function of instruction." When instruction had been completed, the students were tested on their knowledge of math facts.

Note: Data were not normally distributed.

1. Were the data to be related or compared?

2. How many groups were studied? Are these groups dependent or independent?

3. Decide whether or not to use parametric statistics.
   a. What is the dependent variable?
   b. What kind of measurement scale is used?
   If the scale is interval, answer parts c and d.
   c. Are the data normally distributed in all groups?
   d. Are there equal variances in all groups?

4. Identify one statistical test that would be appropriate for analysis. Indicate whether this is a parametric or a nonparametric test.

5. Specify whether there is a need to use follow-up procedures (a post hoc test).

✎ **Exercise 6–10** A high school recently held student council elections. During the campaigning, there was debate about support for male and female candidates for the president of student council. The student council wanted to know if male students supported the male candidate and female students supported the female candidate for president. The null hypothesis stated, "There is no relationship between the gender of the voter and the gender of the candidate."

1. Were the data to be related or compared?

2. How many groups were studied? Are these groups dependent or independent?

3. Decide whether or not to use parametric statistics.
   a. What is the dependent variable?
   b. What kind of measurement scale is used?
   If the scale is interval, answer parts c and d.
   c. Are the data normally distributed in all groups?
   d. Are there equal variances in all groups?

4. Identify one statistical test that would be appropriate for analysis. Indicate whether this is a parametric or a nonparametric test.

5. Specify whether there is a need to use follow-up procedures (a post hoc test).

✎ **Exercise 6–11** A physical educator wanted to compare two types of fitness programs for elementary students, one that occurred outdoors using typical playground equipment and another that occurred indoors using gymnasium equipment. The hypothesis stated, "There is no difference in the scores on the physical fitness test as a function of fitness program." The physical educator matched twenty males and females, ten in each group, for the study and stratified randomly assigned a student from each pair to the outdoor condition and indoor condition. A physical fitness test was given to each student at the completion of the fitness programs.

Data: Total scores on the fitness test—indoors (50, 60, 60, 70, 70, 70, 70, 80, 80, 90); outdoors (55, 65, 65, 75, 75, 75, 75, 85, 85, 95)

Note: Plot frequency histograms of the data for each group to determine if distributions appear normal. Calculate the means and standard deviations.

1. Were the data to be related or compared?

2. How many groups were studied? Are these groups dependent or independent?

3. Decide whether or not to use parametric statistics.
    a. What is the dependent variable?
    b. What kind of measurement scale is used?
    If the scale is interval, answer parts c and d.
    c. Are the data normally distributed in all groups?
    d. Are there equal variances in all groups?

4. Identify one statistical test that would be appropriate for analysis. Indicate whether this is a parametric or a nonparametric test.

5. Specify whether there is a need to use follow-up procedures (a post hoc test).

✎ **Exercise 6–12**   A middle school mathematics teacher was interested in determining the most effective way to teach probability: whole-class instruction/demonstration, whole-class instruction/small-group hands-on activity, or video instruction followed by computer software application. The null hypothesis stated, "There will be no difference in scores on a probability test as a function of the type of instruction." Students were randomly assigned to the mode of instruction. A test on probability was given during the final week of instruction.

Note: Assume that data are normally distributed and group variances are equal.

1. Were the data to be related or compared?

2. How many groups were studied? Are these groups dependent or independent?

3. Decide whether or not to use parametric statistics.
    a. What is the dependent variable?
    b. What kind of measurement scale is used?
    If the scale is interval, answer parts c and d.
    c. Are the data normally distributed in all groups?
    d. Are there equal variances in all groups?

4. Identify one statistical test that would be appropriate for analysis. Indicate whether this is a parametric or a nonparametric test.

5. Specify whether there is a need to use follow-up procedures (a post hoc test).

ANSWERS TO STATISTICAL ANALYSIS EXERCISES

✎ *Exercise 6–1*   Yes, distributions appear normal.

```
                       X
                       X
             X     X   X
     X   X   X     X   X
     12  15  18    21  24
             Instruction
```

Mean = 18; SD = 3.29.

```
                       X
                       X
             X     X   X
     X   X   X     X   X
     9   12  15    18  21
            No Instruction
```

Mean = 15; SD = 3.29.

1. The data were to be compared.

2. There were two groups in the study. The groups were independent.

3. a. The dependent variable is time-on-task.
    b. The interval scale is the type of measurement scale.
    c. Data are normally distributed.
    d. There are equal variances in both groups.

4. An appropriate statistical test would be the independent samples t-test. It is a parametric test.

5. There is no need to use a follow-up test since only two groups are being studied.

✎ *Exercise 6–2*

1. The data were to be compared.

2. There were two groups in the study. These groups were independent.

3. a. The dependent variable is the number of students passing and failing the test.
   b. The nominal scale is the type of measurement scale.

4. An appropriate statistical test would be the chi-square test. It is a non-parametric test.

5. There is no need to use a follow-up test since only two groups are being studied.

✎ *Exercise 6–3*

1. The data were to be compared.

2. There were two groups in the study. These groups were independent.

3. a. The dependent variable is the rank of the choice of urban site.
   b. The ordinal scale is the type of measurement scale.

4. An appropriate statistical test would be the Mann-Whitney test. It is a nonparametric test.

5. There is no need to use a follow-up test since only two groups are being studied.

✎ *Exercise 6–4*

1. The data were to be related.

2. There was one group in the study.

3. a. There is no dependent variable since this is not a causal-comparative study.
   b. There are two measurement scales. Both scales are ordinal scales.
   c. Normal distribution of data is not an issue because of the large N.
   d. Equal variance is not an issue when there is one group.

4. An appropriate statistical test would be the Spearman rank order correlation. It is a nonparametric test.

5. No follow-up test is needed since no comparison is being made.

✎ *Exercise 6–5*

1. The data were to be compared.

2. There were three groups in the study. The groups were independent.

3. a. The dependent variable is the score on the state assessment of educational progress.
   b. The interval scale is the type of measurement scale.
   c. Data are normally distributed.
   d. There are approximately equal variances in the groups.

4. An appropriate statistical test would be the analysis of variance. It is a parametric test.

5. If the null hypothesis is rejected, a post hoc test should be used. There are three groups in the study, and a post hoc test would be needed to determine which groups are significantly different.

✎ *Exercise 6–6*

1. The data were to be related.

2. There was one group in the study.

3. a. There is no dependent variable since this is not a causal-comparative study.
   b. The interval scale is the type of measurement scale.
   c. Normal distribution of data is not an issue because of the large N.
   d. Equal variance is not an issue when there is one group.

4. An appropriate statistical test would be the Pearson product-moment correlation. It is a parametric test.

5. No follow-up test is needed since no comparison is being made.

✎ *Exercise 6–7*

1. The data were to be compared.

2. There were three groups in the study. The groups were independent.

3. a. The dependent variable is the rank of each school according to the number of incidents of violence.
   b. The ordinal scale is the type of measurement scale.

4. An appropriate statistical test would be the Kruskal-Wallis Analysis of Variance of Ranks. It is a nonparametric test.

5.   If the null hypothesis is rejected, a follow-up test should be used. There are three groups in the study, and a Mann-Whitney test could be used to determine which groups are significantly different.

✎ *Exercise 6–8*   No, the distributions do not appear normal.

```
                        X
                        X
        X           X   X
        X   X       X   X
        12  15      18  21
```
Absences of Brothers

Mean = 17; SD = 3.00.

```
        X
        X   X   X   X
        X   X   X   X
        3   6   9   12
```
Absences of Sisters

Mean = 7; SD = 3.46.

1.   The data were to be compared.

2.   There were two groups in the study. The groups were dependent.

3.   a.   The dependent variable is the number of days of absence.
     b.   The interval scale is the type of measurement scale.
     c.   Data are not normally distributed.
     d.   There are approximately equal variances in the groups.

4.   An appropriate statistical test would be the Wilcoxon matched-pairs signed-ranks test. It is a nonparametric test.

5.   There is no need to use a follow-up test since only two groups are being studied.

✎ *Exercise 6–9*

1.   The data were to be compared.

2.   There were three groups in the study. The groups were dependent.

3.   a.   The dependent variable is the number of correct answers on the math facts test.
     b.   The interval scale is the type of measurement scale.

    c.   The data are not normally distributed.

    d.   The variances are not known.

4.   An appropriate statistical test would be the Friedman analysis of variance of ranks. It is a nonparametric test.

5.   If the null hypothesis is rejected, a follow-up test should be used. There are three groups in the study, and a Wilcoxon test could be used to determine which groups are significantly different.

✎ *Exercise 6–10*

1.   The data were to be related.

2.   There was one group in the study.

3.   a.   There is no dependent variable since this is not a causal-comparative study.

    b.   The nominal scale is the type of measurement scale.

4.   An appropriate statistical test could be either the coefficient of contingency or the phi coefficient. These are nonparametric tests.

5.   No follow-up test is needed since no comparison is being made.

✎ *Exercise 6–11*   Yes, the distributions appear normal.

```
                    X
                    X
          X    X    X
     X    X    X    X    X
     50   60   70   80   90
         Indoor Fitness Scores
```

Mean = 70; SD = 10.95.

```
                    X
                    X
          X    X    X
     X    X    X    X    X
     55   65   75   85   95
        Outdoor Fitness Scores
```

Mean = 75; SD = 10.95.

1.   The data were to be compared.

2.   There were two groups in the study. The groups were dependent.

3.   a.   The dependent variable is the score on the fitness test.
     b.   The interval scale is the type of measurement scale.
     c.   Data are normally distributed.
     d.   There are equal variances in both groups.

4.   An appropriate statistical test would be the related samples t-test. It is a parametric test.

5.   There is no need to use a follow-up test since only two groups are being studied.

✎ *Exercise 6–12*

1.   The data were to be compared.

2.   There were three groups in the study. The groups were independent.

3.   a.   The dependent variables are scores on the probability tests.
     b.   The interval scale is the type of measurement scale.
     c.   Data are normally distributed.
     d.   There are equal variances in both groups.

4.   An appropriate statistical test would be the ANOVA. It is a parametric test.

5.   If the null hypothesis is rejected, a post hoc test should be used. There are three groups in the study, and a post hoc test would be needed to determine which groups are significantly different.

SUMMARY

This chapter has provided a systematic way of considering and choosing statistical procedures for data analysis. The statistical procedures discussed here include the most commonly used techniques employed in educational research. Chapter 7 will deal with how we try to make sense of the results of our data analysis and how we use those results to draw conclusions about our experimental hypotheses.

7

INTERPRETING
RESEARCH
RESULTS

INTRODUCTION

Following the analysis of data, the next step for the researcher is to organize and interpret the results of the data collection and analyses. Since the general purpose of conducting a research study is to answer questions in a systematic manner, the interpretation of the results must focus first on the question that was asked, or inferred, in the problem statement.

In order to interpret the results, the researcher must first report them in a clear and understandable manner. Next, the researcher should draw conclusions regarding the various research hypotheses. Finally, the researcher should discuss the implications of the research findings and offer recommendations based on those findings.

REPORTING THE RESULTS

The results of a research study are most useful when they are reported in a clear and comprehensible fashion. This requires the researcher to report the results of the data analysis in text, tables, and graphs.

Since much, if not most, research data today are analyzed using computerized statistical analysis programs, the results of the analysis are generated by the computer. We shall use, as an illustration, the results of a series of Statistical Package for the Social Sciences (Norusis, 1992) analyses of data collected from several groups of students enrolled in a research methods course. From these students, the following data were collected (Note: the Statistical Package for the

Social Sciences variable name is identified in parentheses): height (HEIGHT), weight (WEIGHT), age in months (AGE), month of birth (MONTH), gender (GENDER), undergraduate grade point average (GPA), the miles per gallon of the car most usually driven (MPG), and the section of the class in which the students were enrolled (GROUP). The Statistical Package for the Social Sciences command lines for these data follow:

```
TITLE "Example Data Analyses".
DATA LIST /
        ID 1-3
        HEIGHT 5-6
        WEIGHT 8-10
        AGE 12-14
        MONTH 16-17
        GENDER 19
        GPA 21-23(2)
        MPG 25-26
        GROUP 29-29.
VARIABLE LABELS
        AGE "Age in months"/
        MONTH "Month of birth"/
        MPG "Miles per gallon of car usually driven"/
        GROUP "Class".
VALUE LABELS
        GENDER      1 "Male" 2 "Females"/
        MONTH       1 "January" 2 "February" 3 "March" 4 "April"
                    5 "May" 6 "June" 7 "July" 8 "August" 9 "September"
                    10 "October" 11 "November" 12 "December".
MISSING VALUES
        HEIGHT (99)/WEIGHT TO AGE (999)/MONTH (99)/GENDER (9)/
        GPA TO MPG (999)/GROUP (99).
```

The first three and last two cases from this data set are shown below.

```
BEGIN DATA
001 70 180 292 10 1 310 33 01
002 66 130 280 09 2 309 17 01
003 69 160 300 02 1 330 35 01
.........................
.........................
107 63 112 380 04 2 390 29 07
108 67 130 483 06 2 360 23 07
END DATA.
```

These data are organized according to the Statistical Package for the Social Sciences command lines listed earlier.

To illustrate the form of Statistical Package for the Social Sciences output, let's suppose that we wanted to know the number of male and female students in the sample. The following Statistical Package for the Social Sciences command line would be used:

```
FREQUENCIES VARIABLES=GENDER /STATISTICS=NONE.
```

This would result in the following output from SPSS:

```
GENDER

                                              Cum
Value Label        Value  Frequency  Percent  Percent

Male                  1        43     39.8     39.8
Females               2        65     60.2    100.0
                            -------  -------
                   Total     108     100.0
```

It is from this type of output that the text, tables, and/or graphs will be prepared.

An important element in the interpretation of the results of data analyses is that of sample size. The following section, on degrees of freedom, discusses how information about sample size is interpreted and reported in the discussion of the results of data analysis.

Degrees of Freedom

The size of a research sample has important implications for the validity, and in particular the generalizability, of research results. In general, a researcher is advised to use the largest sample possible (Borg & Gall, 1989).

Sample size information is usually reported as part of the output from most computerized data analyses, and is an important aspect of interpreting and reporting those results. Sample size is often reported as **degrees of freedom** (abbreviated as *df*). Degrees of freedom refers to the number of ways in which the data are free to vary. In general, the degrees of freedom are determined by subtracting the number of restrictions placed on the data from the total number of scores (Wiersma, 1991).

To understand the relationship between degrees of freedom and sample size, consider a relatively simple situation involving three scores, from students A, B, and C. Suppose that all we knew was that the mean of the three scores was 70. The value of the score for student A could be anything. (The same is true, of course, for the value of the scores for students B and C as well.) We might say that the values of the three scores are free to vary. Now suppose we knew that the score for student A was 85, and that the mean for all three scores was 70. The values for the scores for students B and C could still be anything and still result in a mean score of 70. Again, the scores for B and C are still free to vary.

Let's now suppose that we knew that the score for A was 85, the score for B was 60, and the mean was 70. Now the score for student C is no longer free to vary but is fixed at 65. The only way the three scores could have a mean of 70, if two of the scores were 85 and 60, is if the third score is 65. In this set of three scores, two of the scores are free to vary, but once they are "set," the third score is determined, and therefore is not free to vary. We would say that, in this example, we have two degrees of freedom. Degrees of freedom for a sample is simply the number in the sample minus one ($df = n - 1$).

Degrees of freedom can also refer to treatments or groups as well as to a sample. For example, if a researcher is comparing the relative effectiveness of four different methods of instruction, the degrees of freedom for the treatment variable (method of instruction) would be equal to the number of treatments minus one ($4 - 1 = 3$). The determination of df for different analyses will be described in the sections that follow as part of the discussion of reporting results of the analyses.

In the following sections, output from different statistical analyses will be shown, followed by examples of how that output might be presented in text, tables, and/or graphs.

Descriptive Analyses

Suppose we wanted to know the overall average undergraduate grade point average and the overall miles per gallon for our sample, and in addition we wanted to know the standard deviation and the minimum and maximum values for scores in this sample. We could use the following command line to obtain descriptive statistics for the variable GPA:

```
DESCRIPTIVES VARIABLES=GPA MPG /STATISTICS=13.
```

This SPSS command line would result in the following output:

```
Variable     Mean    Std Dev  Minimum   Maximum      N
GPA          3.27       1.01     2.00      4.00     108
MPG         26.11      14.49       10        99     108
```

The text presentation of the descriptive statistics would look something like the following:

> The 108 students in the sample maintain an overall B+ average in their undergraduate studies ($M_{GPA} = 3.27$, SD = 1.01) and usually drive cars that get generally good gas mileage ($M_{MPG} = 26.11$, SD = 14.49).

Presenting the other descriptive statistics in text might become awkward and difficult for the reader to follow. In such cases, presenting the results in a table might be preferable. Since this information is already in a tabular format, the table could be incorporated into the research report almost exactly as it appears in the SPSS output. It is important to note that most research reports that are published in journals or other formats usually conform to a standard editorial style (e.g., the editorial style described in the *Publication Manual of the American Psychological Association)* for tables, figures (which include graphs), as well as text. An example of a table that conforms to this format is shown in Table 7–1.

If the researcher wanted to obtain a frequency distribution for one of the variables, such as GROUP, the following SPSS command would be used:

```
FREQUENCIES VARIABLES=GROUP /STATISTICS=NONE.
```

This would result in the following SPSS output:

```
GROUP     Class


                                          Cum
Value Label              Value Frequency Percent Percent

                           1       17     15.7    15.7
                           2       12     11.1    26.9
                           3       28     25.9    52.8
                           4       18     16.7    69.4
                           5       13     12.0    81.5
                           6        9      8.3    89.8
                           7       11     10.2   100.0
                                 -------  -------
                         Total    108    100.0

Valid cases     108    Missing cases     0
```

These results are not easily presented in text, and although the table is somewhat better, a figure such as a bar graph, such as Figure 7–1, might provide a clearer presentation of these results.

TABLE 7–1   Grade Point Average and Automobile Mileage for Research Students

Variable	N	Mean	SD	Minimum	Maximum
GPA	108	3.27	1.01	2.00	4.00
MPG	108	26.11	14.49	10	44

FIGURE 7–1   Number of Students in Each Class

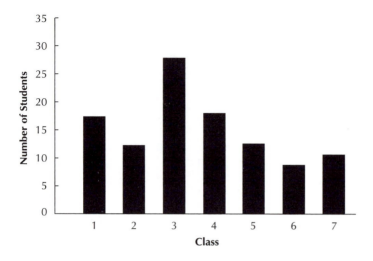

Correlational Analyses

Using the data from our example, let's imagine that the researcher wanted to find out whether or not there was any relationship between students' height and weight, and whether there was any relationship between students' height and their GPA. The null hypotheses for these questions would be as follows:

H_1: There will not be a significant correlation between HEIGHT and WEIGHT.

H_2: There will not be a significant correlation between HEIGHT and GPA.

The following command line would execute a Pearson product-moment correlation to test these hypotheses:

```
CORRELATIONS VARIABLES=HEIGHT WITH WEIGHT GPA/OPTIONS=5.
```

This SPSS command line would result in the following output:

```
Correlations:   WEIGHT      GPA

    HEIGHT        .6998      -.1150
                 (  108)    (  108)
                 P= .000    P= .238

(Coefficient / (Cases) / 2-tailed Significance)
```

Examination of the correlation matrix from the SPSS printout reveals that H_1 would be rejected and that H_2 would not be rejected. (Note that the value of p for the HEIGHT × WEIGHT correlation is shown as .000. This is because SPSS rounds to three significant places after the decimal point. This should be interpreted as $p < .001$.)

An example of a text presentation of these analyses is as follows:

> There was a statistically significant positive correlation between students' height and their weight, $r(107) = + .6998$, $p < .001$, while the negative correlation between height and GPA was not statistically significant, $r(107) = -.1150$, $p = .238$.

Note that in the preceding sample text report, r is the symbol for the coefficient of correlation and the number 107 in parentheses following the r represents the degrees of freedom for this analysis. There were 108 pairs of scores in the correlation analysis, and since the df is the number of pairs minus one, the df for this analysis is 107.

If there were many variables correlated with each other in the analysis, the presentation of the results in a figure containing the correlation matrix might make the presentation clearer. If, for example, the researcher correlated HEIGHT, WEIGHT, GPA, and MPG with each other, we might present the resulting correlation matrix as shown in Table 7–2.

TABLE 7–2   *Correlation Matrix for Selected Variables*

	HEIGHT	**WEIGHT**	**GPA**	**MPG**
HEIGHT	1.0000	.6998	−.1150	−.0297
	(108)	(108)	(108)	(108)
	$p = .000$	$p = .000$	$p = .238$	$p = .761$
WEIGHT	.6998	1.0000	−.2410	−.0898
	(108)	(108)	(108)	(108)
	$p = .000$	$p = .000$	$p = .012$	$p = .358$
GPA	−.1150	−.2410	1.0000	.5500
	(108)	(108)	(108)	(108)
	$p = .238$	$p = .012$	$p = .000$	$p = .000$
MPG	−.0297	−.0898	.5500	1.0000
	(108)	(108)	(108)	(108)
	$p = .761$	$p = .358$	$p = .000$	$p = .000$

Inferential Analyses

The T-Test.
Suppose the researcher in our example wanted to compare men and women students on their height and GPA. The researcher, in this case

would be looking for differences between two independent groups, a group of men and a group of women, and would probably choose an independent samples t-test to decide if the observed differences were statistically significant. The null hypotheses for this situation would be as follows:

H_1:   There will be no significant difference between men and women in height.

H_2:   There will be no significant difference between men and women in GPA.

The SPSS command line for the analyses to test these hypotheses is as follows:

```
T-TEST     GROUPS=GENDER (1,2)/VARIABLES=HEIGHT GPA.
```

This SPSS command line would result in the following output:

Variable	Number of Cases	Mean	SD	SE of Mean
HEIGHT				
Male	43	69.7674	2.689	.410
Females	65	65.0156	2.763	.345

Mean Difference = 4.7518

Levene's Test for Equality of Variances: F= .368   P= .545

Variances	t-test for Equality of Means t-value	df	2-Tail Sig	SE of Diff	95% CI for Diff
Equal	8.82	106	.000	.539	(3.683, 5.821)
Unequal	8.86	91.90	.000	.536	(3.687, 5.817)

Variable	Number of Cases	Mean	SD	SE of Mean
GPA				
Male	43	2.9853	.453	.069
Females	65	3.4551	1.219	.151

Mean Difference = -.4697

Levene's Test for Equality of Variances: F= .590   P= .444

Variances	t-test for Equality of Means t-value	df	2-Tail Sig	SE of Diff	95% CI for Diff
Equal	-2.41	106	.017	.195	(-.855, -.084)
Unequal	-2.82	87.72	.006	.166	(-.800, -.139)

From this SPSS analysis we obtain a considerably more complex printout than in previous analyses. To interpret this printout, let's look at the analysis for HEIGHT in sections. First is the section that simply presents some descriptive statistics about the HEIGHT of males and females in our sample.

Variable	Number of Cases	Mean	SD	SE of Mean
HEIGHT				
Male	43	69.7674	2.689	.410
Females	65	65.0156	2.763	.345

Mean Difference = 4.7518

The information contained in this section is labeled in the headings of the printout table. (Note that SD refers to the standard deviation and SE refers to the standard error). The value of the mean difference is simply the mean height of males minus the mean height of females (i.e., $69.7674 - 65.0156 = 4.7518$).

In the next section, SPSS automatically tests the parametric assumption about equality of variance in the two samples. We can see from the first section that the standard deviations for the males and females are nearly equal (i.e., 2.689 and 2.763, respectively). The Levene's test helps us determine whether the difference between the standard deviations is significant.

Levene's Test for Equality of Variances: F= .368   P= .545

In this case, since the value of $p < .05$, we would not treat the standard deviations as significantly different, and we therefore would accept the assumption of equal variance as being valid.

Even if the difference between the standard deviations for males and females was judged to be significant (and therefore the equal variance assumption is not correct), SPSS automatically provides an alternative test that does not rely on this assumption.

	t-test for Equality of Means				95%
Variances	t-value	df	2-Tail Sig	SE of Diff	CI for Diff
Equal	8.82	106	.000	.539	(3.683, 5.821)
Unequal	8.86	92.90	.000	.536	(3.687, 5.817)

If we decide that the variances (i.e., standard deviations) are *not* significantly different, we would use the "equal variances" row from the printout section above. If, on the other hand, we had decided that the variances were significantly different, we would use the "unequal" row from the printout. In the current example, we would use the "equal" row and decide that the difference between males and females in HEIGHT was statistically significant. Note that in a t-test, the total degrees of freedom equals the sum of the degrees of freedom for each of the two groups, or, $(43 - 1) + (65 - 1) = 106$. The text presentation of these results would say:

> There was a statistically significant difference, $t(106) = 8.82$, $p < .001$, in height between males (mean = 69.7674) and females (mean = 65.0156).

The text presentation for the comparison of male and female GPA scores would say:

> There was a statistically significant difference, $t(106) = 2.41$, $p = .017$, in GPA between males (mean = 2.9853) and females (mean = 3.4551).

One-way ANOVA
When there are more than two groups to be compared, and if the data meet the assumptions of parametric statistics, the researcher would probably use an analysis of variance (ANOVA) as the statistical analysis procedure. Suppose that the researcher in our example was interested in determining whether or not there were differences in height among the seven groups of students. Since there is only one independent variable (GROUP), the researcher would use a one-way ANOVA, using the following SPSS commands:

```
ONEWAY    HEIGHT BY GROUP(1,7)/
          STATISTICS=1/
          RANGES=SNK (.05).
```

These SPSS commands would produce the output shown beginning on the following page. The first part of this output is the ANOVA table, which indicates that the null hypothesis (i.e., there are no differences in height among the groups) should be rejected. Textually, this would be reported as follows:

> There was a statistically significant difference in height among the seven groups, $F(6,100) = 3.98$, $p = .0013$.

In this text report we see the term "$F(6,100)$." This notation is slightly different from that used in the t-test. When conducting between-group comparisons, we must consider the degrees of freedom both between groups and within groups. In a t-test there are never more than two groups; therefore, the between-groups *df* is always 1 (number of groups minus 1) and is usually not stated in a report. The number in parentheses in a t-test is the *df* within groups. In an ANOVA there are often more than three groups. The first number in parentheses after the *F* represents the *df* between groups, and the second number represents the *df* within groups. Since there were seven groups, the *df* between groups is six (number of groups minus 1). The *df* within groups is found by first finding the *df* for each group (n − 1) and then calculating the sum of those numbers. The numbers of people in groups 1 through 7 were 17, 12, 28, 18, 13, 8, and 11. The corresponding degrees of freedom for those groups are 16, 11, 27, 17, 12, 7, and 10. The sum of these numbers is 100, which is the *df* within groups. Another way of determining the *df* within groups is to subtract the number of groups from the number of subjects (e.g., 107 − 7 = 100).

The next section of the output provides some descriptive statistics for the groups in the analysis. The specific statistics that are displayed are controlled by a line in the SPSS command (i.e., STATISTICS = 1). Consult an SPSS manual for the commands needed to display other descriptive statistics.

Since there are so many groups, presentation of these descriptive statistics in text is not practical. A table presenting all or some of this information would be advisable.

```
- - - - - - - - - - O N E W A Y - - - - - - - - - -

    Variable  HEIGHT
   By Variable  GROUP      Class

                        Analysis of Variance

                          Sum of      Mean        F      F
       Source     D.F.    Squares     Squares    Ratio  Prob.

Between Groups      6     263.3479    43.8913    3.9827  .0013

Within Groups     100    1102.0540   11.0205

Total             106    1365.4019
```

```
- - - - - - - - - O N E W A Y - - - - - - - - -
```

Group	Count	Mean	Standard Deviation	Standard Error	95 Pct Conf Int for Mean		Minimum	Maximum
Grp 1	17	68.1176	2.5220	.6117	66.8210 To	69.4143	64.0000	72.0000
Grp 2	12	67.8333	3.2427	.9361	65.7730 To	69.8937	63.0000	73.0000
Grp 3	28	66.6071	3.3592	.6348	65.3046 To	67.9097	58.0000	73.0000
Grp 4	18	68.5000	3.5355	.8333	66.7418 To	70.2582	61.0000	74.0000
Grp 5	13	63.2308	2.6506	.7351	61.6290 To	64.8325	60.0000	71.0000
Grp 6	8	66.2500	3.1960	1.1299	63.5781 To	68.9219	62.0000	71.0000
Grp 7	11	67.1818	4.6004	1.3871	64.0912 To	70.2724	60.0000	73.0000
Total	107	66.9252	3.5890	.3470	66.2373 To	67.6131	58.0000	74.0000

```
- - - - - - - - - O N E W A Y - - - - - - - - -
```

        Variable HEIGHT
     By Variable GROUP   Class

Multiple Range Test

Student-Newman-Keuls Procedure
Ranges for the   .050 level -

        2.82   3.37   3.70   3.93   4.11   4.26

The ranges above are table ranges.
The value actually compared with Mean(J)-Mean(I) is..
        2.3474 * Range * Sqrt(1/N(I) + 1/N(J))

(*) Denotes pairs of groups significantly different at the   .050 level

                        G G G G G G G
                        r r r r r r r
                        p p p p p p p

       Mean   Group   5 6 3 7 2 1 4

      63.2308   Grp 5
      66.2500   Grp 6   *
      66.6071   Grp 3   *
      67.1818   Grp 7   *
      67.8333   Grp 2   *
      68.1176   Grp 1   *
      68.5000   Grp 4   *

The last section of the output contains the results of the post hoc test that was ordered by using the SPSS command: RANGES = SNK (.05). As can be seen in the output, the means for the seven groups are listed in order from lowest to highest on the left. The groups are then identified, in the same order from left to right across the top. This display forms a matrix. The asterisk is used to mark the groups that differ significantly from each other. The output in this section shows that group 5 was significantly different in height from each of the other groups. This finding would be reported as:

The results of a Newman-Keuls post hoc test revealed that group 5, with a mean height of 63.2308, was significantly shorter in height than all of the other groups. No other groups differed from each other significantly in height.

Multiway ANOVA

When there is more than one independent variable, the multiway ANOVA is used. For example, if the researcher wanted to combine the two comparisons done previously (i.e., comparing height as a function of gender and as a function of group), the two-way ANOVA could be employed, using these SPSS commands:

```
ANOVA    HEIGHT BY GENDER(1,2) GROUP (1,7)/
         STATISTICS=3.
```

These SPSS commands would produce the output shown beginning on the next page. The first section of this output consists of the descriptive statistics requested in the analysis. First the overall mean and number of subjects (in parentheses) are provided. Next the means and number of subjects are provided for each gender category, and for each group. Finally, the means and number of subjects are displayed for each gender within each group. If descriptive statistics for this analysis are to be presented, it would be advisable to prepare a table from this section of the SPSS output.

The next section of the SPSS output is the ANOVA table, which indicates that the null hypotheses for both gender and groups should be rejected. This decision is made by checking the significance of F (which is the same as p) for each variable. In the column labeled "Source of Variation," the variables GENDER and GROUP are listed. Following the GENDER line across to the column labeled "Signif of F," we find the value .000. This indicates that the value of p, that is, the probability of obtaining this effect by chance, is very small. In fact, the SPSS output is rounded to three significant numbers after the decimal point, so this finding is reported as follows:

Males (average height = 69.77 inches) were significantly taller than females (average height = 65.02), $F(1,93) = 62.762$, $p < .001$.

Note that since the value of p was rounded to .000, we do not know from this output the exact value of p. Therefore, we can report it as < .001.

In the same fashion, we would decide to reject the null hypothesis regarding differences in height among the seven groups, reporting this finding textually by saying:

There were significant differences in height among the seven groups, $F(6,93) = 3.807$, $p = .015$.

```
             * * *  C E L L   M E A N S  * * *

            HEIGHT
         BY GENDER
            GROUP    Class

TOTAL POPULATION

    66.93
 (   107)

GENDER
         1         2

    69.77     65.02
 (    43) (    64)

GROUP
         1         2         3         4         5         6         7

    68.12     67.83     66.61     68.50     63.23     66.25     67.18
 (    17) (    12) (    28) (    18) (    13) (     8) (    11)

            GROUP
              1         2         3         4         5         6         7
GENDER
         1   70.50     69.43     68.90     70.80     71.00     69.33     69.17

             (   6) (    7) (   10) (   10) (    1) (    3) (    6)


         2   66.82     65.60     65.33     65.63     62.58     64.40     64.80

             (  11) (    5) (   18) (    8) (   12) (    5) (    5)
```

```
        * * *  A N A L Y S I S   O F   V A R I A N C E  * * *

            HEIGHT
         BY  GENDER
            GROUP   Class
```

Source of Variation	Sum of Squares	DF	Mean Square	F	Signif of F
Main Effects	697.174	7	99.596	14.409	.000
GENDER	433.826	1	433.826	62.762	.000
GROUP	116.431	6	19.405	2.807	.015

CONTINUED

Source of Variation	Sum of Squares	DF	Mean Square	F	Signif of F
2-way Interactions	25.385	6	4.231	.612	.720
GENDER GROUP	25.385	6	4.231	.612	.720
Explained	722.560	13	55.582	8.041	.000
Residual	642.842	93	6.912		
Total	1365.402	106	12.881		

Note that the *df* for within groups in this analysis is obtained from the item in the ANOVA table labeled "Residual." Further note that since the value of *F* was statistically significant ($p < .05$) and there were more than two groups, a post hoc test is needed. In order to conduct a post hoc test, the SPSS procedure ONEWAY must be used, as shown earlier in this chapter.

Nonparametric Tests

When the assumptions for parametric tests are not met, a researcher may use nonparametric tests, which rely on less rigid assumptions.

Mann-Whitney Test   Suppose the researcher intended to compare males and females with respect to the miles per gallon of cars they usually drive, and further suppose that the researcher was concerned that the data for the dependent variable, MPG, were significantly skewed (i.e., not normally distributed). Since there are two independent groups, the researcher might choose to analyze the data using the Mann-Whitney test. Note that this test is the nonparametric equivalent of the independent samples t-test. The SPSS command for the Mann-Whitney test is as follows:

```
NPAR TESTS M-W = MPG BY GENDER (1,2).
```

The output from this SPSS analysis follows:

```
- - - - - Mann-Whitney U - Wilcoxon Rank Sum W Test

    MPG       Miles per gallon of car usually driven
  by GENDER

    Mean Rank    Cases

        52.44        43  GENDER = 1  Male
        55.86        65  GENDER = 2  Females
                     --
                    108  Total

                              Corrected for Ties
         U            W          Z      2-tailed P
      1309.0       2255.0     -.5563       .5780
```

This analysis is interpreted and reported exactly the same as the results from the t-test in a previous section of this chapter. We might say:

> A Mann-Whitney test indicated that there was no significant difference in MPG between males and females, $U(106) = 1309.0$, $p = .578$, therefore the null hypothesis was not rejected.

Kruskal-Wallis   Suppose that the researcher is interested in comparing the height of people in the sample as a function of which class (GROUP) they were in. This is the same question that was examined to illustrate the use of the one-way ANOVA earlier in this chapter. Suppose now, however, that the researcher felt that the distribution of data did not satisfy the parametric assumptions. The nonparametric alternative that might be considered is the Kruskal-Wallis test, the command for which follows:

```
NPAR TESTS K-W = HEIGHT BY GROUP (1,7).
```

The output from this SPSS analysis is displayed as follows:

```
- - - - - Kruskal-Wallis 1-way ANOVA

    HEIGHT
by GROUP    Class

   Mean Rank    Cases

       64.03       17    GROUP = 1
       62.13       12    GROUP = 2
       51.84       28    GROUP = 3
       66.58       18    GROUP = 4
       21.58       13    GROUP = 5
       47.31        8    GROUP = 6
       57.73       11    GROUP = 7
                   ---
                   107    Total
                                            Corrected for Ties
      CASES    Chi-Square  Significance   Chi-Square  Significance
        107      20.4153         .0023      20.5747         .0022
```

The results of this nonparametric analysis would be interpreted and reported in the same manner that the comparable parametric one-way ANOVA was reported in a previous section of this chapter. We might say:

> A Kruskal-Wallis one-way ANOVA indicated that there were significant differences in height among the seven groups, $\chi^2 = 20.5747$, $p = .0022$.

Logically, post hoc tests should be done; however, there are no non-parametric post hoc tests. However, as noted in Chapter 6, Huck, Cormier, and Bounds (1974) suggest that the **Wilcoxon** or the **Mann-Whitney tests** could be used for multiple comparisons if the non-parametric ANOVA results in a decision to reject the null hypothesis.

Chi-Square Test   Sometimes the data being analyzed are not able to be analyzed using nonparametric tests since they are not ordinally, but intervally, scaled. For example, if a researcher is interested in finding out if there are differences in the number of people born in each month of the year, the data consist of merely the number of people born during each month. The researcher might expect that the number born in each is the same. The chi-square statistic tests whether there is a significant difference between what was expected by chance and what was actually observed. Note that the df for the chi-square test is the number of categories minus one. In this example, there are twelve categories (the twelve months of the year); therefore, the df for this analysis is 11 (12 − 1). The SPSS command to execute this test is as follows:

```
NPAR TESTS CHISQUARE = MONTH (1,12).
```

The output from this SPSS analysis is shown in the following:

		Cases		
	Category	Observed	Expected	Residual
January	1	7	9.00	-2.00
February	2	9	9.00	.00
March	3	7	9.00	-2.00
April	4	10	9.00	1.00
May	5	10	9.00	1.00
June	6	13	9.00	4.00
July	7	9	9.00	.00
August	8	4	9.00	-5.00
September	9	12	9.00	3.00
October	10	11	9.00	2.00
November	11	6	9.00	-3.00
December	12	10	9.00	1.00

	Total	108		

Chi-Square	D.F.	Significance
8.222	11	.693

The results of this analysis indicate that, by chance, the researcher should have obtained nine cases in each month, but in actuality there were differences between what was observed and what was expected. Those differences were not significant, however, according to the results of the chi-square test, which showed a "Significance" (or p) of .693. The report of this finding might read as follows:

> A chi-square test indicated that the number of people born in each month of the year was not significantly different from what would be expected by chance, $\chi^2(11) = 8.222$, $p = .693$.

DECISIONS ABOUT THE NULL HYPOTHESES

We stated in Chapter 6 that the purpose of conducting a statistical analysis of the data often is to make a decision about whether to reject or not reject the null hypothesis. In conducting research there are two general ways of deciding whether or not to reject the null hypothesis (i.e., deciding whether or not $p < \alpha$). The first way involves the calculation of the value of the statistic being used (e.g., "t" or "F" or "χ^2"). This calculated value is then compared to a critical value of the same statistic from a table of values. If the calculated value of the statistic is *greater than* the critical value in the table, then the researcher should reject the null hypothesis. When this method is used, the research report will typically contain a table of the values being compared, and an asterisk, or series of asterisks, will denote the significance level (e.g., $^* = .05$, $^{**} = .01$). An example of such a table is shown in Table 7–3.

The second way of deciding whether or not to reject the null hypothesis usually involves the use of a computerized statistical analysis program such as SPSS. In these programs the output from the data analysis usually includes the computed value of p. All the researcher has to do is compare the calculated value of p with the predetermined value of α. As explained in Chapter 6, the decision

TABLE 7–3   Height of Males and Females

	N	Mean	t
Females	64	65.02	8.82**
Males	43	69.77	

$^*p < .05$; $^{**}p < .01$; $^{***}p < .001$.

to reject or not reject the null hypothesis is based on a comparison of p with α. The "rule" that we applied was as follows:

if $p \leq \alpha$, reject the null hypothesis

if $p > \alpha$, do not reject the null hypothesis

COMPETENCIES

The exercises in this chapter will provide practice in interpreting the results of a research study. After completing the exercises in this chapter, you will be able to

- Describe research results textually, that is, in the body of a research report

- Decide whether or not to reject the null hypothesis when the research results are described in text

- Interpret the output from computerized statistical analyses and present those results in text

- Decide whether or not to reject the null hypothesis from data presented as output from a computerized statistical analysis program

EXERCISES IN INTERPRETING RESULTS

Two types of exercises are included in this chapter. The first set of exercises will require completing partial summaries of research. The second set will require composing summaries from data presented.

Exercises in Completing Summaries of Research

For each exercise, read the hypothesis. Complete each summary by choosing the correct word or phrase in parentheses or by filling in the blanks, as indicated. Complete the last sentence by summarizing the results of the study.

✎ **Exercise 7–1**   *Hypothesis:* There is no significant difference between the scores that girls and boys receive on the Gesell School Readiness Screening Test (GSRST).

T-Test Results for Gender for GSRST Scores

Groups	Mean	SD	n	t
Female	31.71	4.34	234	1.16*
Male	32.15	4.14	247	

*$p > .05$.

The results for the independent samples t-test are reported in the table presented in Exercise 7–1. The data indicated (a significant difference; no significant difference) at the alpha = (.05; .01) level between the scores that girls and boys received on the GSRST, t (   ) =   , p (>; =; <)   . As a result, the null hypothesis (was; was not) rejected. These results indicated that boys and girls . . .

_____

_____

_____

✎ **Exercise 7–2**   *Hypothesis:* There is no significant relationship between the score a child obtains on the Gesell School Readiness Screening Test (GSRST) and success in school as measured by the reading comprehension section of the Stanford Achievement Test given in the spring of grade one.

Pearson Product-Moment Correlation Coefficient for GSRST Score with Grade One Spring SAT Reading Comprehension Score

$n = 428$	$r = .241*$	1 – tailed

*$p < .001$.

The results of the Pearson product-moment correlation are reported in the table presented in Exercise 7–2. The data indicated that a statistically (significant; nonsignificant) (positive; negative) relationship exists between _____ and _____ as measured by the reading comprehension section of the Stanford Achievement Test given in the spring of grade one, r(   ) =   , p(>; =; <)   . As a result, the null hypothesis (was; was not) rejected. These results indicated that . . .

_____

_____

_____

✎ **Exercise 7–3**   *Hypothesis:*   There is no significant difference between males and females in effective teaching performance.

Effective Teaching Score by Gender

Group	Mean	N
Female	4.2273	5
Male	4.1400	19

Analysis of Variance

Source	Sum of Squares	df	Mean Square	F Ratio	F Prob.
Between groups	.0254	1	.0254	.3215	.5804
Within groups	1.0262	13	.0789		
Total	1.0516	14			

The results of the one-way Anova are reported in the table presented in Exercise 7–3. The data indicated (a significant difference; no significant difference) in gender of the participant between those teachers who were identified as exhibiting effective teaching performance and those teachers who were not identified as exhibiting effective teaching performance, $F($ $) =$, $p (>; =; <)$. As a result, the null hypothesis (was; was not) rejected. These results indicated that . . .

_____

_____

✎ **Exercise 7–4**   *Hypothesis:*   Students who completed the developmental reading course and were retained (continued to be enrolled) in college would not recommend the course to others.

Surveyed Group Who Would Recommend Course to Others by Retention Status

Would Recommend	Retention Status		Total
	Not Retained	Retained	
Yes			
Actual	6	162	178
Expected	(19.2)	(158.8)	87.3%
No			
Actual	6	20	26
Expected	(2.8)	(23.2)	12.7%
Total	22	182	
	(10.8%)	(89.2%)	

Pearson chi square

Value = 4.67992   *df* = 1   Significance = .03052

The results of the independent samples chi-square are reported in the table presented in Exercise 7–4. The data indicated that students who took the course and were retained (recommended; did not recommend) the course at a significantly higher rate than those who were not retained, $\chi^2 =$ ____ , $p (>; =; <)$ ____ . As a result, the null hypothesis (was; was not) rejected. These results indicated that . . .

_____

_____

_____

_____

_____

✎ **Exercise 7–5** *Hypothesis:* There is no difference in pretest and posttest scores of teachers as a function of years of teaching experience on the Stages of Concern Questionnaire.

Kruskal-Wallis One-Way ANOVA for Pre- and Posttest Scores on the First Three Stages of Concern Questionnaire for Years of Teaching Experience (N = 48)

	Chi-Square	Significance	Corrected for Ties	
			Chi-Square	Significance
Stage 0, by years	.5941	.9637	.5941	.9636
Stage 1, by years	7.3479	.1186	7.4065	.1159
Stage 2, by years	7.1197	.1297	7.1352	.1289

The results of the Kruskal-Wallis one-way ANOVA tests are reported in the table presented in Exercise 7–5. The data for stage 0 indicated that there was (a significant difference; no significant difference) between scores on the Stage of Concern Questionnaire as a function of years of teaching experience, $\chi^2 =$ ____ , $df = p (>; =; <)$ ____ . As a result, the null hypothesis (was; was not) rejected. These results indicated that . . .

_____

_____

_____

_____

_____

✎ **Exercise 7–6** *Hypothesis:* There is no significant difference in the attitudes of third-grade students after fifteen weeks of storytelling.

Pretest/Posttest Attitude Scores of Experimental Students

Variable	N	Mean	Standard Deviation	Standard Error
Preattitude	44	31.75	5.310	.800
Postattitude	44	43.04	3.430	.517

(Difference) Mean	Standard Deviation	t Value	df	2-tail Prob.
−11.29	4.386	−17.08	43	<.001

The results of the correlated samples t-test are displayed in the table presented in Exercise 7–6. The data indicated (a significant difference; no significant difference) between the pretest and posttest attitude scores of the students after fifteen weeks of storytelling, *t*(   ) =   , *p*(>; =; <)   . As a result, the null hypothesis (was; was not) rejected. These results indicated that . . .

_____

_____

_____

_____

_____

✎ **Exercise 7–7** *Hypothesis:* There is no significant difference between the computer simulation group and the hands-on group on the 1993 Stanford Achievement Test Science Subtest Scores.

Two-Way ANOVA Summary Table for the 1993 Stanford Achievement Test Science Subtest Scores

Source of Variation	Sum of Squares	df	Mean Square	F	Significance of F
Gender	1132.509	1	1132.509	9.761	.002
Group	6.420	1	6.420	.055	.815
Gender × group	81.519	1	81.519	.703	.404
Residual	9514.286	82	116.028		
Total	10762.093	85	126.613		

The results of the two-way ANOVA are reported in the table presented in Exercise 7–7. The data indicated (a significant difference; no significant difference) in scores on the Stanford Achievement Science Subtest between the computer simulation group and the hands-on group, *F* (   ) =   , *p* (>; =; <)   . As a result, the null hypothesis (was; was not) rejected. These results indicated that . . .

_____
_____
_____
_____
_____

✎ **Exercise 7–8**   *Hypothesis:* There is no significant difference between males and females on the 1993 Stanford Achievement Test Science Subtest Scores.
Refer to the table in Exercise 7–7
The results of the two-way ANOVA are reported in the table presented in Exercise 7–7. The data indicated (a significant difference; no significant difference) in scores on the Stanford Achievement Science Subtest between males and females, $F (\quad) = \quad$, $p (>; =; <)$. As a result, the null hypothesis (was; was not) rejected. These results indicated that . . .

_____
_____
_____
_____
_____

Exercises in Composing Summaries of Research

Read the hypothesis and definitions for each exercise. Then study the results presented in the table. Compose a paragraph that would summarize the results of the research using the format of the summaries in the previous exercises in this chapter.

✎ **Exercise 7–9**   *Hypothesis:* There is no significant difference in retention rate between high-risk students who took EE 102 and those who did not.

Definitions:

High-risk students—college students in a developmental program

Retention to third semester—retained (continued enrollment in college through the third semester); not retained (no longer enrolled in the college where the study was conducted)

EE 102—the developmental reading course

Total High-Risk Students by Retention to Third Semester

Placement Group	Retention to Third Semester		
	Not Retained	Retained	Total
No EE 102			
Actual	345	667	1012
Expected	(308.5)	(703.5)	58%
EE 102			
Actual	187	546	733
Expected	(223.5)	(509.5)	42%
Total	532	1213	1745
	30.5%	69.5%	

Pearson chi square
     Value = 14.76429
       df = 1
Significance = .00012

✎ **Exercise 7–10**   *Hypothesis:* There is no significant relationship between the counselor's satisfaction with work (SW) and satisfaction with supervision (SS).

Definitions:

Satisfaction with work (SW)—an individual's feeling of satisfaction about actual work performed

Satisfaction with supervision (SS)—an individual's feelings of satisfaction concerning reactions toward the immediate supervisor

Summary of the Pearson Correlation between Counselor's Satisfaction with Work (SW) and Satisfaction with Supervision (SS)

	Mean	Standard Deviation
Satisfaction with work	53.850	9.86
Satisfaction with supervision	53.11	9.50

$r_{SW,SS}$ = 0.088; p = 0.420.

✎ **Exercise 7–11**   *Hypothesis:* There is no one stage on the Stages of Concern Questionnaire that has significantly more change of teachers' scores from pretest to posttest as a result of intervention.

Definitions:

Stages of Concern Questionnaire—thirty-five-item Likert scale instrument developed to provide a quick scoring measure of stages of concern (Hall, George, & Rutherford, 1979)

Concern—the composite representation of the feelings, thoughts, and consideration given to a particular issue or task

Stages of concern—questions are clusters in terms of concerns that range from not perceiving innovation as having immediate personal consequences to having a high degree of involvement in innovation; stages range from stage 0 to stage 6

Wilcoxon Matched-Pairs Signed Ranks Test for Pre- and Posttest Scores on the Stages of Concern Questionnaire for Schools

Stage 0		
By school	$z = -1.6603$	2-Tailed $p = .0969$
Stage 1		
By school	$z = -1.0753$	2-Tailed $p = .2822$
Stage 2		
By school	$z = -.9989$	2-Tailed $p = .3178$
Stage 3		
By school	$z = -.6667$	2-Tailed $p = .5050$
Stage 4		
By school	$z = -.4939$	2-Tailed $p = .6214$
Stage 5		
By school	$z = -1.1457$	2-Tailed $p - .2519$
Stage 6		
By school	$z = -.2370$	2-Tailed $p - .8120$

✎ **Exercise 7–12** *Hypothesis:* There is no difference on students' performance scores when immediate and delayed criterion measures are administered.

Definitions:

Pretest/posttest/delayed posttest—fifteen-item multiple-choice test on Pennsylvania's government.

Delayed posttest—administered four weeks after the immediate posttest

Correlated Samples T-Test Differences in Mean Comprehension Scores between Immediate and Delayed Posttests

Difference Mean	Standard Deviation	Corr.	2-Tailed Probability	*t* Value	*df*	2-Tailed Probability
1.5748	2.529	.628	< .001	9.11	213	< .001

✎ **Exercise 7–13**   *Hypothesis:* There is no significant difference in the attitudes of third-grade students after fifteen weeks of storytelling involvement.

Definitions:

Storytelling—the oral interpretation of a literary experience

Attitudes—attitudes about storytelling and writing as measured by a twelve-item survey

Correlated Samples T-Test for Pre- and Posttest Attitude Scores of Experimental Students

Variable	Number	Mean	Standard Deviation	Standard Error
Preattitude	44	31.75	5.310	.800
Postattitude	44	43.04	3.430	.517
(Difference) Mean	Standard Deviation	*t* Value	*df*	2-tail Prob.
11.29	4.386	−17.08	43	< .001

✎ **Exercise 7–14**   *Hypothesis:* There is no significant difference between school board members', principals', and teachers' perceptions of actual teacher participation in shared decision making.

Definition:

Shared decision making—a process by which the members of an organization participate in decision-making decisions that affect the role and function of the organization.

ANOVA Summary Table of Teacher Participation Scores for Teachers, Principals, and School Board Members

Source	*df*	Sum of Squares	Mean Squares	F
Between groups	2	827.83	413.92	11.52*
Within groups	1,144	41,110.86	35.61	
Total	1,146	41,938.70		

*Significant at .05 level.

✎ **Exercise 7–15**   *Hypothesis:* The education level of mentor teachers with noninstructional career plans in the next five years is the same as that of mentor teachers who plan to remain in the classroom.

Definitions:

> Education level—the number of units of graduate credit from an accredited university or college, including degrees

> Mentor teacher—a teacher approved by local school board and paid four thousand dollars as a mentor teacher pursuant to Senate Bill 813

Chi-Square Analysis of Mentor Teacher Career Plans and Education Level (N = 1,305)

Education Level	Plans to Remain in Teaching		Does Not Plan to Remain in Teaching		Total	
	Freq.	Percent	Freq.	Percent	Freq.	Percent
Bachelor's degree	535	(94.5)	31	(5.5)	566	(100.0)
Master's degree	222	(91.4)	21	(8.6)	243	(100.0)
Credits beyond master's	430	(89.8)	49	(10.2)	479	(100.0)
Doctorate degree	14	(82.4)	3	(17.6)	17	(100.0)
Total	1,201	(92.0)	104	(8.0)	1,305	(100.0)

p = .005 for chi-square = 10.451; df = 3.

Note: $p < .05$ implies statistical significance.

ANSWERS TO EXERCISES IN INTERPRETING RESULTS

Answers to Exercises in Completing Summaries of Research

✎ *Exercise 7–1*   The results of the independent samples t-test are reported in the table presented in Exercise 7–1. The data indicated **no significant difference** at the alpha = **.05** level between the scores that girls and boys received on the GSRST, t **(479) = 1.16, p > .05.** As a result, the null hypothesis **was not** rejected. These results indicated that boys and girls **received similar scores on the GSRST, and that how well or poorly a child did was not significantly influenced by gender.**

✎ *Exercise 7–2*   The results of the Pearson product-moment correlation are reported in the table presented in Exercise 7–2. The data indicated that a statistically **significant positive** relationship exists between **a score a child received on the GSRST** and **success in school** as measured by the reading comprehension section of the Stanford Achievement Test given in the spring of grade one, $r(427) = .241, p < .001$. As a result, the null hypothesis **was** rejected. These results indicated that **the GSRST has limited (because the coefficient of correlation is weak) predictive ability. A statistically significant relationship existed between the score a child received on the GSRST and success in school.**

✎ *Exercise 7–3*   The results of the one-way ANOVA are reported in the table presented in Exercise 7–3. The data indicated **no significant difference** in the gender of the participant between those teachers who were identified as exhibiting effective teaching performance and those teachers who were not identified as exhibiting effective teaching performance, $F(1,13) = .321, p > .58)$. As a result, the null hypothesis **was not** rejected. These results indicated that **teaching performance was unaffected by gender.**

✎ *Exercise 7–4*   The results of the independent samples chi-square are reported in the table presented in Exercise 7–4. The data indicated that students who took the course and were retained **recommended** the course at a significantly higher rate than those who were not retained, $\chi^2 = 4.67, p = .030$. As a result, the null hypothesis **was** rejected. These results indicated **that the students who were still enrolled at the university as compared to the students who were no longer enrolled at the university recommended the course as valuable.**

✎ *Exercise 7–5*   The results of the Kruskal-Wallis one-way ANOVA tests are reported in the table presented in Exercise 7–5. The data for stage 0 indicated that there was **no significant difference** between scores on the Stages of Concern Questionnaire as a function of years of teaching experience, $\chi^2 = .594, p = .9637$. As a result, the null hypothesis **was not** rejected. These results indicated that **years of teaching experience did not affect scores at stage 0 on the Stages of Concern Questionnaire.**

✎ *Exercise 7–6*   The results of the correlated samples t-test are displayed in the table presented in Exercise 7–6. The data indicated **a significant difference** between the pretest and posttest attitude scores of the students after fifteen weeks of storytelling, $t(43) = -17.08, p < .001$. As a result, the null hypothesis **was** rejected. These results indicated that **students attitude scores were significantly higher after fifteen weeks.**

✎ *Exercise 7–7*   The results of the two-way ANOVA are reported in the table presented in Exercise 7–7. The data indicated **no significant difference** in scores on the Stanford Achievement Science Subtest between the computer simulation group and the hands-on group, $F(1,84) = .055, p = 8.15.$ As a result, the null hypothesis **was not** rejected. These results indicated **that the computer simulation group and the hands-on group did not significantly differ in their scores on the Stanford Achievement Subtest.**

✎ *Exercise 7–8*   The results of the two-way ANOVA are reported in the table presented in Exercise 7–7. The data indicated **a significant difference** in scores on the Stanford Achievement Science Subtest between males and females, $F(1,84) = 9.76, p = .002.$ As a result, the null hypothesis **was** rejected. These results indicated that **the males and females significantly differed in their scores on the Stanford Achievement Subtest.**

Answers to Exercises in Composing Summaries of Research

✎ *Exercise 7–9*   The results of the independent samples chi-square are reported in the table presented in Exercise 7–9. The data indicated that high-risk students who took EE 102 were retained to their third semester at a significantly higher rate than those who did not enroll in the course, $\chi^2 = 14.76, p = .001.$ As a result, the null hypothesis was rejected. These results indicated that the course, EE 102, was a factor in retention of high-risk students to the third semester.

✎ *Exercise 7–10*   The results of the Pearson correlation are reported in the table presented in Exercise 7–10. The data indicated that a nonsignificant positive relationship exists between a counselor's satisfaction with work and satisfaction with supervision, $r = .088, p = .42.$ As a result, the null hypothesis was not rejected. These results indicated that satisfaction with work and satisfaction with supervision were not significantly related.

✎ *Exercise 7–11*   The results of the Wilcoxon Matched-Pairs Signed Ranks Test for Pre- and Posttest Scores on the Stages of Concern Questionnaire for Schools are reported in the table presented in Exercise 7–11. The data show that there was no significant difference between the pre- and posttest scores of the teachers on each stage of concern. Specifically, for Stage 6, $z = -.2370, p = .812.$ As a result, the null hypothesis was not rejected. These results indicated that teachers did not significantly change their stage of concern for educational innovation as a result of intervention.

✎ *Exercise 7–12*   The results for the correlated samples t-test are reported in the table presented in Exercise 7–12. The data indicated a significant difference between the immediate and delayed posttests results, $t = 9.11$, $df = 213$, $p < .001$. As a result, the null hypothesis was rejected. These results indicated that performance on a delayed posttest differed significantly from performance on the immediate posttest.

✎ *Exercise 7–13*   The results of the correlated samples t-test are reported in the table presented in Exercise 7–13. The data indicated a significant difference between the pretest attitude and the posttest attitude survey, $t (43) = -17.08$, $p < .001$. As a result, the null hypothesis was rejected. These results indicated that students in the group definitely had higher attitude scores following fifteen weeks of involvement in storytelling.

✎ *Exercise 7–14*   The results for the one-way ANOVA are reported in the table presented in Exercise 7–14. The results indicated a significant difference between school board members', principals', and teachers' perceptions of actual teacher participation in shared decision making, $F (2, 1144) = 11.52$, $p < .05$. As a result, the null hypothesis was rejected. The results indicated that the teachers, principals, and school board members do not agree on the extent teachers actually participate in shared decision making. (Note: A post hoc Scheffé's test was used to determine which groups showed a difference because of the significant value of the F ratio. The perceptions of principals were significantly different than those of school board members, and the perceptions of principals were also significantly different than those of teachers at the .05 level.)

✎ *Exercise 7–15*   The results of the independent samples chi-square are reported in the table presented in Exercise 7–15. The data indicated that level of education was a determining factor in career planning. The higher the degree a mentor teacher held, the more likely that he or she planned to leave teaching, $\chi^2 = 10.451$, $p = .005$. As a result, the null hypothesis was rejected. The results indicated that level of education was a significant factor in career decision making.

SUMMARY

This chapter has provided practice in interpreting and reporting the results of data analysis based on typical computer printouts of statistical data analyses. Chapter 8, which follows, will discuss putting all of the parts of the research report together.

8 THE RESEARCH REPORT

INTRODUCTION

The collection, analysis, and interpretation of data are only part of the research process. The results and conclusions are of use only to the researcher unless they are disseminated to a larger audience. Once the analyses of the data and the interpretation of those analyses are finished, the preparation of the research report in a form suitable for publication in a professional journal or presentation at a scholarly conference is the next step.

Before a researcher begins to collect data, or even design a study, it is typical first to examine the existing literature to see what related research has already been done on the topic. The abundance and diversity of literature resources can make this seem a somewhat daunting task; however, the widespread use of computerized databases for beginning this review has become a viable way to manage this task.

In this chapter, we will first discuss the use of computerized databases in reviewing related literature. We shall then describe the parts of a research report and provide a process for critically evaluating research reports.

SEARCHING DATABASES FOR THE LITERATURE REVIEW

An essential part of a research report is the review of literature, which serves to place the current study in a chronological as well as a theoretical context. Traditionally, the process of reviewing the relevant literature for a research study has involved many hours of work in a library during which the researcher painstakingly searched the various abstracts, indexes, and reviews that could contain sources that might be useful. Often this process was slow and frustrating, with many promising sources proving to be irrelevant or unavailable. There was also the possibility that important resources might be overlooked.

To some extent this arduous process has been streamlined through the use of computerized databases, in which printed materials have been stored electronically either in on-line databases or on storage media such as CD-ROM disks. Most university libraries, and increasingly many public libraries, state education departments, and school districts, have access to these databases (Long, Convey, & Chwalek, 1991). Many of the databases are also becoming increasingly accessible through the Internet, which can be accessed through most universities or from commercial on-line services.

Computerized databases allow a researcher to identify potentially relevant sources quickly and efficiently. By using key authors' names, titles, subjects, or descriptors such as keywords and key terms, a researcher can rapidly obtain listings of sources that may be useful in the literature review. The list can be narrowed (i.e., made more specific to include fewer, but more pertinent, sources) or broadened (i.e., made more general to include more sources) by using multiple descriptors with "and" and "or" (known as logical operators) combinations.

Prior to conducting a search of a computerized database, a researcher should have the research problem sufficiently well defined so that appropriate descriptors can be identified. It is also helpful for the researcher to identify several sources that can be expected to be identified in a database search. If these sources are identified through the search, the researcher will have confidence that the search was on target, but if those sources are not identified through the search, the researcher will realize that the search criteria must be modified. In the following sections, the planning and the results of a demonstration search are presented.

Demonstration Search

Suppose a researcher was interested in studying curricula that intend to enhance self-esteem and academic achievement in elementary school students. Realizing that there is probably a large amount of prior research on this topic, the researcher decides to conduct a search of the Educational Resources Information Center (ERIC) database. The ERIC database provides abstracts and other information about many articles and papers that have been published in educational journals or presented at professional conferences. Access to the ERIC database is provided by many university libraries and through some on-line services.

Once the researcher has accessed the ERIC database, the following keyword might be entered to begin the search:

```
NEXT COMMAND: K=SELF ESTEEM
```

After a few seconds of searching, the computer responds:

```
Search Results: 2908 Entries Found
```

Realizing that many authors use the term "self-concept" instead of "self-esteem," the researcher enters "self-concept" as a search keyword.

```
NEXT COMMAND: K=SELF CONCEPT
Search Results: 2889 Entries Found
```

Now the researcher combines the two terms to include all of the articles that mention either "self-esteem" or "self-concept." First the researcher reviews the search process, then uses the logical operator "OR" to combine the two sets of articles. The result, as indicated below, is a larger set of articles than either of the two previous searches, since this set includes any article that mentioned either term.

```
NEXT COMMAND: REVIEW
S1  K =SELF CONCEPT  2889
S2  K =SELF ESTEEM  2908

NEXT COMMAND: K=S1 OR S2
Search Results: 5297 Entries Found
```

Now the researcher decides to enter the term "academic achievement," and then the term "learning." Then these two terms will be combined into a set of articles containing either term.

```
NEXT COMMAND: K=ACADEMIC ACHIEVEMENT
Search Results:  9008 Entries Found

NEXT COMMAND: K=LEARNING
Search Results:  42780 Entries Found

NEXT COMMAND: REVIEW
S1  K =LEARNING  42780
S2  K =ACADEMIC ACHIEVEMENT  9008
S3  K =(SELF CONCEPT) OR (SELF ESTEEM)  5297
S4  K =SELF CONCEPT  2889
S5  K =SELF ESTEEM  2908

NEXT COMMAND: K=S1 OR S2
Search Results: 49070 Entries Found
```

Since the researcher is interested only in elementary schools, the key-word "elementary" is entered.

```
NEXT COMMAND: REVIEW
S1  K =LEARNING OR (ACADEMIC ACHIEVEMENT)   49070
S2  K =LEARNING  42780
S3  K =ACADEMIC ACHIEVEMENT    9008
S4  K =(SELF CONCEPT) OR (SELF ESTEEM)  5297
S5  K =SELF CONCEPT  2889
S6  K =SELF ESTEEM  2908

NEXT COMMAND: ELEMENTARY
Search Results: 57805 Entries Found
```

Now the term "elementary" is going to be combined with the set of articles containing either "learning" or "academic achievement" and the set of articles containing either the terms "self-esteem" or "self-concept." This is done using the logical operator "AND," which will result in the identification of articles that contain all three sets of terms. Since this set of articles must contain all of the defined terms, the resulting set of articles will be smaller than the set of articles containing only one of the included terms.

```
NEXT COMMAND: REVIEW
S1  K =ELEMENTARY     57805
S2  K =(LEARNING OR (ACADEMIC ACHIEVEMENT)   49070
S4  K =LEARNING  42780
S5  K =ACADEMIC ACHIEVEMENT  9008
S6  K =(SELF CONCEPT) OR (SELF ESTEEM)   5297
S7  K =SELF CONCEPT  2889
S8  K =SELF ESTEEM  2908

NEXT COMMAND: K=S1 AND S2 AND S6
Search Results: 771 Entries Found
```

The set of articles that mention "learning" or "academic achievement," "self-esteem" or "self-concept," and "elementary" includes 771 items. The researcher still hasn't included any reference to curriculum, so that term is entered next. Then the set of articles about curriculum is searched to find those that include all of the terms used in the last search.

```
NEXT COMMAND: REVIEW
S1  K =ELEMENTARY AND ((LEARNING OR (ACADEMIC ACHIEVEMENT)) AND ((SELF CONCEPT) OR (SELF ESTEEM)   771
S2  K =ELEMENTARY  57805
S3  K =(LEARNING OR (ACADEMIC ACHIEVEMENT)) AND ((SELF CONCEPT) OR ...  1875
S4  K =LEARNING OR (ACADEMIC ACHIEVEMENT)   49070
S5  K =LEARNING  42780
S6  K =ACADEMIC ACHIEVEMENT  9008
S7  K =(SELF CONCEPT) OR (SELF ESTEEM)   5297
S8  K =SELF CONCEPT  2889
S9  K =SELF ESTEEM  2908

NEXT COMMAND: K=CURRICULUM
Search Results: 28375 Entries Found
```

```
NEXT COMMAND: REVIEW
S1   K =CURRICULUM  28375
S2   K =ELEMENTARY AND ((LEARNING OR (ACADEMIC ACHIEVEMENT)) AND ...  771
S3   K =ELEMENTARY  57805
S4   K =(LEARNING OR (ACADEMIC ACHIEVEMENT)) AND ((SELF CONCEPT) OR ...  1875
S5   K =LEARNING OR (ACADEMIC ACHIEVEMENT)  49070
S6   K =LEARNING  42780
S7   K =ACADEMIC ACHIEVEMENT  9008
S8   K =(SELF CONCEPT) OR (SELF ESTEEM)  5297
S9   K =SELF CONCEPT  2889
S10  K =SELF ESTEEM  2908


NEXT COMMAND: K=S1 AND S2
Search Results: 155 Entries Found
```

Having identified 155 articles that meet the search criteria, the
researcher could list the articles and obtain an abstract and other
information about each. If the researcher decides that the search
could be further narrowed by examining only one subject area, say
reading and language arts, the following commands could be used:

```
NEXT COMMAND: REVIEW
S1   K =CURRICULUM AND (ELEMENTARY AND ((LEARNING OR (ACADEMIC ...  155
S2   K =CURRICULUM  28375
S3   K =ELEMENTARY AND ((LEARNING OR (ACADEMIC ACHIEVEMENT)) AND ...  771
S4   K =ELEMENTARY  57805
S5   K =(LEARNING OR (ACADEMIC ACHIEVEMENT)) AND ((SELF CONCEPT) OR ...  1875
S6   K =LEARNING OR (ACADEMIC ACHIEVEMENT)  49070
S7   K =LEARNING  42780
S8   K =ACADEMIC ACHIEVEMENT  9008
S9   K =(SELF CONCEPT) OR (SELF ESTEEM)  5297
S10  K =SELF CONCEPT  2889
S11  K =SELF ESTEEM  2908


NEXT COMMAND: K=READING
Search Results: 17465 Entries Found


NEXT COMMAND: K=LANGUAGE
Search Results: 24441 Entries Found


NEXT COMMAND: REVIEW
S1   K =LANGUAGE  24441
S2   K =READING  17465
S3   K =CURRICULUM AND (ELEMENTARY AND ((LEARNING OR (ACADEMIC ...  155
S4   K =CURRICULUM  28375
S5   K =ELEMENTARY AND ((LEARNING OR (ACADEMIC ACHIEVEMENT)) AND ...  771
S6   K =ELEMENTARY  57805
S7   K =(LEARNING OR (ACADEMIC ACHIEVEMENT)) AND ((SELF CONCEPT) OR ...  1875
S8   K =LEARNING OR (ACADEMIC ACHIEVEMENT)  49070
S9   K =LEARNING  42780
S10  K =ACADEMIC ACHIEVEMENT  9008
S11  K =(SELF CONCEPT) OR (SELF ESTEEM)  5297
S12  K =SELF CONCEPT  2889
S13  K =SELF ESTEEM  2908
NEXT COMMAND: K=S1 OR S2
Search Results: 36477 Entries Found
```

CONTINUED

```
NEXT COMMAND: REVIEW
S1   K =LANGUAGE OR READING  36477
S2   K =LANGUAGE  24441
S3   K =READING  17465
S4   K =CURRICULUM AND (ELEMENTARY AND ((LEARNING OR (ACADEMIC ...  155
S5   K =CURRICULUM  28375
S6   K =ELEMENTARY AND ((LEARNING OR (ACADEMIC ACHIEVEMENT)) AND ...  771
S7   K =ELEMENTARY  57805
S8   K =(LEARNING OR (ACADEMIC ACHIEVEMENT)) AND ((SELF CONCEPT) OR ...  1875
S9   K =LEARNING OR (ACADEMIC ACHIEVEMENT)  49070
S10  K =LEARNING  42780
S11  K =ACADEMIC ACHIEVEMENT  9008
S12  K =(SELF CONCEPT) OR (SELF ESTEEM)  5297
S13  K =SELF CONCEPT  2889
S14  K =SELF ESTEEM  2908

NEXT COMMAND: K=S1 AND S4
Search Results:  46 Entries Found
```

The researcher has now identified forty-six articles that seem to meet the established criteria. A partial listing of the articles, as they appear on the computer display, is shown below.

```
NUMBER:   DATE:    TITLE:                                          AUTHOR:
1         1994     Self-Perceptions of Preparedness for Teach      Lang, Catherine
2         1994     The Gifted Learning Disabled Student
3         1994     Valued Youth Program: Dropout Prevention S      Montecel, Maria Ro
4         1994     Freedom Fighters: Affective Teaching of th      Cecil, Nancy Lee
5         1994     Culturally Responsive Curriculum.               Abdal-Haqq, Ismat
6         1994     Sex Can Wait: An Abstinence-Based Sexualit      Young, Michael
7         1993     Transitional Intervention Program (Project      Choonoo, John
8         1993     A Multicultural Model for Rural At-Risk St      Bloodsworth, Gasto
9         1993     Strategy Instruction in a Literature-Based      Block, Cathy Colli
10        1993     Accelerating the Learning of At-Risk Stude      Ramaswami, Soundar
11        1993     100 Great Ideas                                 Rice, Julie
12        1993     Quien Soy Yo?/All about Me. Learning throu
13        1993     Research Symposium. Teacher Education in R
14        1993     Personal Change                                 Bretherton, Di
```

Suppose that the researcher now wants to look more closely at article 10. By simply entering that number, the following information is displayed:

```
NEXT COMMAND: 10
Brief View
ACCESSION #: ED364640
AUTHOR(S): Ramaswami, Soundaram.
TITLE: Accelerating the Learning of At-Risk Students: An Evaluation of Project ACCEL.
PUBLISHED: 1993
INSTITUTION: Newark Board of Education, NJ. Office of Planning, Evaluation and Testing.
MAJOR SUBJECTS: Academic Achievement. Acceleration (Education). Attitude Change. Elementary School
    Students. High Risk Students. Low Achievement.
MINOR SUBJECTS: Grade 6. Grade 7. Grade Repetition. Intermediate Grades. Junior High Schools.
    Junior High School Students. Parent Attitudes. Program Effectiveness. Program Evaluation.
    School Districts. Self Esteem. Student Attitudes. Teacher Attitudes. Urban Schools.
```

```
MAJOR IDENTIFIERS: Project ACCEL NJ.
MINOR IDENTIFIERS: Newark School System NJ.
ABSTRACT: Project Accelerated Curriculum Classes Emphasizing Learning (ACCEL) was implemented by
the Newark School District (New Jersey) in the 1989-90 school year in response to the ineffective
practice of retaining underachieving students.  The innovative approach of accelerated learning was
made available to retained sixth and seventh grade students.  These students were allowed to skip a
grade if they met the academic requirements stipulated by the district for promotion.  This report
is organized into five sections: principles of Accelerated Learning and an overview of Project ACCEL;
(2) results from teacher survey; (3) results from student and parent surveys; (4) results of the
Achievement Test; and (5) conclusions and recommendations.  Responses of the 11 teachers who replied
clearly point to beneficial effects of the program on student self-esteem, in spite of some program
implementation problems.  Responses of ACCEL students and 154 non-ACCEL students support positive
effects of the program  on student attitudes and educational goals.  Survey replies of 131 parents
also indicate constructive changes in student attitudes. Achievement test score improvements for
reading and language and a non-significant improvement in mathematics indicate that the program is
effective in improving academic achievement.  Recommendations are made for program improvement.
Three figures, 1 chart, and 22 tables present study data.  An appendix contains the surveys.
(Contains 7 references.)
PUBLICATN TYPE: Reports - Evaluative.  Tests/Questionnaires.
LANGUAGE: English
PAGES; FICHE: 132
PRICE CODE: EDRS Price - MF01/PC06 Plus Postage.
GEOGR. SOURCE: U.S.  New Jersey.
CLEARINGHOUSE#: UD029622
RIE/CIJE ISSUE: RIEAPR94
```

If the researcher wishes to obtain the entire article, the "ACCESSION #" will be useful. The "ED" prefix to the accession number indicates that the article is stored on microfiche by ERIC. Most university libraries have the ERIC microfiche documents as part of their collections. Procedures for retrieving, viewing, and copying these documents may be obtained by consulting with the reference librarian at the university library.

Some ERIC documents will have the prefix "EJ" as part of the accession number. This indicates that the article appeared in a published journal. The name, volume and number, and all other relevant bibliographic information for the document will be included in the ERIC summary. Check with the university librarian for information about the availability of journals containing articles with the "EJ" prefix.

There are other computerized databases that may contain documents a researcher in the field of education may find useful. The search process for most databases is similar to the process described here, but a consultation with the university librarian is recommended.

Once all of the articles and other documents that will constitute the literature review have been collected and examined, they will be discussed in the research report. The following section discusses the literature review and other parts of the research report.

PARTS OF THE RESEARCH REPORT

It should be kept in mind that the primary purpose of the research report is to disseminate the results of the study and thereby share the work with the researcher's professional community (Hopkins, 1992). Most research articles that are published in the field of education conform to the editorial style of the American Psychological Association (APA, 1994). The parts of a research report described in the following are consistent with that editorial style with one exception. The literature review is typically included as part of the introduction in an article prepared according to APA style. It is discussed separately here in order to clarify its purpose and contents.

Abstract

The abstract is a brief yet thorough summary of the contents of a research report. Most journals require an abstract, which is often used by abstracting services. The abstract enables readers quickly to get a sense of what the article is about in order to decide whether it is relevant to their needs.

Introduction

The main part of a research report begins with a section that identifies the research question or problem being studied and briefly describes the general approach to how that question or problem will be examined. The introduction should clearly

- State the purpose of the study

- Identify the research hypotheses

- Explain the significance of the study

- Define any special terms or concepts used in the study

- Describe any limitations of the study

In most research articles the introduction, which because it comes first is not labeled, also includes a discussion of how the study relates to previous work in the field and how the hypotheses to be tested are related to appropriate theory. This aspect will be discussed in the following section on the literature review.

Literature Review

The literature review in a research article or report differs from that in an academic thesis or dissertation. In a research article, relevant literature should be discussed in a manner that assumes a knowledgeable audience. In a thesis or dissertation, the literature review is more comprehensive and exhaustive. In both cases, the literature review serves to place the current study in a chronological as well as a theoretical context. The literature to be reviewed should include, as appropriate, both relevant theories and relevant research studies. The reader should find a connection between the theories on which the study is based, and a connection between prior related research and the current study.

It is important to identify and discuss not only theories and research that support the hypotheses of the study but also those that might offer alternate points of view. This is especially important in areas where there is controversy or lack of agreement on a theoretical or methodological perspective.

Method

The underlying premise for this section is that all aspects of the study should be described in a way that will enable a reader to conduct an identical study, or replication, based on the information provided. The method section should provide a description of how the study was carried out, including detailed descriptions of the participants, apparatus, and procedures. The method section is usually divided into subsections that describe each of these aspects.

Participants

This section should contain a description of the population to which the results are intended to be generalized, the people who actually participated in the study, and how they were identified, chosen, and assigned to different aspects of the study. This description should include relevant demographic information about the participants, and should also include such things as whether the participants were volunteers or were compensated in some manner. If some of the original participants did not complete the study, the number and reasons for withdrawal should be identified. Finally, all of the procedures involving participants must reflect that they were treated in accordance with appropriate ethical standards. The topic of ethics in research will be discussed more fully in Chapter 9.

Apparatus
This section describes any equipment, materials, instruments, or other apparatus used in the study. The description of items must be sufficiently specific to enable a reader to know exactly what was used.

Procedure
Here the researcher describes each step that was used in carrying out the study. Again, this section should tell the readers what was done and how it was done so that they could duplicate the researcher's efforts should they attempt to replicate the study.

Results

Having described, in the method section, the data that are to be collected, the sample from whom the data will be obtained, and the procedures for the actual collection of data, the task of the researcher in this section is to report the results of the data collection and analysis. It is important to understand that this section does not include any interpretation of the data, merely the objective report of the results. In other words, the results section deals with "what" was found, but not with "why."

Keeping in mind that the purpose for collecting and analyzing data was to test a hypothesis or answer a research question, the results should be organized according to the way the hypotheses or research questions were stated in the introduction. The findings related to each hypothesis or research question must be addressed, including those hypotheses and questions for which the results were contrary to what was expected. The main findings should be stated first, and then the researcher should report the results in sufficient detail to make it clear how the conclusions (to be discussed later) were made. To provide that detail, this section often includes a combination of tables and graphs intermixed with explanatory text.

Discussion

Here is where the researcher interprets, evaluates, and discusses the results of the research study, especially as they pertain to the original hypotheses and research questions. Usually, the researcher will review the hypothesis or research question and the results that are relevant to it, indicating whether or not the results were consistent with what was expected. When the results are consistent with what was expected, the researcher should relate those findings to the theory and prior research that were presented in the review of the literature. If the results are unexpected, either by being the opposite of what was expected or inconclusive, the researcher should attempt to explain why. The reasons for unexpected results generally fall into two categories.

First, there could be methodological aspects that account for the inconsistency. For example, the researcher may have expected, based on the review of the literature, that an instructional treatment would improve achievement scores. The finding that there was no such improvement might be due to the way achievement was measured. In other words, the instrument for measuring achievement may have been invalid.

A second category of reasons for unexpected results may be theoretical. Hypotheses are often logically deduced from theories, based on certain assumptions. It could be that the assumptions on which the theory is based were not warranted in this study. For example, suppose that a theory, which predicts the effectiveness of an instructional activity, is based on the assumption that the students will be motivated to learn. Further suppose that the researcher realizes, after completing the data collection, that there was a distraction in the school that undermined the students' motivation. This might account for a finding that the activity was not effective, even though all of the literature suggested that it should be.

In the first situation, there may be nothing wrong with the theory that led to the researcher's expectations. The problem was in the way the researcher carried out the study and, in particular, in the way a variable was measured. In the second situation, the researcher may not have had any methodological problems but inadvertently overlooked an essential theoretical consideration, namely, motivation of the students. In either case, the researcher might consider and recommend additional future research to address the question.

The discussion section usually includes recommendations, either for practice or for future research or both, depending on the nature of the findings and the implications that can be drawn from them. When all of the hypotheses have been discussed and recommendation have been made, this section often closes with a brief summary of the study and its findings.

References

All sources cited, quoted, or referred to in the paper should be listed in the reference section. This provides the documentation needed for a reader to judge the adequacy of the theoretical and empirical basis for the research. Conversely, all sources listed in the reference section should be cited, quoted, or referred to in the body of the report. This means that the reference section is not an exhaustive bibliography of sources related to the topic but a list of sources that were actually used by the researcher.

Since references should be listed in a way that makes them accessible to the reader, and since these references may come from a wide variety of sources, it is important that the writer of a research report use a standard format for citing references. As mentioned earlier, most research reports in education use the citation style described in the fourth edition of the *Publication Manual of the American Psychological Association* (APA, 1994).

Appendixes

If a researcher uses materials for which a detailed description is needed, that detail is usually included in an appendix rather than in the body of the paper. This reduces the possibility that such detail will distract a reader from the main ideas presented in the research report. Examples of such materials would include unpublished tests (including technical data on norms and validation), researcher-designed treatments, or the detailed description of a unique setting or arrangement. Tests, materials, equipment, or other materials that are published or generally available should be described in the method section, with appropriate referral to an entry in the reference section.

CRITICAL EVALUATION OF A RESEARCH REPORT

Unlike many academic activities, research methodology does not consist only of a set of facts to be understood and recalled. It consists instead of a set of skills that can be applied to the solution of problems. The process of analyzing and critiquing a research study can be broken down into a series of steps that are listed here in the form of a series of questions. You can answer these questions to help you evaluate a research report or article.

1. Problem statement
   a. Is the problem stated clearly enough for you confidently to restate it in your own words?
   b. Is the problem feasible?
   c. Does the problem have sufficient theoretical value?
   d. Does the problem have sufficient practical value?

2. Variables
   a. Are the independent and dependent variables clearly identified?
   b. Are there any important variables that should have been included but were not?

3. Hypotheses
   a. Are the experimental (or null) hypotheses stated clearly?
   b. Is each hypothesis supported by sufficient literature or argument?
   c. Are the hypotheses consistent with the research design?

4. Literature review
   a. Is the context of the problem clear?
   b. Are relevant theories and research cited to support the hypotheses?
   c. Are theories and research cited relevant to the variables used?

5. Operational definitions
   a. Are all variables operationally defined?
   b. Are the operational definitions sufficiently unambiguous?

6. Measurement and manipulation of variables
   a. Are the manipulations of all independent variables clear?
   b. Are the measurements of dependent or predictor/criterion variables reliable?
   c. Are the manipulations of all independent variables and the measurements of dependent or predictor/criterion variables valid?

7. Research design
   a. Is the design stated sufficiently clearly so that you could diagram it?
   b. Is the design adequate to test the stated hypotheses?
   c. Is the sample adequate and representative?
   d. Are there any sources of bias that were not controlled?
   e. Is the design internally valid?
   f. Is the design externally valid?

8. Statistics
  a. Are the descriptions clear for all statistical tests that were used?
  b. Are the statistical tests used appropriate and relevant to the stated hypotheses?
  c. Are there other statistical analyses that should have been done instead of or in addition to those actually done?
  d. Are the presentations of the results of the data analyses sufficiently clear?
  e. Are the tables, graphs, and figures clear and adequately labeled?

9. Findings and conclusions
  a. Are the findings and conclusions stated clearly?
  b. Are the findings and conclusions related to the problem as stated?
  c. Are the findings and conclusions related to the stated hypotheses?
  d. Is there an adequate and convincing interpretation of the findings?
  e. Are there alternative explanations for the findings?
  f. Are there recommendations for future related research?

10. References
  a. Are all citations listed in the reference list?
  b. Is the reference list complete and up-to-date?

These questions can be answered informally or in a formal narrative critique. If you are quantitatively oriented, you can use the questions as the basis for a checklist when you evaluate a research article. A sample of such a checklist is provided in Table 8–1.

COMPETENCIES

The exercises in this chapter will provide practice in critiquing and preparing the various parts of a research report. After completing the exercises in this chapter, you will be able to

- Expand a computerized database search using the "OR" logical operator

- Narrow a computerized database search using the "AND" logical operator

- Recognize the parts of a research report
- Systematically evaluate the adequacy of a research report

TABLE 8–1   *Research Article Evaluation Checklist*

1.	Problem statement	5	4	3	2	1	NA
2.	Variables	5	4	3	2	1	NA
3.	Hypotheses	5	4	3	2	1	NA
4.	Literature review	5	4	3	2	1	NA
5.	Operational definitions	5	4	3	2	1	NA
6.	Measurement and						
	manipulation of variables	5	4	3	2	1	NA
7.	Research design	5	4	3	2	1	NA
8.	Statistics	5	4	3	2	1	NA
9.	Findings and conclusions	5	4	3	2	1	NA
10.	References	5	4	3	2	1	NA

For the items on this checklist, a five-point rating scale is used. The following criteria should be applied when using this scale:

5	Outstanding	It is as good or as clear as possible; it could not be done better.
4	Good	It is certainly well done but leaves a little room for improvement.
3	Adequate	It is marginal but acceptable, leaving clear room for improvement.
2	Substandard	It is not up to the standard of clarity or acceptability; it leaves much room for improvement.
1	Inadequate	It is unacceptable and would require considerable revision to reach minimum acceptability.
NA	Not applicable	The criteria cannot be applied, either because they are irrelevant or because the section being critiqued is absent.

EXERCISES IN CONDUCTING A SEARCH OF A COMPUTERIZED DATABASE

✎ **Exercise 8–1**   A researcher is interested in investigating how combinations of text and pictures influence learner performance on an assembly task. More specifically, the researcher is interested in determining whether different types of pictures, when used in combination with text, affect the speed or accuracy of assembly performance, and whether any effect is related to the cognitive style of the learner. The researcher would like to identify between five and ten relevant articles for the literature review.

1. List some descriptors, or keywords, that the researcher should use in conducting a computerized search of the ERIC database. Be sure to consider synonyms for keywords where appropriate.

2. The following lines depict the results of several search entries:

```
NEXT COMMAND: K=TEXT
Search Results: 6051 Entries Found

NEXT COMMAND: K=PICTURE
Search Results: 1396 Entries Found

NEXT COMMAND: K=ILLUSTRATION
Search Results: 334 Entries Found

NEXT COMMAND: REVIEW
S1   K =ILLUSTRATION  334
S2   K =PICTURE  1396
S3   K =TEXT  6051
```

How should the researcher narrow the search to include only articles that relate to pictures or illustrations, and that also relate to text? List the specific commands that follow:

```
NEXT COMMAND:
```

3. Next the researcher searched for the keywords "cognitive style," "assembly," "performance," "assembly speed," and "assembly accuracy." The following output shows the commands that the researcher entered, as well as the results.

```
NEXT COMMAND: K=COGNITIVE STYLE
Search results: 1893 Entries Found

NEXT COMMAND: K=ASSEMBLY
Search Results: 585 Entries Found

NEXT COMMAND: K=PERFORMANCE
Search Results: 13509 Entries Found

NEXT COMMAND: ASSEMBLY SPEED
Search Results: 3 Entries Found

NEXT COMMAND: ASSEMBLY ACCURACY
Search Results: 3 Entries Found

NEXT COMMAND: REVIEW
S1   K =ASSEMBLY ACCURACY  3
S2   K =ASSEMBLY SPEED  3
S3   K =PERFORMANCE  13509
S4   K =ASSEMBLY  585
S5   K =COGNITIVE STYLE  1893
S6   K =(ILLUSTRATION OR PICTURE) AND TEXT  136
S7   K =ILLUSTRATION OR PICTURE  1718
S8   K =ILLUSTRATION  334
S9   K =PICTURE  1396
S10  K =TEXT  6051
```

How would the researcher proceed next, given the purpose of the study and the search results so far? What commands should be used?

4. Assume that the researcher obtained the following results. What is a reasonable next step? What commands should be used?

```
NEXT COMMAND: REVIEW
S1   K =ASSEMBLY ACCURACY AND ((ILLUSTRATION OR PICTURE) AND TEXT)   1
S2   K =ASSEMBLY SPEED AND ((ILLUSTRATION OR PICTURE) AND TEXT)   1
S3   K =PERFORMANCE AND ((ILLUSTRATION OR PICTURE) AND TEXT)   0
S4   K =ASSEMBLY ACCURACY   3
S5   K =ASSEMBLY SPEED   3
S6   K =PERFORMANCE   13509
S7   K =ASSEMBLY   585
S8   K =COGNITIVE STYLE   1893
S9   K =(ILLUSTRATION OR PICTURE) AND TEXT   136
S10  K =ILLUSTRATION OR PICTURE   1718
S11  K =ILLUSTRATION   334
S12  K =PICTURE   1396
S13  K =TEXT   6051
```

5. Assume that the researcher combined S8 with S9 using the "AND" as shown in the following, and decided that 7 "hits" were enough. What commands might follow?

```
NEXT COMMAND: K =S8 AND S9
Search Results: 7 Entries Found
```

NUMBER	DATE	TITLE:	AUTHOR:
1	1990	The Role of Pictures in Learning Biology	Reid, David
2	1990	Proceedings of Selected Research Paper Pre	Simonson, Michael
3	1990	A Synthesis of Social Cognition and Writing	Bonk, Curtis J
4	1989	The Durability of Picture Text Procedural	Ausel, Dennis
5	1989	Facilitating Children's Comprehension thro	Townsend, Michael
6	1988	"Johnny the Rat": Using the Child as Our I	Schoen, Bev
7	1988	Picture Books as Contexts for Literary, Ae	Kiefer, Barbara

RESEARCH REPORT EXERCISES

Exercise 8–2   Read the following research report, "The Effects of Picture Format and Cognitive Style on Time and Accuracy of Assembly Performance." Then critique this report by answering the questions that follow. Paragraphs in the report have been numbered for reference.

The Effects of Picture Format and Cognitive Style on Time and Accuracy of Assembly Performance

(1) Pictorial depictions, such as photographs, illustrations, cartoons, and schematics, have been widely used in virtually every area of printed communication. A child's first books are almost always filled with colorful pictures and, as the child's skill and sophistication as a reader increases, pictures are commonly used to complement or supplement the text. Even adult reading materials often have pictures to accompany text. Given the widespread

use of pictures, one might have expected to find a sizable body of research that explains how pictures are used to transmit information to a reader. One might also have expected such research to have provided a precise description of how different types of pictures affect the learning performance of different users.

(2) Unfortunately, these expectations have not been realized and, generally, the research which has examined the uses of pictures has yielded inconclusive and occasionally contradictory results. Some of these studies found that pictures helped comprehension (Halbert, 1943; Weintraub, 1966; Findahl, 1971; Gombrich, 1972; Kennedy, 1974; Lesgold, DeGood, & Levin, 1976; Denburg, 1976), while other studies (Fries, Fries, Wilson, & Rudolph, 1965; Chall, 1967; Samuels, 1970) reported that pictures actually interfered with comprehension, and still others (Miller, 1938; Vernon, 1953, 1954; Koenke, 1968) found that the addition of pictures to text made no difference in comprehension.

(3) There are several explanations for lack of definitive research findings in this area. First, the materials used in many of these studies are never identified or adequately described. Thus it is difficult, if not impossible, to replicate these studies. Second, there was considerable inconsistency among these studies in the way that comprehension and memory were measured. It is difficult, therefore, to compare or contrast the findings of the studies or to generalize from the collective results. Third, these studies generally failed to consider the question of how differences among readers interact with the kind of pictures employed. Most theories of cognitive processing suggest that the reader-material interaction is an important aspect of comprehension and memory. The research reported in this paper was designed to address some of the inadequacies in prior research.

(4) Pictures can be of different kinds, ranging from photographs to line drawings to cartoons. For the research reported here, simple line drawings (e.g., see Bieger & Glock, 1986) were used since they are typical of the pictures that accompany most assembly instructions. Pictures can also vary in their structure. For example, assembly pictures are often either sequential, that is, depicting a series of subassemblies, one at a time; or composite, that is, depicting a finished product, but with the parts projected or "exploded." Crandell and Bieger (1987) found that sequential and composite pictures have different effects on performance. In this research both sequential and composite pictures were used.

(5) A critical shortcoming of much previous research centers on its failure to consider differences among individual users of the materials. One relevant dimension on which users differ is

that of cognitive style (Witkin, 1950). Some people are able to process information independent of the field or context in which it is embedded, while others are distracted by the embedding context. This study examined how this variable interacted with picture type to affect performance.

METHOD

(6) The independent variables were kind of picture (sequential or composite), cognitive style of the reader (field-independent or field-dependent), and gender. The dependent variable was assembly performance (i.e., speed and accuracy of performance). A criticism of much prior research has been the use of widely different methods of assessing comprehension. This research addressed that deficiency by using actual performance to assess comprehension. That is, the time to complete an assembly and the accuracy of the assembly were the principal dependent variables used throughout this study. This approach is consistent with the recommendations of some researchers (e.g., Stone, 1977) who argued that performance adds the element of "task realism" to the assessment of comprehension, and that time and number of errors are valid indices of comprehension of procedural information capable of being measured in a highly reliable manner.

Subjects

(7) Thirty-four undergraduate communications media majors volunteered to participate in the study. They were identified as being either field-independent or field-dependent and were then randomly assigned to one of the two picture type groups.

Materials

(8) Identification of cognitive style was done using the Embedded Figures Test (Witkin, Oltman, Raskin, & Karp, 1971). The assembly task was chosen from the Fisher-Technik 100 Model Kit and will be similar to assemblies used by Stone (1977), Crandell (1979), and Bieger and Glock (1984, 1986).

(9) Sequential and composite pictures were prepared by a professional technical illustrator according to the specifications of the researchers using the techniques for information content analysis described by Bieger and Glock (1984).

Procedures

(10) Subjects were given one of two sets of instructional stimuli. One set consisted of pictorial assembly instructions consisting

of a series of sequential pictures, while the other set consisted of a detailed composite picture. The subjects were instructed to complete the assembly by following the instructions, and their performances were timed, videotaped, and scored for accuracy using a standard scoring protocol.

RESULTS

(11) The speed and accuracy data from this research were analyzed separately using $2 \times 2 \times 2$ (cognitive style × picture type × gender) ANOVAs. These analyses revealed significant differences in speed of assembly for both picture type and cognitive style. The results are summarized in the following table.

Mean Performance Scores

	Picture Type		
	Composite	Sequential	Prob.
Time engaged in task (seconds)	985.72	671.60	.034
Accuracy score (max = 19)	13.11	12.40	.623
(*n*)	(18)	(15)	

	Cognitive Style		
	Field Dependent	Field Independent	Prob.
Time engaged in task (seconds)	1030.78	617.53	.002
Accuracy score (max = 19)	11.11	14.80	.023
(*n*)	(18)	(15)	

	Gender		
	Male	Female	Prob.
Time engaged in task (seconds)	859.25	817.85	.882
Accuracy score (max = 19)	13.75	11.31	.252
(*n*)	(20)	(13)	

Note: There were no significant interactions.

(12) The subjects using the sequential picture completed the assembly in significantly less time ($F(1,25) = 5.027$, $p = .034$) than those using the composite pictures (671.60 seconds vs. 985.72 seconds). Those subjects identified as being field-

independent completed the assembly significantly faster ($F(1,25) = 11.716$, $p = .002$) than those identified as field-dependent (617.53 seconds vs. 1030.78 seconds). There were no significant differences between male and female subjects, nor were there any interactive effects.

(13) The analyses also indicated significant ($F(1,25) = 5.826$, $p = .023$) differences in accuracy scores between field-independent subjects (14.80) and field-dependent subjects (11.11). There were no significant differences in accuracy attributable to different picture types or between males and females, nor were there any interactions.

(14) A Pearson's Product-Moment correlation between time and accuracy indicated a coefficient of correlation of $r = -.48$, $p = .002$, indicating that those subjects who had the highest accuracy scores also tended to complete the assembly faster.

DISCUSSION

(15) The results described above indicate that different pictures affect performance differently and that field-independent subjects perform at a higher level (i.e., faster and more accurately) than field-dependent subjects. It was predicted, but not confirmed, that there would be a two-way interaction between picture type and cognitive style. It was expected that field-dependent subjects would be more adversely affected, in both speed and accuracy, by the composite picture than would the field-independent subjects. The data indicated, however, that the effect of the different pictures was the same for both categories of cognitive style.

(16) The results of this study confirm the differential effect of composite and sequential pictures (Crandell & Bieger, 1987) and further demonstrate that processing style differences (e.g., cognitive style) and other aspects of individual differences can affect performance. These results add to a growing body of data accumulated from research that is attempting to understand how stimulus variables and individual characteristics of learners interact to affect performance.

REFERENCES

Bieger, G. R., & Glock, M. D. (1984). The information content of picture-text instructions. *Journal of Experimental Education, 53,* 68–76.

Bieger, G. R., & Glock, M. D. (1986). Comprehension of operational, spatial, and contextual information in pictures and texts. *Journal of Experimental Education, 54,* 181–188.

Chall, J. S. (1967). *Learning to read: The great debate.* New York: McGraw-Hill.

Crandell, T. L. (1979). *The effects of cognitive style elements on the comprehension of reading procedural information in picture-text amalgams.* Unpublished doctoral dissertation, Cornell University.

Crandell, T. L., & Bieger, G. R. (1987). *Technical communication: Taking the user into account.* Paper submitted for publication.

Denburg, S. (1976). The interaction of picture and print in reading instruction (abstracted report). *Reading Research Quarterly, 12,* 176–189.

Findahl, D. (1971). *The effect of visual illustration upon perception and retention of news programmes.* Sveriges Radio, Audio Programme Research Department.

Fries, C., Fries, A., Wilson, R., & Rudolph, M. (1965). *To teach reading: A manual and guide for a basic reading series.* Ann Arbor: University Press.

Gombrich, E. (1972). The visual image. *Scientific American, 227,* 82–96.

Halbert, M. (1943). An experimental study of children's understanding of instructional materials. *Bureau of School Service,* University of Kentucky, *15,* 7–59.

Kennedy, J. M. (1974). *A psychology of picture perception.* Washington, DC: Jossey-Bass Publishers, Inc.

Koenke, K. R. (1968). *The role of pictures and readability in comprehension of the main idea of a paragraph.* Paper presented at the annual meeting of the American Educational Research Association, Chicago.

Lesgold, A., DeGood, H., & Levin, J. (1976). *Pictures and young children's prose learning: A supplementary report.* Pittsburgh: LRDC.

Miller, W. A. (1938). Reading with and without pictures. *Elementary School Journal, 38,* 676–682.

Samuels, S. J. (1970). Effects of pictures on learning to read, comprehension, and attitudes. *Review of Educational Research, 40,* 397–407.

Stone, D. E. (1977). *Comprehension of information in picture-text amalgams in procedural texts.* Unpublished doctoral dissertation, Cornell University.

Vernon, M. D. (1953). The value of pictorial illustration. *British Jrnl. of Educ. Psychology, 23,* 180–187.

Vernon, M. D. (1954). The instruction of children by pictorial illustration. *British Journal of Educational Psychology, 24,* 171–179.

Weintraub, S. A. (1966). Illustrations for the beginning reader. *Reading Teacher, 20,* 61–67.

Witkin, H. A. (1950). Individual differences in ease of perception of embedded figures. *Journal of Personality, 19,* 1–15.

Witkin, H. A., Oltman, P. K., Raskin, E., & Karp, S. A. (1971). *A manual for the Embedded Figures Test.* Palo Alto, CA: Consulting Psychologists Press.

QUESTIONS

1. Problem statement
   a. Is the problem stated clearly enough for you confidently to restate it in your own words? If yes, restate it. If not, explain.
   b. Is the problem feasible? If not, explain.
   c. Does the problem have sufficient theoretical value? Explain.
   d. Does the problem have sufficient practical value? Explain.

2. Variables
   a. Are the independent and dependent variables clearly identified? Identify them and the paragraph where they are found.
   b. Are there any important variables that should have been included but were not? If yes, list them and indicate how they should be used.

3. Hypotheses
   a. Are the experimental (or null) hypotheses stated clearly? Identify the paragraph where they are found. State the hypotheses.
   b. Is each hypothesis supported by sufficient literature or argument? Identify the paragraphs where support for each hypothesis is found.
   c. Are the hypotheses consistent with the research design? Explain.

4. Literature review
   a. Is the context of the problem clear? Identify paragraphs that specify the context of the problem.
   b. Are relevant theories and research cited to support the hypotheses? Identify paragraphs in which these theories and research are cited.
   c. Are theories and research cited relevant to the variables used? Identify paragraphs in which these theories and research are cited.

5. Operational definitions
   a. Are all variables operationally defined? Identify the variables and paragraphs where they are operationally defined.
   b. Are operational definitions sufficiently unambiguous? If not, explain.

6. Measurement and manipulation of variables
   a. Are the manipulations of all independent variables clear? If not, explain. Identify the paragraphs where manipulations of independent variables are described.
   b. Are the measurements of dependent or predictor/criterion variables reliable? If yes, identify the paragraph in which reliability is documented.
   c. Are the manipulations of all independent variables and the measurements of dependent or predictor/criterion variables valid? If yes, identify the paragraphs in which validity is documented.

7. Research design
   a. Is the design stated sufficiently clearly so that you can diagram it? Diagram the design. (Refer to Chapter 3 to review diagramming of research designs.)
   b. Is the design adequate to test the stated hypotheses? If not, explain.
   c. Is the sample adequate and representative? If not, explain. Identify the paragraph that describes the sample.
   d. Are there any sources of bias that were not controlled? If yes, name them.
   e. Is the design internally valid? Address potential issues of internal validity.
   f. Is the design externally valid? Address potential issues of external validity.

8. Statistics
   a. Are the descriptions clear for all the statistical tests that were used? If not, explain. Identify the paragraphs that describe the statistical tests that were used.
   b. Are the statistical tests used appropriate and relevant to the stated hypotheses? If not, explain.
   c. Are there other statistical analyses that should have been done instead of or in addition to those actually done? If yes, name the statistical analyses and give your rationale.
   d. Are the presentations of the results of the data analyses sufficiently clear? If not, explain.
   e. Are the tables, graphs, and figures clear and adequately labeled? If not, explain.

9. Findings and conclusions
   a. Are the findings and conclusions stated clearly? If not, explain.
   b. Are the findings and conclusions related to the problem as stated? If not, explain.
   c. Are the findings and conclusions related to the stated hypotheses? If not, explain.

   d. Is there an adequate and convincing interpretation of the findings?
       If not, explain.
   e. Are there alternative explanations for the findings? If yes, state
       them.
   f. Are there recommendations for future related research? Identify
       the paragraph in which recommendations for future related
       research are described.

10. References
   a. Are all citations listed in the reference list? If not, explain.
   b. Is the reference list complete and up-to-date? If not, explain.

✎ **Exercise 8–3**   Read the following research report, "Differences in Perception of Children's Developmental Level as a Function of the Child's Gender." Then critique this report by answering the questions that follow.
Paragraphs in the report have been numbered for reference.

Differences in Perceptions of Children's Developmental Level as a Function of the Child's Gender

   (1) One of the most persistent findings in a variety of educational and behavioral research studies is that of differences
between males and females. One can almost guarantee significant
differences by examining the scores on any of several measurements and then comparing scores between men and women or
between boys and girls. The nature, source, and implication of
those observed differences continue to be a matter of dispute.

   (2) Much has been written about gender differences in
behavior and performance and the importance of *social shap-
ing* in fostering and perpetuating those differences. Social shap-
ing refers to how a person learns, in this case to be feminine or
masculine, according to the expectations and values communicated by various aspects of culture and society. A key element
in the gender role socialization of children is the extent to which
other people (e.g., parents, teachers, siblings, neighbors) perceive boys and girls differently, and as a consequence treat them
differently. It has been clearly shown (Rosenthal & Jackson,
1971) that one's perception that children are different is subtly
(and often blatantly) translated into differential treatment of
those children.

   (3) What are these expectations about gender that might
lead to certain altered perceptions and hence to different performance? If, for example, a teacher believes that it is not as
necessary for a girl to develop her motor coordination as a boy,
the girl may be perceived by the teacher as being aggressive

rather than athletic. Likewise, a young boy who is particularly artistic may be viewed in a negative light by a teacher who feels that it is inappropriate for boys to express their artistic abilities. Such attitudes and opinions held by parents, teachers, or other people significant in the lives of children can seriously inhibit the development of children. There is a considerable body of research to suggest that different expectations for boys and girls may lead to different judgments of the ability of boys and girls, even at very young ages.

(4) The purpose of this study was to investigate whether or not people's perceptions and judgments about a child's behavior and performance are affected by whether they believe they are observing a boy or a girl.

METHOD

Subjects

(5) The sample consisted of one hundred undergraduate university students from two academic majors: elementary education and communications media. Students volunteered to participate in the study as one of several alternatives from which they could choose which could satisfy a course requirement.

Materials

1. (6) *Videotape*—A videotape was made of a two-year-old boy engaged in a variety of "play" activities. The activities were carefully selected to include a variety of easily observable instances of specific behaviors. For example, the child was asked to point to his "nose," "eyes," and "knee," and was asked to name his "ear," "cheeks," and "chin" when these were touched by the adult in the videotape. Care was taken to include *male-stereotypic* (e.g., throwing a ball), *female-stereotypic* (e.g., answering a question about a story), and *neutral* (e.g., referring to a hidden object) activities. The classification of these items was validated during pilot testing of the materials. The child's appearance leaves his gender ambiguous, and there is no reference to his name or gender in the taped episode. Three versions of the videotape have been prepared, with the only difference among them being the title frame. In the first version, the title frame will state, "Two-year-old child"; the second title frame will state, "Two-year-old boy"; and the third will state, "Two-year-old girl."

2. (7) *Developmental checklist*—A developmental checklist was constructed which asks observers to rate (as Well Below Average, Below Average, Average, Above Average, or Well Above

Average) the developmental level of a child's behavior with respect to the chronological age of the child. The areas of observation and the items on this checklist were derived from the set of behaviors described in the *Yellow Brick Road Manual* (Kallstrom, 1975), which is a series of activities designed to assess the motor, perceptual, and linguistic functioning of preschool children. The items on the checklist were designed specifically to assess the behaviors depicted on the videotape; therefore, the items were categorized according to the broad area of performance and further classified as stereotypically masculine, stereotypically feminine, or gender neutral. Items include:

A. Verbal Ability
   1. Vocabulary
   2. Comprehension
   3. Clarity of Speech
   4. Structure

B. Physical Ability
   1. Coordination
   2. Strength
   3. Fine Motor Skills
   4. Gross Motor Skills

C. Cognitive/Intellectual Skills
   1. Colors
   2. Counting
   3. ABCs
   4. Object Recognition
   5. Memory
   6. Object Permanence

D. Social/Emotional
   1. Attention
   2. Autonomy/Initiative
   3. Assertiveness
   4. Independence
   5. Attachment
   6. Following Instructions

Procedure

(8) Classes were randomly assigned to view one of the three videotape versions. The observers were given identical instructions, namely, that they were to observe the tape and rate the behaviors exhibited as being Well Below Average, Below Average, Average, Above Average, or Well Above Average for a two-year-old, using the developmental checklist described earlier.

(9) The observer's gender was also recorded and used in the subsequent analyses as a possible independent variable.

RESULTS

(10) Ratings were tabulated for each item and for each category, and descriptive statistics were calculated.

(11) Mean ratings for each item were compared among observers in the three videotape version groups (i.e., "male," "female," "gender unspecified"), and for each of the categories of activity (i.e., "Language," "Cognitive," "Physical," and "Social/Emotional") using a two-way ANOVA (Gender of Rater × Perceived Gender of Child).

(12) In the "gender unspecified" condition, all but three of the raters indicated the gender of the child as a female, although the child was actually a male. This was probably due to the fact that the child had shoulder-length curly hair, which gave him the appearance of a girl. Comparisons of developmental ratings were made between raters in the "male" condition and those in the "unspecified" condition who indicated that the child was a male, but there were no significant differences between these groups. A similar comparison was made between raters in the "female" condition and those in the "unspecified" condition who indicated that the child was a female, but, again, there were no significant differences between these groups.

(13) A two-way ANOVA was used to test for differences in developmental ratings as a function of the child's perceived gender and as a function of the gender of the rater. The interaction between rater gender and child's perceived gender was also examined. There were no statistically significant differences between male and female raters in any category of developmental ratings or in the overall developmental rating.

(14) There were statistically significant differences between raters who perceived a male and those who perceived a female in two areas: Language and Physical development. Those who thought they were viewing a boy rated the child more advanced physically, but less advanced in language than those who thought that the child was a girl. There were no significant differences in any other areas. Table 1 provides the mean ratings in all areas, and Figure 1 illustrates this finding. Note that the **lower** the score, the more **advanced** the child was judged to be.

(15) **TABLE 1   Developmental Level as a Function of Perceived Gender of the Child**

	Perceived Gender of Child		
Area of Development	**Male**	**Female**	**p**
Language	12.23	9.63	<.001
Cognitive	15.28	15.90	.169
Physical	9.50	10.73	.005
Social	15.25	16.25	.036
Overall	52.25	52.51	.741

Note: The lower the score, the more advanced the child was judged to be.

(16) *FIGURE 1   Developmental rating*

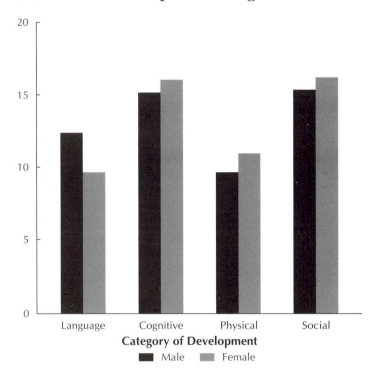

Category of Development
■ Male   ■ Female

(17) There were also significant interactions between Rater's Gender and Perceived Gender of the Child in ratings of Physical, Social, and Overall development. The mean ratings for these interactions are provided in Tables 2 through 4. These interactions are also graphically illustrated in Figures 2 through 4.

(18) *TABLE 2   Interaction between Rater's Gender and Perceived Gender of the Child in Ratings of Physical Development*

	Rater's Gender	
Child's Perceived Gender	**Male**	**Female**
Male	9.57	9.46
Female	9.64	11.55

Note: This two-way interaction was significant, $F(1,87) = 4.7$, $p = .033$.

FIGURE 2   *Physical development interaction*

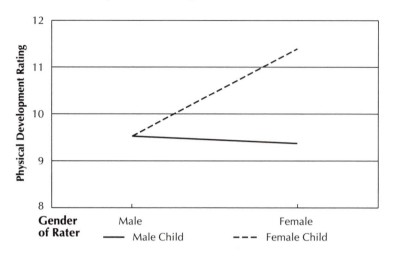

**Gender
of Rater**   Male   Female
——— Male Child   - - - Female Child

(19) **TABLE 3   *Interaction between Rater's Gender
and Perceived Gender of the Child in
Ratings of Social Development***

	Rater's Gender	
Child's Perceived Gender	**Male**	**Female**
Male	9.57	9.46
Female	9.64	11.55

Note: The two-way interaction was significant, $F(1,87) = 4.7$, $p = .008$.

FIGURE 3   *Social development interaction*

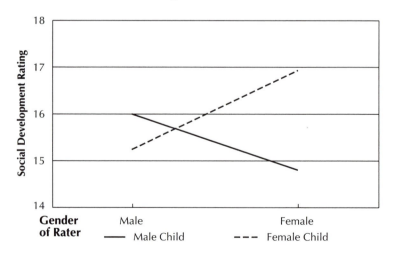

**Gender
of Rater**   Male   Female
——— Male Child   - - - Female Child

(20) **TABLE 4**   *Interaction between Rater's Gender and Perceived Gender of the Child in Ratings of Overall Development*

Child's Perceived Gender	Rater's Gender	
	Male	Female
Male	52.86	51.92
Female	49.86	54.52

Note: The two-way interaction was significant, $F(1,87) = 4.7$, $p = .047$.

FIGURE 4   *Overall development interaction*

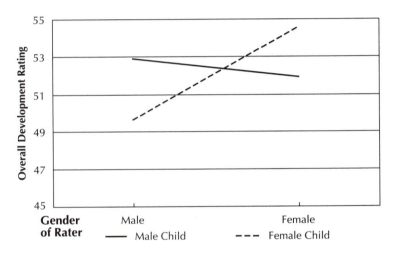

DISCUSSION

(21) By analyzing the results of the study, several interesting observations can be made. There were statistically significant differences between raters who perceived a male and those who perceived a female in two areas: Language and Physical Development. It was found that those who thought they were viewing a boy perceived him to be more advanced physically but less advanced in language. Likewise, those who thought they were viewing a girl rated the subject as being less advanced physically but above average in language skills. This finding reinforces the idea that people stereotype boys as being better at physical tasks, while girls are seen as being better in verbal tasks or academic subjects like reading.

(22) Analysis of the two-way interactions (Perceived Gender of Child × Rater's Gender) revealed that if the rater was male, there was no difference between his ratings of perceived males and females. However, female raters generally perceived a female subject as being less advanced in terms of physical development. In social development, a crossover in perceptions was observed. Male raters perceived a female subject as being more socially advanced, while the female raters generally rated a male subject as being more advanced in social development. Overall, this same pattern was observed. Male raters tended to perceive a female subject as being above average in most areas, while female raters perceived a male subject as being above average in more areas.

(23) In future studies, currently being planned, we intend to refine and extend the study reported here. The addition of the videotape of a second child is planned, perhaps using a female child whose appearance does not suggest one gender or the other. Also, a more careful analysis of the stereotypicality of the activities is planned.

(24) The question of how people's perceptions of a young child are influenced by their gender expectations continues to be worthy of study. Understanding of this phenomenon will add to our understanding of the relationship between gender and development. By learning more about the way people perceive boys and girls as being different, we may gain additional insight into the influence of our perceptions on children's development and performance.

REFERENCES

Bem, S. L. (1981). *Bem Sex-Role Inventory*. Palo Alto, CA: Consulting Psychologists Press.

Kallstrom, C. (1975). *Yellow Brick Road*. Austin, TX: Learning Concepts.

Rosenthal, Robert, and Jackson, Lenore (1971). Pygmalion in the classroom. In Melvin Silberman (Ed.) *The experience of schooling*. New York: Holt, Rinehart, and Winston.

QUESTIONS

1. Problem statement
   a. Is the problem stated clearly enough for you confidently to restate it in your own words? If yes, restate it. If not, explain.

     b. Is the problem feasible? If not, explain.

     c. Does the problem have sufficient theoretical value? Explain.

     d. Does the problem have sufficient practical value? Explain.

2. Variables
   a. Are the independent and dependent variables clearly identified? Identify them and the paragraphs where they are found.
   b. Are there any important variables that should have been included but were not? If yes, list them and indicate how they should be used.

3. Hypotheses
   a. Are the experimental (or null) hypotheses stated clearly? Identify the paragraphs where they are found. State the hypotheses.
   b. Is each hypothesis supported by sufficient literature or argument? Identify the paragraphs where support for each hypothesis is found.
   c. Are the hypotheses consistent with the research design? Explain.

4. Literature review
   a. Is the context of the problem clear? Identify paragraphs that specify the context of the problem.
   b. Are relevant theories and research cited to support the hypotheses? Identify paragraphs in which these theories and research are cited.
   c. Are theories and research cited relevant to the variables used? Identify paragraphs in which these theories and research are cited.

5. Operational definitions
   a. Are all the variables operationally defined? Identify the variables and paragraphs where they are operationally defined.
   b. Are operational definitions sufficiently unambiguous? If not, explain.

6. Measurement and manipulation of variables
   a. Are the manipulations of all independent variables clear? If not, explain. Identify the paragraph where manipulations of independent variables are described.
   b. Are the measurements of dependent or predictor/criterion variables reliable? If yes, identify the paragraph in which reliability is documented.
   c. Are the manipulations of all independent variables and the measurements of dependent or predictor/criterion variables valid? If yes, identify the paragraphs in which validity is documented.

7. Research design
    a. Is the design stated sufficiently clearly so that you can diagram it? Diagram the design. (Refer to Chapter 3 to review diagramming of research designs.)
    b. Is the design adequate to test the stated hypotheses? If not, explain.
    c. Is the sample adequate and representative? If not, explain. Identify the paragraphs that describe the sample.
    d. Are there any sources of bias that were not controlled? If yes, name them.
    e. Is the design internally valid? Address potential issues of internal validity.
    f. Is the design externally valid? Address potential issues of external validity.

8. Statistics
    a. Are the descriptions clear for all the statistical tests that were used? If not, explain. Identify the paragraphs that describe the statistical tests that were used.
    b. Are the statistical tests used appropriate and relevant to the stated hypotheses? If not, explain.
    c. Are there other statistical analyses that should have been done instead of or in addition to those actually done? If yes, name the statistical analyses and give your rationale.
    d. Are the presentations of the results of the data analyses sufficiently clear? If not, explain.
    e. Are the tables, graphs, and figures clear and adequately labeled? If not, explain.

9. Findings and conclusions
    a. Are the findings and conclusions stated clearly? If not, explain.
    b. Are the findings and conclusions related to the problem as stated? If not, explain.
    c. Are the findings and conclusions related to the stated hypotheses? If not, explain.
    d. Is there an adequate and convincing interpretation of the findings? If not, explain.
    e. Are there alternative explanations for the findings? If yes, state them.
    f. Are there recommendations for future related research? Identify the paragraph in which recommendations for future related research are described.

10. References
    a. Are all citations listed in the reference list? If not, explain.
    b. Is the reference list complete and up-to-date? If not, explain.

ANSWERS TO EXERCISE IN CONDUCTING A SEARCH OF A COMPUTERIZED DATABASE

✎ *Exercise 8–1*

1. Keywords: text, picture, illustration, performance, assembly, assembly speed, assembly accuracy, cognitive style

2. The researcher should use the "OR" logical operator to combine the keywords "picture" and "illustration." Next the researcher should use the "AND" operator to merge the picture/illustration terms with the keyword "text." The commands to do this, and the results, are shown in the following:

    ```
    NEXT COMMAND: REVIEW
    S1  K =ILLUSTRATION  334
    S2  K =PICTURE  1396
    S3  K =TEXT  6051

    NEXT COMMAND: K=S1 OR S2
    Search Results: 1718 Entries Found

    NEXT COMMAND: REVIEW
    S1  K =ILLUSTRATION OR PICTURE  1718
    S2  K =ILLUSTRATION  334
    S3  K =PICTURE  1396
    S4  K =TEXT  6051

    NEXT COMMAND: K=S1 AND S4
    Search Results: 136 Entries Found
    ```

3. The researcher might try to combine S1 with S6, S2 with S6, and S3 with S6 using the "AND" logical operator. The results of that effort are shown in the following:

    ```
    NEXT COMMAND: K=S1 AND S6
    Search Results: 1 Entries Found

    NEXT COMMAND: K=S2 AND S6
    Search Results: 1 Entries Found

    NEXT COMMAND: K=S3 AND S6
    Search Results: 0 Entries Found
    ```

4. Since the searches described too few articles, the researcher might consider searching for a combination of the keyword "cognitive style" (S8) with the combined terms identified as "S9." The results of that search are shown in the following:

    ```
    NEXT COMMAND: K =S8 AND S9
    Search Results: 7 Entries Found
    ```

5. The researcher could merely press the number corresponding to the article that was of further interest. For example, if the researcher wanted to see more about the second article, more information would be obtained by pressing "2" and the ENTER key, with the results shown in the following:

```
NUMBER          DATE      TITLE:              AUTHOR:
  1             1990      The Role of Pictures in Learning Biology      Reid, David
  2             1990      Proceedings of Selected Research Paper Pre     Simonson, Michael
  3             1990      A Synthesis of Social Cognition and Writing    Bonk, Curtis J
  4             1989      The Durability of Picture Text Procedural      Ausel, Dennis
  5             1989      Facilitating Children's Comprehension thro     Townsend, Michael
  6             1988      "Johnny the Rat": Using the Child as Our I     Schoen, Bev
  7      1988            Picture Books as Contexts for Literary, Ae          Kiefer, Barbara
NEXT COMMAND: 2
Brief View


ACCESSION#: ED323912
AUTHOR(S): Simonson, Michael R., Ed. Hargrave, Connie, Ed.
TITLE: Proceedings of Selected Research Paper Presentations at the Convention of the
       Association for Educational Communications and Technology and Sponsored by the Research
       and Theory Division (Anaheim, California, January 31-February 4, 1990).
PUBLISHED: 1990
INSTITUTION: Iowa State Univ. of Science and Technology, Ames. Coll. of Education.
NOTE: For the individual papers, see IR 014 536-582. For the proceedings of the 1989 conference,
see ED 308 805.
MAJOR SUBJECTS: Cognitive Processes. Cognitive Style. Educational Technology. Instructional
Design.
Media Research.
MINOR SUBJECTS: Educational Media. Hypermedia. Instructional Development. Intermode Differences.
Learner Controlled Instruction. Learning Strategies. Research Methodology. Visual Learning.
MINOR IDENTIFIERS: Media Characteristics.
ABSTRACT: Current issues in educational communications and technology are addressed in this
collection of 47 conference papers in which research reports predominate. Topics discussed
include factors related to the learner, e.g., learning strategies, information processing,
spatial ability, cognitive style, and cognitive strategies. Presentation format and media and
stimulus characteristics are also addressed, including illustration types, graphics in
courseware design, text layout variables, feedback, and synthesizing strategies. Several papers
examine educational media such as videodiscs, videotapes, and microcomputers. Additional papers
discuss the design of instructional visuals, the use of video to study cognition, learner versus
program control of interactive media, trends and issues in educational technology, assessment of
structural knowledge, applications of hypermedia, distance education for teacher training,
facilitating the acquisition of clinical reasoning skills, Kuhnian paradigms in educational
technology research, and advancements in instructional design theory. References and data tables
are included with many papers. Author and descriptor indexes are provided.
PUBLICATN TYPE: Collected Works - Proceedings. Opinion Papers. Reports - Research.
LANGUAGE: English
PAGES; FICHE; 8
PRICE CODE: EDRS Price - MF04/PC30 Plus Postage.
GEOGR. SOURCE: U.S. Iowa.
CLEARINGHOUSE#: IR014535
RIE/CIJE ISSUE: RIEFEB91
```

The researcher could continue this process to identify the articles that were relevant and could then obtain those articles from the library. If the articles identified here were sufficient, the search process would end, but if more articles are needed, the search could be broadened using appropriate keywords.

ANSWERS TO RESEARCH REPORT EXERCISES

✎ *Exercise 8–2*   "The Effects of Picture Format and Cognitive Style on Time and Accuracy of Assembly Performance"

1. Problem statement
   a. Is the problem stated clearly enough for you confidently to restate it in your own words? If yes, restate it. If not, explain.
      Yes. Research on how pictures affect comprehension is inconclusive.
   b. Is the problem feasible? If not, explain.
      Yes.
   c. Does the problem have sufficient theoretical value? Explain.
      Yes, cognitive processing theory suggests that interaction with components of text is important to comprehension and memory.
   d. Does the problem have sufficient practical value? Explain.
      Yes, for instructors and textbook publishers.

2. Variables
   a. Are the independent and dependent variables clearly identified? Identify them and the paragraph where they are found.
      Yes. Independent variables: picture format and cognitive style; dependent variable: assembly performance. Paragraph 6.
   b. Are there any important variables that should have been included but were not? If yes, list them and indicate how they should be used.
      No.

3. Hypotheses
   a. Are the experimental (or null) hypotheses stated clearly? Identify the paragraph where they are found. State the hypotheses.
      Hypotheses are implied in the discussion, paragraph 15. Hypotheses: Assembly performance is not a function of cognitive style; assembly performance is not a function of picture format; assembly performance is not a function of gender.
   b. Is each hypothesis supported by sufficient literature or argument? Identify the paragraphs where support for each hypothesis is found.
      Yes. Paragraphs 1–5.
   c. Are the hypotheses consistent with the research design? Explain.
      Yes. Paragraph 6 discusses variables.

4. Literature review
   a. Is the context of the problem clear? Identify paragraphs that spec-
      ify the context of the problem.
      Yes. Paragraphs 1–5.
   b. Are relevant theories and research cited to support the hypothe-
      ses? Identify paragraphs in which these theories and research are
      cited.
      Yes. Paragraphs 1–5.
   c. Are theories and research cited relevant to the variables used?
      Identify paragraphs in which these theories and research are
      cited.
      **Yes. Theories and research are cited for all variables, except
      gender, in paragraphs 1–5.**

5. Operational definitions
   a. Are all the variables operationally defined? Identify the variables
      and paragraphs where they are operationally defined.
      **Yes. Picture format, paragraph 4; cognitive style, paragraph
      5; assembly performance, paragraph 10.**
   b. Are operational definitions sufficiently unambiguous? If not,
      explain.
      Yes.

6. Measurement and manipulation of variables
   a. Are the manipulations of all independent variables clear? If not,
      explain. Identify the paragraph where manipulations of indepen-
      dent variables are described.
      Yes. Paragraph 10.
   b. Are the measurements of dependent or predictor/criterion vari-
      ables reliable? If yes, identify the paragraph in which reliability is
      documented.
      Reliability of assembly performance is not discussed.
   c. Are the manipulations of all independent variables and measure-
      ments of dependent or predictor/criterion variables valid? If yes,
      identify the paragraphs in which validity is documented.
      **Yes. Manipulations of independent variables: picture for-
      mat (paragraph 9) and identification of cognitive style
      (paragraph 8) seem valid. Measurement of the dependent
      variable: assembly performance (paragraph 10) seems valid.**

7. Research design
   a. Is the design stated sufficiently clearly so that you can diagram it?
      Diagram the design.
      Yes.

Posttest-only control group design

$$R \begin{cases} X_1 \rightarrow O_1 \\ X_2 \rightarrow O_2 \end{cases}$$

    b.   Is the design adequate to test the stated hypotheses? If not, explain.
        Yes.

    c.   Is the sample adequate and representative? If not, explain. Identify the paragraph that describes the sample.
        No. Paragraph 7; the sample is neither adequate nor representative, since the sample consists of volunteers.

    d.   Are there any sources of bias that were not controlled? If yes, name them.
        Yes. The sample was composed of volunteers.

    e.   Is the design internally valid? Address potential issues of internal validity.
        Selection—students were volunteers; however, they were randomly assigned. Instrumentation—measurement procedures are not described sufficiently to determine if instrumentation is a threat to internal validity; however, a standard scoring protocol was used.

    f.   Is the design externally valid? Address potential issues of external validity.
        Effects of experimental arrangements—participants may have been aware that they were involved in a study. Experimenter effects—it is not known how many researchers were involved in conducting the study.

8.   Statistics

    a.   Are the descriptions clear for all statistical tests that were used? If not, explain. Identify the paragraphs that describe the statistical tests that were used.
        Yes. Paragraphs 11–14.

    b.   Are the statistical tests used appropriate and relevant to the stated hypotheses? If not, explain.
        Yes.

    c.   Are there other statistical analyses that should have been done instead of or in addition to those actually done? If yes, name the statistical analyses and give your rationale.
        No.

d. Are the presentations of the results of the data analyses sufficiently clear? If not, explain.
Yes.

e. Are the tables, graphs, and figures clear and adequately labeled? If
not, explain.
Yes.

9. Findings and conclusions

a. Are the findings and conclusions stated clearly? If not, explain.
Yes.

b. Are the findings and conclusions related to the problem as stated?
If not, explain.
Yes.

c. Are the findings and conclusions related to the stated hypotheses?
If not, explain.
Yes.

d. Is there an adequate and convincing interpretation of the findings?
If not, explain.
Yes.

e. Are there alternative explanations for the findings? If yes, state
them.
No.

f. Are there recommendations for future related research? Identify
the paragraph in which recommendations for future related
research are described.
No. There were no recommendations for future research.

10. References

a. Are all citations listed in the reference list? If not, explain.
Yes.

b. Is the reference list complete and up-to-date? If not, explain.
No, the most recent reference is dated 1986.

✎ *Exercise 8–3* "Differences in Perceptions of Children's Developmental
Level as a Function of the Child's Gender"

1. Problem statement

a. Is the problem stated clearly enough for you confidently to restate
it in your own words? If yes, restate it. If not, explain.
**Yes. Different expectations for boys and girls may influence
the judgments of the abilities of boys and girls.**

b. Is the problem feasible? If not, explain.
Yes.

c. Does the problem have sufficient theoretical value? Explain.
**Yes. There has been research that attempts to explain the
effects of gender on social interactions.**

      d.   Does the problem have sufficient practical value? Explain.
          Yes. For individuals who interact with children—teachers and parents

2. Variables
      a.   Are the independent and dependent variables clearly identified? Identify them and the paragraphs where they are found.
          Yes. Independent variable: videotape of play activities, paragraph 6; dependent variable: developmental checklist, paragraph 7.
      b.   Are there any important variables that should have been included but were not? If yes, list them and indicate how they should be used.
          No.

3. Hypotheses
      a.   Are the experimental (or null) hypotheses stated clearly? Identify the paragraph where they are found. State the hypotheses.
          Hypotheses are implied in paragraphs 4 and 13. Judgments about a child's behavior and performance are not a function of perception of the child's gender; Judgments about a child's behavior and performance are not a function of the rater's gender.
      b.   Is each hypothesis supported by sufficient literature or argument? Identify the paragraphs where support for each hypothesis is found.
          Yes. Gender issues are discussed in paragraphs 1–3.
      c.   Are the hypotheses consistent with the research design? Explain.
          Yes. Gender of the child and gender of the rater are factored in a two-way ANOVA; paragraph 11.

4. Literature review
      a.   Is the context of the problem clear? Identify paragraphs that specify the context of the problem.
          Yes. Paragraphs 1–3.
      b.   Are relevant theories and research cited to support the hypotheses? Identify paragraphs in which these theories and research are cited.
          Yes. Paragraphs 1–3.
      c.   Are theories and research cited relevant to the variables used? Identify paragraphs in which these theories and research are cited.
          Yes. Paragraphs 1–3.

5. Operational definitions
      a.   Are all variables operationally defined? Identify the variables and paragraphs where they are operationally defined.
          Yes. Videotape of play activities, paragraph 6; developmental checklist, paragraph 7.
      b.   Are operational definitions sufficiently unambiguous? If not, explain.
          Yes.

6. Measurement and manipulation of variables
    a. Are the manipulations of all independent variables clear? If not, explain. Identify the paragraph where manipulations of independent variables are described.
        Yes. Videotape of play activities, paragraph 6
    b. Are the measurements of dependent or predictor/criterion variables reliable? If yes, identify the paragraph in which reliability is documented.
        Yes. Developmental checklist, paragraph 7. The items of the checklist were derived from the *Yellow Brick Road Manual;* however, reliability is not documented.
    c. Are the manipulations of all independent variables and the measurements of dependent or predictor/criterion variables valid? If yes, identify the paragraphs in which validity is documented.
        Yes. The manipulation of the independent variable: videotape of play activities (paragraph 6) seems valid. The measurement of the dependent variable: developmental checklist (paragraph 7) seems valid.

7. Research design
    a. Is the design stated sufficiently clearly so that you could diagram it? Diagram the design.
        Yes.
        Posttest-only control group design

        $$R \begin{cases} X_1 \rightarrow O_1 \\ X_2 \rightarrow O_2 \\ X_3 \rightarrow O_3 \end{cases}$$

    b. Is the design adequate to test the stated hypotheses? If not, explain.
        Yes.
    c. Is the sample adequate and representative? If not, explain. Identify the paragraphs that describe the sample.
        No. The sample was composed of volunteers in intact classes. However, they were randomly assigned to treatments, paragraphs 5 and 8.
    d. Are there any sources of bias that were not controlled? If yes, name them.
        The sample was composed of volunteers.
    e. Is the design internally valid? Address potential issues of internal validity.

> **Selection—students were volunteers in intact classes; however, they were randomly assigned.**
> **Instrumentation—measurement procedures are not described sufficiently to determine if instrumentation is a threat to internal validity**

    f.   Is the design externally valid? Address potential issues of external validity.

> **Effects of experimental arrangements—participants may have been aware that they were involved in a study**
> **Experimenter effects—it is not known how many researchers were involved in conducting the study**

8.   Statistics

    a.   Are the descriptions clear for all the statistical tests that were used? If not, explain. Identify the paragraphs that describe the statistical tests that were used.
       Yes. Paragraphs 11–20.

    b.   Are the statistical tests used appropriate and relevant to the stated hypotheses? If not, explain.
       Yes.

    c.   Are there other statistical analyses that should have been done instead of or in addition to those actually done? If yes, name the statistical analyses and give your rationale.
       No.

    d.   Are the presentations of the results of the data analyses sufficiently clear? If not, explain.
       Yes.

    e.   Are the tables, graphs, and figures clear and adequately labeled? If not, explain.
       Yes.

9.   Findings and conclusions

    a.   Are the findings and conclusions stated clearly? If not, explain.
       Yes.

    b.   Are the findings and conclusions related to the problem as stated? If not, explain.
       Yes.

    c.   Are the findings and conclusions related to the stated hypotheses? If not, explain.
       Yes.

    d.   Is there an adequate and convincing interpretation of the findings? If not, explain.
       Yes.

e. Are there alternative explanations for the findings? If yes, state them.
    No.
f. Are there recommendations for future related research? Identify the paragraph in which recommendations for future related research are described.
    Yes. Paragraph 23.

10. References
    a. Are all citations listed in the reference list? If not, explain.
        Yes.
    b. Is the reference list complete and up-to-date? If not, explain.
        The reference list could be expanded. References are not current. The most recent reference is dated 1981.

SUMMARY

This chapter has provided practice in conducting a computerized database search to prepare a review of the literature. Also, a systematic approach for reviewing and evaluating a research report was described, and practice was provided in reviewing and critiquing a research report. In Chapter 9 a variety of ethical considerations that are related to the entire process of conducting educational research are discussed, and practice is provided in identifying and resolving ethical issues.

9 | ETHICAL CONSIDERATIONS

INTRODUCTION

All research studies must be conducted in an ethical manner. This obvious statement means that all phases of a research study, from planning and design to reporting, must be conducted in accordance with accepted standards of ethical behavior. Most institutions or agencies that conduct research have organized review committees that examine proposed research studies to make sure that the procedures and methods are consistent with recognized ethical standards.

Since much research in education involves the study of people, and in particular children, special care must be taken to ensure that the participants are treated fairly and ethically in all respects. The following sections present various steps that will help a researcher comply with recognized ethical standards. Before beginning a research study, a researcher should first consult with an appropriate individual, committee, or review board to make sure that all proposed methods and procedures ensure the ethical treatment of participants.

STEPS TO ENSURE ADHERENCE TO ETHICAL STANDARDS

During Participant Recruitment and Selection

Obtain Informed Consent
The guiding principle here is that participation in a research study must be voluntary. This means that all participants must be informed

about the purpose of the study and any risk they may encounter, and must freely agree to participate. When the participants are minors, informed consent from their parents or guardians must be obtained. Although it is generally not legally required, it is reasonable to obtain informed consent from participating minors themselves as well. Informed consent should be obtained in writing, usually by having the participant and parent (or guardian) sign a form that describes the relevant information and clearly describes what will be done if they choose not to participate or if they choose to withdraw during the study. A sample informed consent form is shown in Figure 9–1.

Provide Information about the Study   Before prospective participants can consider volunteering for a study, they must know what it is they are being asked to do. The researcher must provide as much information as possible to allow participants to make a free and informed choice. Such information should include descriptions of the precise nature of participation, the duration of the participation, the nature of the data to be collected, how the data will be stored and reported, the nature of any possible risk to which participants might be exposed, and how participants can withdraw once the study has begun.

Explain the Nature of Any Risk   Inform participants about any potential risk they might encounter or be exposed to during the study. All risks should, of course, be minimized, but sometimes they cannot. The researcher should explain clearly what risks exist, what measures have been taken to minimize risk, and what procedures will be followed if a risk results in actual harm. "Risk" should be construed to include any physical, mental, social, or psychological harm that could reasonably be anticipated as a possible outcome or consequence of participating in the study. While educational research typically does not involve the use of instruments that could cause physical harm, some educational interventions might present some psychological risk. Such risks must be revealed as part of the process of obtaining informed consent.

Eliminate Coercion   In order to volunteer freely to be part of a study, potential participants must feel that they are under no pressure to participate. If, for example, a child is asked by a teacher or school administrator to take part in a study, the child (or parent) might feel that he or she *must* participate. A researcher should

FIGURE 9–1   Sample Informed Consent Form

You are invited to participate in this research study. The following information is provided in order to help you make an informed decision whether or not to participate. If you have any questions about any aspect of this study, or the information in this form, please do not hesitate to ask. You are eligible to participate because you are a student in *Introduction to Education (ED 101)* at State University.

The purpose of this study is to compare the effectiveness of and student preferences for computerized assisted instruction (CAI) versus lecture as a teaching technique. Participation in this study will require approximately 90 minutes of your time and is not considered a part of ED 101. Participation or nonparticipation will not affect the evaluation of your performance in this class. First you will take a pretest, consisting of 20 multiple-choice questions. Next, you will be randomly assigned (similar to the flip of a coin) to either a 50-minute CAI class or a 50-minute lecture class on lesson planning. Both the CAI class and the lecture class will have the same educational objectives and will cover the same material. At the end of the CAI class or the lecture class, you will be asked to complete a posttest consisting of 20 multiple-choice questions. Finally, you will be asked to complete an attitude questionnaire about your educational experience in this study.

Your scores on the tests will be correlated with your SAT scores. Therefore, we ask your permission to obtain your SAT scores from your admissions file. There are no known risks or discomforts associated with this study.

You may find the learning experience enjoyable, and the information may be helpful to you when you study lesson planning in *Curriculum Planning (ED 102)*. The information gained from this study may help us to better understand the effectiveness of CAI versus lecture as a teaching technique and learning format preference.

Your participation is *voluntary*. You are free to decide not to participate in this study or to withdraw at any time without adversely affecting your relationship with the researchers or with the University. Your decision will not result in any loss of benefits to which you are otherwise entitled. If you choose to participate, you may withdraw at any time by notifying the Project Director (at the address or phone number below) or by informing the person administering the tests. Upon your decision to withdraw, all information pertaining to you will be destroyed. If you choose to participate, all information will be held in strict confidence and will have no bearing on your academic standing or services you receive from the University. Your response will be considered *only in combination* with those from other participants. The information obtained in the study may be published in scientific journals or presented at scientific meetings, but your identity will be kept strictly confidential.

If you are willing to participate in this study, please sign the statement below and deposit it in the designated box by the door. Take the extra unsigned copy with you. If you choose not to participate, deposit the unsigned copies in the designated box by the door.

Thank you for considering participating in this study.

Project Director: I. M. Curious, Professor of Education State University, Collegetown, USA, Telephone (555) 555-5555

- -

I have read and understand the information on the form and I consent to volunteer to be a participant in this study. I understand that my responses are completely confidential and that I have the right to withdraw at any time. I have receive an unsigned copy of this Informed Consent Form to keep in my possession.

Name (PLEASE PRINT) ———————————————   Telephone No. ————————

Signature ———————————————————————

employ procedures that eliminate all forms of coercion and the perception of coercion. For example, the researcher could get permission from school authorities to contact the students and parents directly. Then the informed consent letters could be returned directly to the researcher so that the teacher will not know who did and who did not agree to participate. The procedures that are used to eliminate any possible coercion should be explained clearly and thoroughly in a cover letter that accompanies the request for informed consent to participate in the study.

Inform Participants That Illegal Behavior Must Be Revealed
Confidentiality of data and information, discussed later, is an important ethical consideration. However, researchers also have a responsibility to report certain information, even if it is obtained during "confidential" data collection. For example, suppose that a researcher learns, during the course of an interview, that a child has been sexually molested. The researcher is obligated to report that information to the authorities. Prior to starting a study, a researcher who plans to collect data that might reveal illegal behavior should inform potential participants that any such illegal behavior must and will be reported to the authorities.

Avoid Deception   Most educational research studies are straightforward, and deception can easily be avoided completely. Sometimes, however, having complete information about a study could alter participants' responses. In such cases there might be some justification for withholding information or deceiving participants, as long as the deception or lack of information does not present any risk. The use of deception is very controversial. Before using any deception in a study, Diener and Crandall (1978) recommend that researchers carefully weigh the value of the research against the detrimental effects of the deception. In addition, they argue that researchers should not use deception when participants might be exposed to risk. Finally, they suggest that participants should be fully debriefed following a study in which deception was used.

During Treatment and Data Collection

Cause No Harm   Most educational research poses little risk to participants. Although all potential risks that might exist must be revealed during the informed consent process, the researcher is still ethically obligated to minimize any potential risk. It is important, as part of the process of obtaining informed consent, that the procedures for eliminating or minimizing risk are thoroughly explained.

Maintain the Confidentiality of Data   Confidentiality of data is one of the main areas of concern to educational researchers. No one, other than the researcher and a few coinvestigators, should have access to the data. The data should be collected in a manner that ensures that they cannot be linked to specific participants; once collected, the data should be kept in a secure location. This is especially true when the data are collected in a manner that allows participants to be identified easily. The issue of confidentiality is closely related to that of anonymity, discussed in the following section.

Maintain Participant Anonymity   One way to maintain data confidentiality is to have participants furnish information anonymously. If anonymous responses are not possible or practical, an identifier (such as a number) can be used to code responses so that the names can be eliminated when all data have been collected. Having a third party select the sample and collect the data using an identifier system can further protect participant anonymity. The issues of confidentiality and anonymity apply to institutions, schools, and classes as well as to individuals.

Maintain the Integrity of Data   Storing data in locked cabinets or closets protects against any violations of confidentiality and also helps protect against the falsification and contamination of data. Some forms of data, such as videotapes or audiotapes, require special care since identities are more difficult to hide in such media.

Train Assistants   Besides being a good general practice for maintaining the validity and reliability of research procedures, training all data collectors and other assistants helps maintain adherence to ethical standards.

Avoid Invasions of Privacy   Researchers should not ask questions, or generally collect data, that are not essential to the purpose of the study. Many of the risks associated with privacy can be eliminated by following the procedures discussed earlier for maintaining confidentiality and anonymity.

Permit Participants to Withdraw   Participation in a research study is completely voluntary. Even if someone agrees to participate in a study, the researcher must recognize that participant's right to withdraw at any time. The researcher is obligated to inform participants of this right and to describe the procedures by which they can withdraw from the study. Further, the researcher must ensure that participants who withdraw are not penalized in any way, and that the fact of their withdrawal should be held in confidence. Any data that were collected prior to withdrawal may not be included in the study, and the procedures for destroying or eliminating such data should be fully explained.

During Data Analysis and Interpretation

Maintain Participant Anonymity   The steps to maintain anonymity, discussed earlier, are applicable and perhaps even more important during the analysis, interpretation, and reporting of the results of a study.

Maintain the Integrity of the Data   In addition to the procedures described earlier, the researcher should make sure that appropriate and relevant analysis techniques are used, and that the conclusions and recommendations drawn from the study are appropriate and do not pose any risk to individuals or groups.

During Follow-up or Debriefing

Provide Information about the Study   It is generally a good practice to debrief participants following a study. It is essential that this debriefing include any information that may have been withheld initially, or, if deception was used, that the deceptive practice is revealed. Additionally, it is a good practice to offer to provide a summary of the results and conclusions of the study, when they become available, to the participants.

Provide Opportunity to Receive Beneficial Treatment   Many times a researcher investigating the value of a new technique or treatment will use a control group, or a group that receives a placebo or standard treatment. If the data show that the new technique or treatment is beneficial to the participants, the researcher then has an ethical obligation to offer that technique or treatment to those participants who were in other groups. For example, if the results of a study show that students who were instructed in mathematics using computers, reached higher levels of achievement, the researcher should arrange additional instruction, using computers for those participating students who were taught using less beneficial techniques.

Submit the Research for Publication   A researcher may want to submit a study for publication. A manuscript should be submitted to one publisher at a time. If the manuscript is rejected by that publisher, it may be submitted to another.

COMPETENCIES

The exercises in this chapter will provide practice in identifying and addressing various ethical issues in conducting educational research. After completing the exercises in this chapter, you will be able to

- Identify the need for consideration of various ethical issues

- Describe a course of action to address a specified ethical issue

- Determine when steps need to be taken to address ethical considerations

- Describe specific techniques for avoiding ethical problems at various stages of the research process

EXERCISES IN ETHICAL STANDARDS

The following exercises provide practice in addressing ethical standards when conducting research. The first set of exercises will require consideration of an ethical standard at a specific point in the research. The second set will require consideration of all ethical standards related to each study.

Exercises in Addressing Specific Ethical Standards

Below are some research situations in which ethical considerations need to be addressed at a specific point in the process of conducting research. The specific point is marked with an asterisk. Address only those ethical considerations that pertain to the issues mentioned in the description of the proposed research. Determine which action or actions need to be taken by the researcher.

✎ **Exercise 9–1**   A researcher plans to videotape children at play on the school playground as part of a study on peer relationships among preschool children.

   *During participant recruitment and selection

✎ **Exercise 9–2**   A researcher plans to score holistically pieces of writing from his freshman college writing class. The results of the study will be presented at a professional conference.

   *During participant recruitment and selection

✎ **Exercise 9–3**   A study is being planned to compare alcohol consumption between students who have taken the Prom Promise Pledge and those who have not at a large rural high school. The results of the study will be reported to the school newspaper.

   *During participant recruitment and selection

   *During data analysis and interpretation

✎ **Exercise 9–4**   Literature has shown promise for a new technique for enabling students who fall behind in reading achievement to reach appropriate levels within one year of intense use of the technique. A study is being planned to assess this technique. One group of students will have intense application of the technique; a control group will be involved in traditional techniques to improve reading achievement.

   *During follow-up or debriefing

✎ **Exercise 9–5**   A school administration is interested in teachers' responses to the national standards that have been developed by professional associations. The purpose of the study is to determine if there is a commitment to adopting the standards for the fine arts; however, the administration does not want to reveal the purpose of the study at this time.

   *During follow-up or debriefing

✎ **Exercise 9–6**   Several researchers will be involved in the treatment phase of a study on physical fitness.

   *During treatment and data collection

✎ **Exercise 9–7**   A college nutrition professor is interested in studying the effects of weight loss on temperament. The treatment, a rigorous diet and physical exercise, will continue for six months.

> *During participant recruitment and selection

> *During treatment and data collection

✎ **Exercise 9–8**   A university professor is nearing the time when she will be reviewed for tenure. She has no publications, which are required for acquiring tenure. She has just finished a research study and written a manuscript describing the study and results, which yielded no significant differences. Since time is crucial, she decides to alter slightly the data and submit the manuscript to several journals in the field.

> *During data analysis and interpretation

> *During follow-up or debriefing

✎ **Exercise 9–9**   A driver-training teacher plans to study the effects of a program that includes simulation exercises, which have embedded driver education theory. This program will be compared to the typical driver-training program that has considerable classroom instruction before practice on the road. Adult students in the simulation program will have actual driving experience sooner than students in the traditional classroom setting.

> *During participant recruitment and selection

✎ **Exercise 9–10**   A researcher has collected data over a period of three months. For ease of access to the data, he has stored the data in the main office in a shoebox.

> *During treatment and data collection

Exercises in Addressing Multiple Ethical Standards

For each research study, discuss ethical considerations before, during, and after the study to ensure adherence to ethical standards.

✎ **Exercise 9–11**   Early childhood specialists have noted that there might be a relationship between health care education of parents and children and school attendance. A researcher has received a grant to provide health care education for parents and children. Health care education sessions will be videotaped. During data collection, parents will be asked to reveal their family incomes. The request to respond to a question about family income will not be explained in the consent form. Children in a control group and their parents will not receive health care education.

1. During participant recruitment and selection
2. During treatment and data collection
3. During data analysis and interpretation
4. During follow-up or debriefing

Exercise 9–12 A college president proposes redistributing money for athletics so that more funding is spent for tutoring athletes. She has requested that a researcher study this increase in funding for tutorial services to determine if there is an effect on grade point averages of athletes. Athletes will be randomly assigned to one of two conditions: traditional tutoring or extensive tutoring.

1. During participant recruitment and selection
2. During treatment and data collection
3. During data analysis and interpretation
4. During follow-up or debriefing

Exercise 9–13 A high school faculty has decided to study the effects of the use of primary source materials and trade books on attitude toward social studies. Since the current social studies textbooks are five years old, it would be convenient to try an approach to teaching that utilizes materials other than text materials. However, new texts will be purchased for use with a control group.

1. During participant recruitment and selection
2. During treatment and data collection
3. During data analysis and interpretation
4. During follow-up or debriefing

Exercise 9–14 Attrition among faculty has been higher than normal in a school district. The administration thinks that possibly there is not enough support for teachers. It was decided to develop a teacher center, which would support the professional development of teachers. The administration would like to study the effects of the teacher center on retention of teachers. One-half of the teachers in the district will be assigned to participation in the teacher center. The other teachers, who will be in the control group, will not have teacher center experience.

1. During participant recruitment and selection

2. During treatment and data collection

3. During data analysis and interpretation

4. During follow-up or debriefing

Exercise 9–15   Traditionally, vocational technical schools have had job placement offices to assist graduates in finding employment. Administrators of one county vocational technical school are interested in arranging for students to have access to an on-line directory of available positions rather than the services of a job placement office. They want to compare placement rates using the on-line service with the number of placements through job placement offices of other county schools. If successful, the administrators plan to publish the results of the studies in several vocational education journals.

1. During participant recruitment and selection

2. During treatment and data collection

3. During data analysis and interpretation

4. During follow-up or debriefing

ANSWERS TO EXERCISES IN ETHICAL STANDARDS

Answers to Exercises in Addressing Specific Ethical Standards

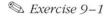 *Exercise 9–1*

*During participant recruitment and selection

> Parents of participants would need to be informed of the study and sign consent forms for their child to participate; participants also should sign consent forms. This should include consent to be video-taped.

> Participants should be informed that they can withdraw from the study at any time.

✎ *Exercise 9–2*

*During participant recruitment and selection

> Participants would need to be informed of the study and sign consent forms to participate.

> Participants cannot be required to participate because they are in the researcher's class; coercion must be avoided.

> Participants should be informed that they can withdraw from the study at any time.

✎ *Exercise 9–3*

*During participant recruitment and selection

> Parents of participants would need to be informed of the study and sign consent forms for their child to participate; participants also should sign consent forms.

> Participants should be informed that they can withdraw from the study at any time.

> Participants should be informed that illegal behavior, such as under-age drinking, must be reported to authorities.

*During data analysis and interpretation

> Names should be removed from the data, and the data aggregated to maintain confidentiality and anonymity.

✎ *Exercise 9–4*

*During follow-up or debriefing

> Results of the study should be shared with the participants.

> Participants who were in the control group should have the same opportunity to improve their reading achievement as the experimental group, if the results of the treatment prove to be beneficial.

✎ *Exercise 9–5*

*During follow-up or debriefing

> When results of the study are shared with teachers, the administration should reveal the purpose of the study and the impact of the results on this purpose.

✎ *Exercise 9–6*

*During treatment and data collection

Researchers should be trained so that treatment is uniform and consistent.

✎ *Exercise 9–7*

*During participant recruitment and selection

Participants would need to be informed of the study and sign consent forms to participate.

Participants should be informed that they can withdraw from the study at any time.

Participants in the study's treatment component should be informed of the potential risks of a rigorous diet and physical exercise.

*During treatment and data collection

Participants can withdraw from the treatment using the procedures outlined in the consent form and their data will be destroyed.

Data should be kept confidential and secured at all times.

✎ *Exercise 9–8*

*During data analysis and interpretation

Data should not be falsified.

*During follow-up or debriefing

A manuscript should be submitted to only one prospective publisher at a time.

✎ *Exercise 9–9*

*During participant recruitment and selection

Participants would need to be informed of the study and sign consent forms to participate.

Participants should be informed that they can withdraw from the study at any time.

Participants in the simulation component of the study should be informed of the potential risks of on-the-road practice that occurs sooner than in traditional driver training.

✎ *Exercise 9–10*

*During treatment and data collection

Data should be kept confidential and secured at all times.

Answers to Exercises in Addressing Multiple Ethical Standards

✎ *Exercise 9–11*

1. During participant recruitment and selection

    Parents of participants would need to be informed of the study and sign consent forms for themselves and their child to participate; minors also should sign consent forms. This should include consent to be videotaped.

    Participants should be informed that they can withdraw from the study at any time.

2. During treatment and data collection

    Data should be kept confidential and secured at all times.

    The camera for videotaping should not be hidden.

    Participants can withdraw from the treatment using the procedures outlined in the consent form, and their data will be destroyed.

    Privacy should not be invaded by asking questions of a sensitive nature, such as family income, without prior consent.

3. During data analysis and interpretation

    Names should be removed from the data and data aggregated to maintain confidentiality and anonymity.

4. During follow-up or debriefing

    Results of the study should be shared with the participants.

    Participants, parents and children, who were in the control group should have the same opportunity for health care education as the experimental group, if the treatment results are beneficial.

✎ *Exercise 9–12*

1. During participant recruitment and selection

    Athletes and tutors would need to be informed of the study and sign consent forms to participate.

Participants should be informed that they can withdraw from the study at any time.

2. During treatment and data collection

    Tutors should be trained so that treatment is uniform and consistent.

    Data should be kept confidential and secured at all times.

    Participants can withdraw from the treatment using the procedures outlined in the consent form, and their data will be destroyed.

3. During data analysis and interpretation

    Names should be removed from the data, and the data aggregated to maintain confidentiality and anonymity.

4. During follow-up or debriefing

    Results of the study should be shared with the participants.

    Participants who were in the control group should have the same opportunity for extensive tutoring as the experimental group, if the results of the treatment prove to be beneficial.

✎ *Exercise 9–13*

1. During participant recruitment and selection

    Parents of participants would need to be informed of the study and sign consent forms for their child to participate; participants also should sign consent forms.

    Participants should be informed that they can withdraw from the study at any time.

    Participants cannot be required to participate because they are in a class where research is being conducted; coercion must be avoided.

2. During treatment and data collection

    Teachers should be trained so that treatment is uniform and consistent.

    Data should be kept confidential and secured at all times.

    Participants can withdraw from the treatment using the procedures outlined in the consent form, and their data will be destroyed.

3. During data analysis and interpretation

    Names should be removed from the data, and the data aggregated to maintain confidentiality and anonymity.

4. During follow-up or debriefing

Results of the study should be shared with the participants.

✎ Exercise 9–14

1. During participant recruitment and selection

Teachers would need to be informed of the study and sign consent forms to participate.

Participants should be informed that they can withdraw from the study at any time.

2. During treatment and data collection

Data should be kept confidential and secured at all times.

Participants can withdraw from the treatment using the procedures outlined in the consent form, and their data will be destroyed.

3. During data analysis and interpretation

Names should be removed from the data and data aggregated to maintain confidentiality and anonymity.

4. During follow-up or debriefing

Results of the study should be shared with the participants.

Participants who were in the control group should have the same opportunity to participate in the teacher center as the experimental group, if the results of treatment prove to be beneficial.

✎ Exercise 9–15

1. During participant recruitment and selection

Parents of participants must be informed of the study and sign the consent forms for their child to participate; children also should sign consent forms.

Participants must be informed that they can withdraw from the study at any time.

2. During treatment and data collection

Data should be kept confidential and secured at all times.

Participants can withdraw from the treatment using the procedures outlined in the letter of consent, and their data will be destroyed.

3. During data analysis and interpretation

    Names should be removed from the data and data aggregated to maintain confidentiality and anonymity.

4. During follow-up or debriefing

    Results of the study should be shared with the participants.

    A manuscript should be submitted to only one prospective publisher at a time.

SUMMARY

Ethical considerations should permeate all phases and aspects of educational research. This chapter has provided practice in identifying and addressing ethical considerations in the conduct of educational research. As a researcher prepares to conduct a study, plans to address ethical considerations should be addressed as soon as possible. Consultation with appropriate committees or review boards during the planning stage is highly recommended.

REFERENCES

American Psychological Association. (1994). *Publication Manual of the American Psychological Association* (4th ed.). Washington, DC: American Psychological Association.

Berg, Bruce. (1989, 1994). *Qualitative research methods for the social sciences.* Boston: Allyn and Bacon.

Bogdan, R. C., & Biklen, S. K. (1992). *Qualitative research for education* (2nd ed.). Boston: Allyn and Bacon.

Borg, W. R., & Gall, M. D. (1989). *Educational research: An introduction* (5th ed.). New York: Longman.

Bracht, G. H., & Glass, G. V. (1968). The external validity of experiments. *American Educational Research Journal, 5,* 437–474.

Campbell, D., & Stanley, J. (1966). *Experimental and quasi-experimental designs for research.* Chicago: Rand McNally.

Diener, E., & Crandall, R. (1978). *Ethics in social and behavioral research.* Chicago: University of Chicago Press.

Fisher, R. A. (1951). *The design of experiments* (6th ed.). New York: Hafner Publishing Company.

Fraenkel, J. R., & Wallen, N. E. (1993). *How to design and evaluate research in education* (2nd ed.). New York: McGraw-Hill.

Gay, L. R. (1992). *Educational research: Competencies for analysis and application* (4th ed.). New York: Merrill.

Hall, G. E., George, A. A., & Rutherford, W. L. (1979). *Measuring stages of concern about the innovation: A manual for use of the SoC questionnaire.* Austin, TX: Research and Development Center for Teacher Education.

Hopkins, D. (1992). *A teacher's guide to classroom research.* Philadelphia: Open University Press.

Kerlinger, F. (1986). *Foundations of behavioral research* (3rd ed.). Fort Worth, TX: Holt, Rinehart, and Winston.

Long, T. J., Convey, J. J., & Chwalek, A. R. (1991). *Completing dissertations in the behavioral sciences and education.* San Francisco: Jossey-Bass.

Nurosis, M. J. (1992). *SPSS/PC+ Base System Users Guide. Version 5.0.* Chicago: SPSS Inc.

Popham, W. J., & Sirotnik, K. A. (1967). *Educational statistics: Use and interpretation* (2nd ed.). New York: Harper and Row.

Rosenthal, R. (1966). *Experimenter effects in behavioral research.* New York: Appleton-Century-Crofts.

Rosenthal, Robert, & Rosnow, Ralph L. (1991). *Essentials of behavioral research: Methods and data analysis* (2nd ed.). New York: McGraw-Hill.

Roethlisberger, F. S., & Dickson, W. J. (1939). *Management and the worker.* Cambridge, MA: Harvard University Press.

Saslow, C. A. (1982). *Basic research methods.* Reading, MA: Addison-Wesley.

Scheffé, H. (1955). *The Analysis of Variance.* New York: John Wiley and Sons, Inc.

Sowell, E. J., & Casey, R. J. (1982). *Analyzing educational research.* Belmont, CA: Wadsworth.

Tuckman, B. (1994). *Conducting educational research* (4th ed.). New York: Harcourt, Brace, Jovanovich.

Wiersma, W. (1995). *Research methods in education* (6th ed.). Boston: Allyn and Bacon.

I N D E X